Demons of the Mind

Demons of the Mind

Psychiatry and Cinema in the Long 1960s

Tim Snelson, William R. Macauley and David A. Kirby

EDINBURGH
University Press

Edinburgh University Press is one of the leading university presses in the UK. We publish academic books and journals in our selected subject areas across the humanities and social sciences, combining cutting-edge scholarship with high editorial and production values to produce academic works of lasting importance. For more information visit our website: edinburghuniversitypress.com

Grateful acknowledgement is made to the sources listed in the List of Illustrations for permission to reproduce material previously published elsewhere. Every effort has been made to trace the copyright holders, but if any have been inadvertently overlooked, the publisher will be pleased to make the necessary arrangements at the first opportunity.

Edinburgh University Press Ltd
13 Infirmary Street
Edinburgh EH1 1LT

Typeset in 11/13 Arno Pro by
IDSUK (DataConnection) Ltd, and
printed and bound in Great Britain

A CIP record for this book is available from the British Library

ISBN 978 1 4744 8641 5 (hardback)
ISBN 978 1 4744 8643 9 (webready PDF)
ISBN 978 1 4744 8644 6 (epub)

Contents

List of figures   vi

Acknowledgements   viii

Introduction: psychiatry, cinema and the long 1960s   1

1   Morally acceptable madness: psychiatry, Catholics and censorship at the Legion of Decency   10

2   The BBFC's 'psychiatrist friends': psychiatric consultation and the British censors   42

3   Freud goes to Hollywood: translating psychoanalysis to cinema   65

4   Mad housewives and women's liberation: the psychiatric reinvention of the 'woman's film'   94

5   Radical collaborations: 'anti-psychiatry' on-screen   124

6   Aetiology of a murder: forensic psychiatry and the evolution of true crime   151

Conclusion: aftershocks   177

Notes   184

Index   218

Figures

I.1 Dr Richman provides a psychiatric explanation for Norman
     Bate's crimes in *Psycho* (1960)   2

1.1 A scene from *Shock Corridor* (1963) condemned by the
     Legion of Decency as being only included in the film for
     sensationalistic reasons   29

1.2 The Legion of Decency's concerns regarding this scene from
     Through a Glass Darkly (1961) was outweighed by their trust
     in filmmaker Ingmar Bergman   32

1.3 Scenes involving real patients in *A Child is Waiting* (1963)
     caused disagreement between the Legion of Decency and the
     Legion's French equivalent, Office Catholique International
     du Cinema   36

2.1 The NAMH called on the BBFC to cut scenes from
     Borderlines (1963)   52

2.2 The spectator is encouraged to experience Carole's psychotic
     episode in *Repulsion* (1965)   59

3.1 *A Clinical Lesson at the Salpêtrière*, 1887, by André Brouillet   74

3.2 John Huston restaged and updated Brouillet's painting to
     include a male patient for *Freud* (1962)   75

3.3 The ambiguous, abstracted background for *Freud*'s foreword   81

3.4 The theatrical staging of the therapy scenes in *Pressure Point*
     (1962)   83

3.5 Douglas Slocombe's innovative technique for therapy scenes, shot
     through a manipulated glass photographic plate   85

3.6 *Freud*'s orthochromatic dream sequence draws links between
    Freud and Cecily's dreams and reminiscences   86

4.1 Journalist Alistair Cooke directly addresses the cinema audience
    in the introduction to *The Three Faces of Eve* (1957)   107

4.2 Dr Luther, and the spectator, meet Eve Black for the first time
    in *The Three Faces of Eve*   108

5.1 An agitated Kate Winter is interviewed by an off-screen
    psychiatrist in the opening of *In Two Minds* (1967)   135

5.2 At the end of *In Two Minds*, the editing cross-cuts to Kate's
    ECT treatment, filmed on location at Shenley Hospital   137

5.3 Janice settles into a Villa 21-inspired experimental ward in
    Family Life (1971)   144

6.1 The superimposition of Smith's abusive father over bullying
    accomplice Hickock visualises the killer's psychological
    motivations in *In Cold Blood* (1967)   166

6.2 The reflection of rain on the window suggests tears on
    Perry Smith's cheeks, as he awaits execution   168

6.3 *In Cold Blood*'s final scene sends out a clear anti-capital
    punishment message that is absent from Capote's novel   169

Acknowledgements

The research for this book was made possible by funding from the Arts and Humanities Research Council (Grant No. AH/P005136/1) and constitutes part of 'Demons of the Mind: The Interactions of the "Psy" Sciences and Cinema in the Sixties', a research project based at the University of East Anglia and the University of Manchester. This work was also supported, in part, by the Wellcome Trust (Grant No. 100618) through an Investigator Award titled 'Playing God: Exploring the Intersections between Science, Religion and Entertainment Media.' We would like to thank the British Science Association who were partners on the project and who programmed Demons of the Mind events for a number of their national and regional science festivals. We would also like to thank a number of people who helped with and contributed to this project, including the Steering Group which comprised: Professor Mark Jancovich (University of East Anglia), Dr Rhodri Hayward (Queen Mary University), Dr Tim Boon (the Science Museum) and Ivvet Modinou (formerly of the British Science Association, now at the Simons Foundation).

We would like to thank all the contributors to our project symposium, particularly those who published their papers in our December 2021 special issue of *History of the Human Sciences*: Dr Laura Tisdall, Dr Amy C. Chambers, Dr Sophia Satchell-Baeza and Dr Katie Joice. Thanks also to those who offered support and advice on emergent ideas for the book, including Professor Melanie Williams, Professor Julian Petley, Professor Keith Johnston and the late Professor Martin Barker, an important and inspiring scholar and mentor to many in the field. He will be deeply missed. Thanks also to the late Tony Garnett, who was extremely generous with his time and interest in our project. He was a kind and inspirational man. Thank you also to his collaborator, Ken Loach, who was very gracious in agreeing to be involved in the project research and dissemination.

This book would not have been possible without the incredible support and expertise of a range of curators, archivists and librarians, who provided us with generous, skilful assistance and enrichment of the research for this book. This includes: Genevieve Maxwell, Bijan and all at the Margaret Herrick Library, Beverly Hills, California; Kate Collins and all at the David M. Rubenstein Rare Book and Manuscripts Library, Duke University, Durham, North Carolina; Jacob Smith at the British Board of Film Classification (BBFC) Archive, London; Nigel Good and all at the British Film Institute (BFI) National Archive, Berkhamsted; the staff of the BFI Reuben Library, BFI Southbank, London; Jeff Walden and all at the BBC Written Archives, Reading; Sam Maddra and all at the R. D. Laing Collection, University of Glasgow Library, Glasgow; staff at the Wellcome Collection Archive and Library, London; and the librarians at the Catholic University of America, Washington DC, where the Legion of Decency collections are held.

Thanks also to the Science Museum Group (SMG), who are co-investigators on the AHRC follow-on-funding project, Objects of the Mind (Grant No. AH/W002140/1). In particular, in addition to Tim Boon, we would like to thank current and ex-SMG staff members Toni Booth, Annie Jamieson, Efram Sera-Shriar, Geoff Belknap, Natasha McEnroe, Selina Hurley, Katie Maggs, Harriet Cash and Pippa Hough. Also, thanks to project partners StudioCanal, especially Massimo Moretti, and INTO Film, especially Ani Bailey.

A big thanks to Mark Dishman for all his editing on the book, you are a star. And to Ricky Foyle for the amazing cover. Thanks also to Gillian Leslie, Sam Johnson, Grace Balfour-Harle and Lyn Flight at Edinburgh University Press for all their support and patience in waiting for this book.

Finally, we would individually like to thank family members and friends for their support, interest and perseverance. David would like to thank Laura Gaither for all her help with his contribution to the book. Ray would like to express heartfelt thanks to his partner Laima Lisauskienė for her abiding support, understanding, and incisive advice on his research and writing for the book. Tim would like to send love and thanks to his wife Lucy and daughter Frida for all their love, support, ideas and patience, and also thank his parents and parents-in-law for their help and support whist he has been seemingly endlessly writing for this book.

Introduction: psychiatry, cinema and the long 1960s

On a Universal-Revue Studio set in early 1960, actor Simon Oakland, portraying forensic psychiatrist Dr Richman, enters the Office of the Chief of Police where a group of law enforcement officers and family members wait expectantly. They want an explanation for the horrors, involving their town and their loved ones that have just been revealed to them. When asked, 'Did he talk to you?', a pensive Richman equivocally responds 'No.' He pauses, then explains that he 'got the whole story, but not from Norman', he 'got it from the Mother', or, more precisely, 'the Mother-part of Norman'. Norman's mother is long dead, the first of her psychotic son's numerous victims. The camera pans to follow Oakland's psychiatrist as he embarks on a 5-minute explanation of this most unusual case history, elucidating that Norman's psychosis stemmed from the over-involvement of his mother – referred to as 'a clinging, demanding woman' – following his father's death, and Norman's resultant jealousy when, after many years, she detaches from him and takes up a lover: the trigger for his murder of both mother and lover (see Figure I.1). Norman's resultant dissociative behaviour – switching to the alternative personality of his mother to 'give her half his life, so to speak' – allowed him to assuage the guilt for these crimes, but also triggered more psychotic behaviour when 'reality came too close, when danger or desire threatened that illusion'. Before reaching for a congratulatory cigarette, Richman concludes his explanation that the 'battle' for Norman's mind is over, and the mother's 'dominant personality has won'. On the assistant director's shout of 'cut', the film's famous director walks over to the man playing the psychiatrist, shakes his hand and says, 'Thank you very much Mr Oakland. You've just saved my picture.'[1]

Figure I.1 Dr Richman provides a psychiatric explanation for Norman Bate's crimes in *Psycho* (1960)

In books and articles on the relationships between psychiatry and cinema, particularly in and around the 1960s, it is hard to avoid this film, this scene and, indeed, this potentially apocryphal account of its production and censorship. Alfred Hitchcock's *Psycho* (1960) has been hailed as pioneering in its use of the cinematic apparatus to allow the spectator to experience and even empathise with its protagonist's psychotic episodes. Alternately, it has been decried as the film that established a troubling link between certain dissociative mental health conditions and violent behaviour (lead character Norman Bates is typically 'diagnosed' as a paranoid schizophrenic or as suffering from multiple personality disorder, now dissociative identity disorder). Norman (as portrayed by Anthony Perkins) is also understood as establishing the trope of the pitiable psychopath – the product of parental over-attachment or abandonment, or both – that has become a mainstay of popular film and television. *Psycho* not only established representational conventions of the serial killer and slasher film genres, but has been seen also as contributing to wider media and public discourse about the origin and dangers of mental illness, including the promulgation of 'psycho' as a common and almost invariably pejorative label. Because of these widespread influences and circulations, *Psycho* is the film we have screened and discussed most with mental health professionals, survivors, service-users, film critics, academics and the public for events for the Demons of the Mind project from which this book derives.[2] It certainly speaks to some of the key themes and findings of our project: the cinematic use of psychiatric authority (both on- and off-screen), shifting censorship contexts and concerns, worries over the influence of depictions of mental illnesses, technological and stylistic innovations for evoking altered states of consciousness, and so forth.

But *Psycho* is just one of many films that were produced and circulated during the 1960s that engage with issues of mental health in diverse and often contradictory ways. *Psycho* is itself a complex cultural and historical entity that raises as many questions about causes and conceptions of mental illness as it answers. Is Norman the dysfunctional creation of a tyrannical Mother, or is Mother an elaborate fantasy created by a calculating and murderous Norman? This is an issue that has divided critics since the film was first released. Is 'the Mother-part of Norman' a reliable narrator from whom to get the 'whole story'? Is the domineering and prudish Mother of *Psycho* a personality fabricated by Norman – a projection, perhaps, of his own disgust, shame and guilt, rather than the introjection of the real Mrs Bates' voice? Norman's version of his Mother does not necessarily correspond with other clues regarding her parenting history. Maybe she was a caring or, to quote paediatrician and psychoanalyst Donald Winnicott, 'good-enough mother'. Film scholar Tom Bauso goes further in claiming the 'murdered, buried, resurrected, stuffed, carried about the house, and spoken for' Mrs Bates as the 'archetypal unacknowledged victim of American cinema'.[3] The scene following Dr Richman's explanatory speech serves to underscore the unreliability of the testimony of the 'Mother-part of Norman', as her/his voiceover assuring us that 'Why, she wouldn't even harm a fly' is undercut by the brief superimposition of a grinning skull over Norman's face and then a dissolve to his/her victim's car – owned by lead character Marion Crane with her brutalised body in the boot – being pulled from the swamp. Even this one scene from this one film, therefore, belies the difficulty in unpacking the complex mediations and cross-pollinations of psychiatric and cinematic ideas and technologies in and across what Arthur Marwick identifies as the 'long 1960s'.[4]

Marwick identifies this period, of approximately 1958–1974, as one of 'interaction and acceleration' of political, economic, social and (counter) cultural movements, activities and ideas, ones that emerged in the fifties but became 'powerful practicalities in the Sixties'.[5] We identify the long 1960s, additionally, as a period of intense struggles over competing claims and understandings of the human mind, with psychologists, psychiatrists and psychoanalysts in deep conflict or, in some instances, uneasy alliances. This was the period of professional and public disputes over key developments in the 'psy' sciences (psychiatry, psychology, psychoanalysis), such as the clinical use of anti-psychotic and psychotropic drugs;[6] theories on the role of genetics and personality used to diagnose and treat behaviour labelled as deviant, psychotic or criminal;[7] theories of child development and attachment;[8] conformity, obedience and bystander apathy;[9] psychology's contribution to defining sexuality, gender and women's oppression;[10] the popularisation of psychotherapy;[11] and emergence of the 'anti-psychiatry' movement.[12]

It was also a period in which cinema and other popular media became preoccupied with the *Demons of the Mind*, with horror, science-fiction, crime, melodrama and thriller films, in particular, becoming key ways in which psychological concepts were disseminated as well as debated within the public sphere. Hollywood and British cinema invested heavily financially and creatively in exploring psychological ideas in overlapping cycles of genre films. Many were Anglo-American co-productions featuring the two countries' most celebrated directors and stars (Hitchcock, William Wyler, Otto Preminger, Joseph Losey, Lawrence Olivier, Noel Coward, Audrey Hepburn) and luminaries of New Hollywood and the British New Wave (Robert Altman, Peter Bogdanovich, Jack Clayton, Karel Reisz, Mia Farrow). These also spanned and hybridised a wide range of genres and explored a range of psychological themes and conditions: child development (*Bad Seed* (1956), *Peeping Tom* (1960), *Children of the Damned* (1964), *The Mind of Mister Soames* (1970), *The Beguiled* (1971), *Unman, Wittering and Zigo* (1971), *Child's Play* (1972), *Demons of the Mind* (1972)); motherhood and attachment (*The Innocents* (1961), *Inside Daisy Clover* (1965), *Bunny Lake is Missing* (1965), *Rosemary's Baby* (1968), *Secret Ceremony* (1968), *Trog* (1970), *The Exorcist* (1973)); legal understandings of insanity (*Compulsion* (1959), *Anatomy of a Murder* (1959), *In Cold Blood* (1967)); psychogenetics (*Twisted Nerve* (1968), *Goodbye Gemini* (1970), *The Other* (1972) *Sisters* (1973)); psychopathy, sociopathy and personality disorders (*Psycho* (1960), *Cape Fear* (1962), *Marnie* (1964), *The Collector* (1965), *The Psychopath* (1966), *The Boston Strangler* (1968), *10 Rillington Place* (1971), *Asylum* (1972)); schizophrenia (*David and Lisa* (1962), *Lilith* (1964), *The Third Secret* (1964), *Repulsion* (1965), *Images* (1972)); multiple personality disorder (*Lizzie* (1957), *The Three Faces of Eve* (1957), perhaps also *Psycho*); authoritarianism and obedience (*Lord of the Flies* (1963), *Punishment Park* (1971), *A Clockwork Orange* (1971), *The Wicker Man* (1973)); psychotropic drugs (*The Trip* (1967), *Psych Out* (1968), *The Big Cube* (1969), *Performance* (1970)); 'talk therapies' (*Freud* (1963), *The Caretakers* (1963), *Pressure Point* (1963)); anti-psychiatry (*Morgan: A Suitable Case For Treatment* (1966), *In Two Minds* (1967), *Family Life* (1971)), and so forth.

In discussing historical representation of mental illness in film, academic and critical debate has been dominated by a focus on the misleading correlation between mental illness and violent crime. This is perhaps understandable given the historical over-emphasis on violent psychopathic characters in Hollywood films and, more recently, television. From Hitchock's *The Lodger* (1927) to Norman Bates, from Hannibal Lector to the *Joker* (2019), the cinematic psychopath – usually male, often sexually motivated and, more recently, super-intelligent – has predominated. As a result, discussions of popular films within psychiatric journals have focused mostly on criticism of the over-emphasis on and misleading representation of psychopathy onscreen.[13] Although depictions of psychopaths and the links between mental illness and violent crime appeared from the silent era (and, of course, have a long history of antecedents conveyed in other media such as literature, theatre and television), the long 1960s period is the period that really established the model for the cinematic psychopath with Norman Bates. The success of *Psycho* prompted a cycle of cheap imitators in both America and Britain, such as *Maniac* (1963), *Paranoiac* (1963), *The Psychopath* (1966), which reproduced narrative and character traits of the earlier film. The pressbook for *Paranoiac* references *Psycho*, in stressing that this new film would resonate with current tastes – 'thrill movies that deal with the criminal subconscious are very much in demand' – but also positioned it as the continuation of a wider current 'trend' in psychological films that included *David and Lisa* and John Huston's *Freud*.[14]

The *Paranoiac* pressbook makes a distinction here between 'trends' and 'cycles', and their relationship to genre categories. As Tino Balio demonstrates, analysis of trade presses in the Classical Studio era highlights that producers, distributors and exhibitors understood films in terms of 'trends' and 'cycles'. Production trends operated as broader more enduring categories, some of which corresponded to generic definitions with which we are familiar – such as musicals and comedies – but others which transgressed genre categories and were defined by broad themes or production values, such as the enduring trend of the 'prestige picture'.[15] Trends are then broken down into component production cycles, which are shorter-lived and more responsive to, for example, imitating recent box-office successes or tapping into timely subjects and topical issues.[16] As the pressbook suggests, *Paranoiac* is most certainly part of a responsive cycle of 'Psycho' pictures, but can also be understood in the context of a wider trend across the long 1960s, of films dealing with psychiatric themes. In the midst of these converging Hollywood cycles, film scholar Stephen Farber made a case for a 'New American Gothic' – spanning films as diverse as *Lilith*, *The Collector*, *Bunny Lake is Missing* and *Inside Daisy Clover* – which he suggested combined elements of conventional psychological drama with 'Gothic excess' to 'achieve unexpected, trenchant insights' into psychological issues and experiences.[17]

A more holistic and historical understanding of these trends and cycles – across the long 1960s, across generic boundaries, across national cinemas, across specific diagnosis and conditions – is a key aim of *Demons of the Mind*. A key academic text that previously sought to explore psychiatric and cinematic relationships in a more detailed way, is the 1987 monograph *Psychiatry and the Cinema* co-authored by brothers Krin and Glen O. Gabbard, the former being a film studies scholar and the other a practicing psychiatrist. The book remains useful in its mapping of key historical shifts in representations from silent through classical and post-classical Hollywood cinema, and introduced key ideas such as the narrative trope of the 'cathartic cure' as discussed in Chapter 3.[18] However, the book separates rather than synthesises its authors' professional expertise in splitting the monograph into two parts: 'The Psychiatrist in the Movies' and 'The Psychiatrist at the Movies'. The first section maps the shifting depiction of psychiatrists and their methods in Hollywood films (on the whole celebrating the positive depiction of the professions in Hollywood's 'Golden Age' and bemoaning the mid-1960s shift towards more critical and thereby damaging depictions in later films). The second section offers psychoanalytically informed readings of a selection of these films with the aim of revealing their true or hidden meanings. Gabbard and Gabbard, therefore, separate and arguably hierarchise the(ir) two fields of expertise, understanding the influence of psychiatric ideas on cinema as unilinear, rather than seeking to understand the reciprocal or, perhaps, non-linear flow and reshaping of scientific knowledge and creative ideas.

Our tighter focus on the long 1960s timeframe, rather than the entire twentieth century, allows us to reflect on and interrogate evidence relating to this period of complex convergence and contention both within and between psy professions and cinema. Whilst there has been some interesting recent work on Hollywood depictions of psychiatric and psychotherapeutic practices at this time, they retain the focus on representation rather than material interaction.[19] *Demons of the Mind* is not just about the ways in which filmmakers interpreted and incorporated psy practitioners and theories into their films but, rather, on how filmmakers and 1960s cinema culture more generally constituted a marshalling and merging of psychological and creative expertise to both communicate and critique established (that is, conventional, hegemonic) and emergent modes of disciplining and governance associated with the psy sciences both on- and off-screen. Across the chapters of this book, we demonstrate the mid-1950 to mid-1970s as a period of significant co-production and contestation of scientific knowledge when both orthodox and progressive psychiatrists, child psychologists and leading psychoanalysts were employed as paid consultants on films and television; psy professionals were directly involved in making confidential decisions on censorship, classification and revision of scripts for the British Board of Film Censors (BBFC); a New York psychoanalyst was appointed to head up America's reoriented Classification and Rating Administration (CARA) as it shifted from a religious to psychiatric basis for decision-making; mental health organisations launched their own filmmaking training and production wings; Hollywood films dealing with mental institutions were screened in the US Congress and cited in the passing of major mental health legislation; and psychologists took up roles as film critics for the middle-brow press because of the increasing prevalence of psychological and psychedelic themes on screen.

Central to our research, like Marwick's, are ideas of 'interaction and acceleration'. We identify a number of different modes of interaction between medical and media spheres in and between the British and American contexts we are focusing upon, and the acceleration of trends emerging in the late 1950s (the liberalisation of censorship, for example) that made these interactions possible. In the first instance, we can understand interaction in terms of films being based on real case histories or other psychiatric texts. Whilst films had been (loosely) based on real cases prior to the late 1950s, this trend was certainly accelerated in the long 1960s period, with films being more explicitly based upon recent authenticated case histories and identified as such in their credits and promotion. The films that are the focus of three of the subsequent case study chapters, *The Three Faces of Eve*, *Freud* and *In Two Minds/Family Life*, are based on psychiatric case histories. What for us is also interesting is that, within the process of adaptation, there are interactions of this dominant psychiatric mode of writing with the respective Hollywood and British film genres and traditions: the 'woman's film', the biopic, the social realist drama. All of these films, and others in the book, also involve significant interactions of professional expertise in their conception, production, mediation and reception. As the chapters will highlight, the scientific consultation on these films went well beyond 'fact checking', often involving creative collaboration that shaped the content and style of the films in profound and, at times, unexpected ways. Whilst some of this creative interaction was sought by the filmmakers, others were brokered by the 'censors' – both the BBFC and the Production Code Administration (PCA) – as mechanisms to allow films based on contentious sources or subject matter to be depicted. In the process, these interactions not only shaped the individual films but also reshaped censorship policy, as Chapters 2 and 3 demonstrate. Even the conservative Catholic Legion of Decency, while initially seeing these films as a challenge to religious authority, resultantly began to shift and nuance its priorities and policies in the 1960s (see Chapter 1).

As these issues of censorship attest, the emergence of this greater psychiatric realism necessitated complex institutional relationships and alliances to enable production, but also promoted the practical use of film as a mode of mental health awareness, consciousness raising and political intervention, as well as a form of entertainment. Some of these relationships were more formalised, such as the British National Association for Mental Health's formation of the Mental Health Film Council, which sought not only to influence and intervene in commercial films, but also trained psy professionals to make their own, to counter perceived psychiatric misinformation within these entertainment films (as discussed in Chapter 2). However, as Chapters 5 and 6 highlight, this also involved political cooperation between progressive film-makers and progressive psy professionals who saw film as a synergistic means to raise awareness, even mobilise mass audiences. This included the British anti-psychiatry films, discussed in Chapter 5, which were made in collaboration with radical psychiatrists who wished to challenge the hegemonic bio-medical approaches to treating mental illness in Britain. Also, the Hollywood true crime film *In Cold Blood* (1967), discussed in Chapter 6, which, through an alliance with a group of reformist forensic psychiatrists, who saw all crime as motivated by treatable mental illnesses, sought to spread a controversial 'anti-punishment' message.

A number of these films also involved innovations in film and sound technologies to represent psychological states and authentic phenomeno-logical experiences, many of which were developed through interactions between expertise, techniques and technologies from medical and media fields. This included the innovative cinematic techniques for represent-ing regression and dreams discussed in Chapter 3, which sought to move beyond cinematic clichés and instil a sense of psychological realism into depictions of characters' inner worlds. In addition, new and emergent psy-chological theories and practices allowed for more discursive modes of character development and perceptual experiments on-screen, including non-linear narratives and expository forms, experimental sound design and compositional styles. Whilst filmmakers sought to use these innovations to represent patients' psychiatric experiences – both positive and negative – most of the films we analysed omitted direct input of patient or service-user experience and expertise. This is a serious oversight, which, in the early 1970s, helped to mobilise mental health movements to fight the omission or misrepresentation of their experiences, as discussed in Chapter 4.

In order to do justice to these complex convergences and contentions across a range of professional fields, a shifting psychological and political terrain, and two national contexts, we have, for *Demons of the Mind*, fos-tered an interaction between scholars in the fields of film studies, history of science and medicine, and science communication. There is overlap in the rationale if not terminology of the methods employed by the science communication and media scholars which have been used in the project. Science communication's circuit of mass communication and film studies' historical reception studies approaches seek to understand the complex interactions between processes of production, circulation and reception.[20] The former approach understands cultural texts as vehicles of scientific communication that can significantly impact cultural meanings of science. The latter understands cultural texts as contested spaces in which divergent cultural concerns and ideological interests compete and intersect during the specific material conjunctures of their production, mediation and consumption. A further unifying factor across our work is the belief in the value of the archive as a concrete mechanism to illuminate the complex contestations and cross-pollinations within and between the psy sciences, cinema and wider popular culture. To illuminate the complex discursive struggles enacted within the processes of production, mediation and consumption, as well as within the film texts themselves, later chapters will, having provided wider context, focus in on one or two case study films and analyse them in real depth.

More broadly, *Demons of the Mind* seeks to make a significant contribution to film studies in its ambition to understand and interrogate 1960s film culture's fixation with the psychological not as unconscious meanings or subject positions, but rather as a conscious and vigorously contested intermediation of medical, psychological, and psychiatric discourses and practices. Even for a perceived 'schlocky' horror film such as Hammer's *Paranoiac*, the promotion for this film, 'aimed at the arm-chair-psychiatrist', interpellates a psychologically sophisticated audience who will appreciate the film's 'clinical basis' in the classical theories of nineteenth-century German psychiatrist Richard von Krafft-Ebing, but also employs psychoanalytic concepts to explain 'the behaviour pattern as Freud might have put it' of audiences using films like *Paranoiac* to engage in self-analysis. Another pressbook article explains that nowadays the 'vocabulary of the man in the street includes complexes, traumas and phobias . . . One thing appears to be clear. The psyche is fascinating, probably because it concerns intimately everyone's own self.'[21] *Demons of the Mind* – which takes its name from a subsequent Hammer film that combines classic Gothic horror elements and X-rated gore with 'very serious' psychiatric history – seeks, like these Hammer films, to engage its knowledgeable audience by finding novel ways of interrogating the intersections between the fields of psychiatry and cinema.[22]

1

Morally acceptable madness: psychiatry, Catholics and censorship at the Legion of Decency

Hollywood's self-censorship organisation, colloquially known as the Hays Office, was established by Hollywood in 1922 as a response to protests by the Catholic Church and other religious organisations over what they considered to be immoral content in movies.[1] The ineffectiveness of the Hays Office led to religious groups again pushing for a governmental censorship organisation in the late 1920s. In 1930, studio heads agreed to abide by a code of standards called the Motion Picture Production Code, which was written by two prominent Catholics.[2] The Hays Office initially took a very lenient approach to the Production Code. From the perspective of religious protestors, the failure of the Hays Office to rigorously enforce the Production Code meant that movies were just as morally problematic as they were before its adoption. The Catholic Church had taken a particular interest in the moral status of movies. They threatened to form their own censorship group if the studios did not start adhering to the Production Code. This pressure led to the formation of the Production Code Administration (PCA) in 1934 run by the tough-minded Catholic Joseph Breen. But even the formation of the PCA, with the Catholic Breen in charge, could not prevent the Catholic Church from establishing its own censorship organisation, the Catholic Legion of Decency in 1934.[3]

The Legion of Decency's primary means for compelling studios to modify their scripts was their film classification system, which advised Catholics as to a film's moral acceptability. After receiving the PCA's seal of approval, studios would then submit their films to the Legion for classification prior to their theatrical release. Initially the Legion had four levels of classification: A-1 (morally unobjectionable for general audiences); A-2 (unobjectionable for adults); B (morally objectionable in part); and C (condemned).[4] Studios believed that a B or C classification would seriously affect their box office by driving significant numbers of Catholics away from the film, and they were willing to negotiate with the Legion to avoid this.[5] Studios' approaches included sending scripts for approval before filming and submitting completed films for review, which often involved recommendations of scenes to cut. The Legion wanted to make sure that film content was morally appropriate or, at the very least, make sure the texts were not blasphemous, indecent or legitimating what they considered to be dangerous ideas. Their concerns about morality were not limited to non-verbal, visual aspects such as sex and violence. The Legion was just as concerned with the portrayal of less tangible elements whose meanings were open to interpretation. These concerns encompassed representations associated with science, including the social, political and cultural aspects of scientific practice and knowledge.

The psy sciences were a topic of great concern to the Legion because psychiatry and psychoanalysis were historically problematic for the Catholic Church.[6] From the 1920s, Catholics associated psychiatry exclusively with the work of Sigmund Freud. The Church's initial hostility was grounded in the fact that Freud was extremely hostile to religion in his writing. Freud considered religious belief to be a kind of neuroses. Catholics also bristled at Freud's supposed 'pan-sexualism'. They considered the focus on sex in Freud's theories as an affront to a Christian sense of decency and threatened the foundation of sexual morality. In addition, the science of psychiatry made claims in areas that were already occupied by Catholic religious traditions. They believed that psychiatry not only took positions on fundamental issues of human nature and our place in the cosmos, but also on how we should act, think and feel.

Catholic critics also attacked psychiatry for its supposed determinism that was anchored in the drives-based model of the human psyche and which clashed with the axiom of moral responsibility for one's actions promulgated within Catholic doctrine. They believed that the 'irreligious materialism' of Freud's theories left no room for free will, morality or God. Many Catholic philosophers believed that psychology was strongly tied to an immaterial soul. Thus, that the nature of the subject matter made a scientific approach to psychiatry impossible, labelling psychiatry as 'psychology without a soul'.[7] Moreover, Catholics had long denied the notion of madness or mental illness in general where these conditions were instead claimed to be the result of moral weakness or demonic possession. Catholics associated psychiatry as a science largely with the method of psychoanalysis established by Freud. The Church felt that psychiatrists were claiming the psychoanalyst's couch as a replacement to the priest's confessional. So, they asserted the superiority of the sacrament of confession to solve personal problems rather than psychoanalysis. Catholics worried that through psychoanalysis psychiatrists were attempting to relieve patients of all sense of guilt without any admission of sin and depriving them of the guidance of a Christian conscience. This concern made Catholics very suspicious of psychiatry and outright hostile to psychoanalysis.

Catholic hostility towards the psy sciences, and especially psychoanalysis, took root in the 1920s and became accepted as unofficial Catholic 'doctrine' through the 1930s. This antipathy was evident in the Legion of Decency's classifications of films incorporating psychiatric themes from the 1930s through to the early 1950s. Before the mid-1950s, movie depictions that directly included psychiatry and psychoanalysis automatically received an 'adults only' classification and several were given B classifications indicating that they were morally objectionable in part. The Legion found Alfred Hitchcock's classic psychoanalytic film *Spellbound* (1945) to be objectionable merely because 'the story accepts a Freudian theory of psychoanalysis which is utilised as an important element in plot development and treatment'.[8] Likewise, they considered the British film *The Seventh Veil* (1945) to be morally objectionable because its psychoanalytic solution to a woman's acute depression and suicidal thoughts lacked 'adequate moral compensation'.[9] This suicidal character may have been cured of her delusions, but for the Legion this was not an acceptable narrative unless she was also put on the pathway to righteousness, which is something they believed that psychoanalysis could not do. In another case, the Legion objected to *Possessed* (1945) not because it involved a schizophrenic married woman trying to rekindle an adulterous affair and killing her former lover. Instead, the Legion considered the film problematic because its psychiatrist character characterised demonic possession as a disease of the mind.[10]

The Legion's reaction to cinematic stories about the psy sciences changed significantly after Pope Pius XII's 1953 speech at the Fifth International Congress on Psychotherapy and Clinical Psychology.[11] In his address Pope Pius declared that the principles of psychiatry and psychology could be reconciled with the doctrines of Catholic faith. The Church realised that psychiatrists could separate Freud's personal opinions about religion from his scientific theories, as well as segregating psychotherapy from Freud's deterministic philosophy.[12] In addition, Catholic psychiatrists distinguished between 'neurotic guilt' that occurred in the absence of wrongdoing and 'moral guilt' that was the result of moral transgressions. Psychiatrists could relieve a person of neurotic guilt, but moral guilt could be removed only through confessional absolution. Essentially, the Church was ready to acknowledge the benefits of psychotherapies in treating mental illnesses. They were also willing to admit that mental illnesses were real conditions that were not caused by moral failings or demonic possessions. The one area of the psy sciences that Catholic leaders were unwilling to accept was psychoanalysis. In fact, the Catholic governing body, the Holy See, published a denunciation of psychoanalysis in 1961 that prohibited Catholics, both analysts and patients, from utilising it as a psychotherapy.[13]

In this chapter we explore the negotiations between the Legion of Decency and film studios in the 1960s to understand their struggle over what constituted acceptable stories about the nature of human behaviour and the psy sciences as a personal, social, political and cultural force. After Pope Pius' 1953 speech, the Legion no longer considered stories involving psychiatry or psychology to be inherently problematical. But institutional and cultural changes in the 1950s and 1960s led to them changing their opinion of what constituted an appropriate story involving the psy sciences.[14] The Legion's censorship decisions for post-1953 films illustrate the Catholic Church's continuing conflict with the moral implications of psychiatric narratives. Film narratives including the psy sciences may have become acceptable to the Catholic Church, but they still wanted to control how psychiatric stories were told in movies. By controlling cinematic stories relating to psychiatry, the Legion of Decency believed they could regulate the meaning of the psy sciences themselves. The battle over cinematic depictions of psychiatry in the long 1960s was a battle over the impact of film on the public's belief systems and the wider cultural meanings of the psy sciences.

Rejecting 'inappropriate' cinematic narratives about the psy sciences

The Legion of Decency did not embrace every film with psychiatric or psychological themes after 1953. The Legion's response to the psy sciences post-1953 indicates that the Catholic Church remained conflicted about the moral implications of cinematic narratives about psychiatry and psychology. The 1957 film *I Was a Teenage Werewolf* illustrates their concern over the implications of psychiatric theories about inherited animalistic behaviours. The Legion gave the movie a B rating because it 'tends to give credence to certain philosophical theories whose acceptance can lead to serious moral harm'.[15] In the movie, a scientist explains that his goal is to use psychiatric techniques to regress a teenager back to an earlier evolutionary state of humanity:

> DR BRANDON: Through hypnosis, I'm going to regress this boy back . . . back into the primitive past that lurks within him. I'll transform him and release the savage instincts of life hidden within.
> DR WAGNER: And then?
> DR BRANDON: Then I'll be judged a benefactor. Mankind is on the verge of destroying itself. The only hope for the human race is to hurl it back to its primitive dawn . . . to start all over again.

Several other films of this period involved scientists using hypnosis to release humanity's inherited but submerged animal instincts. The scientist in *Blood of Dracula* (1957), for example, argues that these inherited bestial behaviours are an untapped psychiatric potential that represent 'a power strong enough to destroy the world buried within each of us', which can only be accessed through hypnotic experiments. As in *I Was a Teenage Werewolf*, she uses hypnotic experiments to unleash this psychiatric power in her teenage assistant who then kills several classmates. The Legion gave the film a B classification because the 'film tends to give credence to an erroneous philosophy of the origins of human life'.[16]

It might seem surprising for the Legion to respond so negatively to such absurd low-budget horror films, especially since the Catholic Church had significantly shifted its views on the psy sciences. But the Catholic Church's acceptance of psychiatric narratives was conditional; they accepted these explanations only as long as psychiatric theories did not make claims that it could explain human actions beyond simplistic behaviours and severe mental illnesses. Pope Pius XII explained in his 1953 address on psychotherapy that the Church was concerned when psychological science 'encroaches on the moral domain' and claims 'control of the conscience and of the soul'.[17] In these cases the pope said that the Church would not accept any psychiatric explanations that would 'lower man, in the concrete, along with his personal character, to the level of the brute'.[18] This meant that while the Church accepted the notion that mental illnesses were legitimate medical conditions they did not like any assertion that human behaviours were the result of inherited animal instincts. Suggesting that inherited animalistic elements in the human psyche could explain sinful behaviours such as murder or adultery, as the characters in these films do, was certainly an unacceptable interpretation of the psy sciences for the Legion.

The scientists' use of hypnosis to 'regress' their teenage subjects in both films points to a link between psychology and Darwinism. The theory of evolution is a fundamental assumption for modern psychology. Darwin's writings were a major influence on the field of psychology and on Sigmund Freud's theories. According to Lucille Ritvo, Freud made it clear that Darwinian theory was 'essential to psychoanalysis' and that it 'has always been present in Freud's writings, albeit never explicitly'.[19] Frank J. Sulloway similarly argues that 'Freud, ethology, and sociobiology share a common evolutionary heritage.'[20] Freud derived concepts such as the libido, id and psychosexual stages from the Darwinian notion that behaviours are the result of a few basic animal instincts produced by natural selection to facilitate survival. As with the pope's guarded acceptance of clinical psychology and psychotherapy in 1953, his 1950 papal encyclical acknowledged biological evolution as consistent with Catholic theology.[21] So, the linking of evolutionary thought with the psy sciences was not inherently problematic. However, these two movies advanced the idea that human behaviours were fundamentally driven by inherited animal instincts. The Catholic Church considered that notion to be a particularly alarming misapplication of Darwinian-informed psychiatric thought.[22]

The Catholic Church took issue with any scientific explanation, including those coming from the psy sciences, which removed personal responsibility from an individual's actions. For Catholics, sinful actions stem from choices made using God's gift of free will.[23] They are not, as scientists in these films claimed, the product of 'primitive instincts' inherited from our animal ancestors. From the Legion of Decency's perspective, these fictional scientists appeared to be offering absolution to sinners using scientific explanations based on Darwinian-informed psychiatry. The fact that these were frivolous low-budget horror films made the underlying ideas more worrisome. The Catholic Church viewed these as exploitation films aimed squarely at teenagers who might not be able to think through the moral implications of this philosophical position. After 1953, the Church may have become more open to the psy sciences, but combining psychiatric explanations with human evolution in film narratives was too dangerous even in 'grade-Z' movies like *I Was A Teenage Werewolf* and *Blood of Dracula*.

Free will and the threat of psychiatric essentialism

The Legion found the idea of inherited animal instincts disturbing because it represented an essentialist explanation for human behaviour. Despite the Church's growing acceptance of psychotherapy, they still saw a strain of biological essentialism in mainstream psychiatry where psychology becomes destiny rather than one determinant among many for a person's behaviour.[24] This meant that the Legion was vigilant in denouncing cinematic stories where scientific explanations made a character's actions seem inevitable rather than voluntary. One reviewer's comments about *The Mark* (1961), for example, illustrates how Catholic concerns about psychiatry, mental health and free will actually reflected the larger question of free will and sin, 'Where does "free-will" stop and "sickness" begin? And if that be admitted in this connection, could not it be transferred to other moral transgressions?'[25] Catholicism is a religion built around sin. Sin requires free will. By showing that people are not always in control of their behaviours the psy sciences cast doubt upon the notion of free will and, thus, called into question a major component of Catholic belief.

The Legion's reaction to the prologue for the 1962 bio-pic *Freud* illustrates their concern about films embracing psychiatric essentialism. Given the Church's historic antipathy to Freud and his ideas, *Freud*'s production studio, Universal-International Pictures, was concerned about receiving a potential B or C classification from the Legion. The studio screened the completed film for the Legion's reviewers with instructions to let them know if anything needed to be changed to avoid those classifications. The assistant executive secretary of the Legion at the time, Father Patrick J. Sullivan, relied on the opinion of psychiatrist Father William Bier to guide his decisions about requiring changes.[26] Overall, Bier was pleased with the film's handling of Freud's ideas calling it 'a superior film, competently directed'. The only problem he had with *Freud* was the narrated prologue opening the film. He believed that the prologue was 'not well done' because it 'contains the gratuitous suggestion of a conflict between the unconscious and human freedom, which is neither true nor necessary for the film'.

The prologue's conceit was to contextualise Freud alongside two other famous scientists whose work altered humanity's conception of itself, Copernicus and Darwin. The original prologue mentioned Copernicus destroying humanity's geocentric view, Darwin placing humanity within the animal kingdom, then said:

> Before Sigmund Freud, man believed that what he said and did were the products of his conscious will – but the great psychologist demonstrated the existence of another part of our mind which functions in darkest secrecy and requires our blind obedience.[27]

For Bier, the prologue's claim that humans are 'blindly obedient servants of [their] unconscious' made the entire film unacceptable. He told Sullivan that the prologue was crucial to how audiences would interpret the depiction of Freud's work in the film because it served 'as an editorial [setting] the tone of the picture'.[28] Therefore, the Legion requested a revised prologue that removed the words 'requires our blind obedience' and replaced them with 'can even rule our lives'. For Universal-International Pictures this seemed like a minor alteration and one they were more than willing to make to avoid a B or C. For the Legion, however, the new prologue made it clear that Freud's ideas may have identified a new factor in shaping human behaviour, but his scientific concepts did not negate free will.

The 1956 film *The Bad Seed* took an extreme position in the debate over nature versus nurture. The film is based on the 1954 novel *The Bad Seed*, which was written in the style of 'literary naturalism' that interpreted human behaviour in deterministic, biological terms.[29] Naturalist novels eschewed environmental explanations and focused on hereditary lineages as the sole cause of aberrant human behaviour. The film portrays an eight-year-old girl, Rhoda, as someone without a conscience who either directly kills or causes the death of at least three people. The film makes it clear that her sociopathic nature is entirely due to genetics rather than her upbringing. In fact, the film stacks the deck against nurture by establishing that the murderous Rhoda was raised in an almost perfect environment. She has two financially stable and happily married parents that dote on her. The film then establishes the overriding importance of heredity in determining behaviour by introducing a famous mystery author who tells Rhoda's mother, Christine, that many criminologists and behavioural scientists promote the idea of inherited criminal tendencies. He further claims that most female murderers start young and come from advantageous backgrounds. Ultimately, Christine learns that she was adopted and that her biological mother was a notorious female serial killer. Christine concludes that Rhoda inherited her biological grandmother's genetic propensity for murder and that no upbringing would have prevented the girl's homicidal nature.

The Hays Office was initially very concerned about studios turning this story into a film.[30] The theme of heredity and criminality was not an issue for them. Instead, they were concerned with a young girl being shown as a murderer and the impact they believed this depiction would have on young viewers.[31] Ultimately, the Hays Office approved the script after the studio changed the original ending so that the girl was punished by an act of God. Although this ending may have solved the issue of copy-cat child murderers it left the theme of heredity equalling destiny intact. The Legion had issues with depicting a child murderer on screen, but they also expressed concern about the film's message about violence and genetics.

A series of articles about the film in Catholic newspapers and magazines, including *America*, *The Catholic Messenger* and *The Pilot*, explained in detail why the idea of inherited criminality was problematic for Catholic viewers.[32] Monsignor Thomas J. Riley used his 'Theology for Everyman' column in *The Catholic Messenger* to address the theological implications of *The Bad Seed*'s science in a piece titled 'Can We Inherit Criminal Compulsions?'[33] He explains that according to Catholic theology 'free will' is the 'basis of morality'. But we can be said to have free will only if our actions are determined solely by our conscious choices. If human behaviour is based on our genetic makeup, then free will cannot exist because our actions would no longer be based on intentional choices. They would instead be determined by our genetic propensities. In the context of *The Bad Seed*, Rhoda clearly broke the law and committed horrific deeds. But if the film's psychiatric explanation was true, then we could not claim that her actions were immoral because she could not have voluntarily resisted her genetic propensity for murder. Riley argued that the idea that someone's genetics would impel them to kill, especially a small child, was impossible to reconcile with the centrality of free will in Catholic theology. For Catholics sin is a choice, not a genetic predisposition.

Riley made it clear, however, that the Church's rejection of genetic determinism in *The Bad Seed* was not meant to be an endorsement of the idea
that a person's developmental environment determined their psychological
makeup. From a Catholic perspective, individuals who embrace environmental explanations for human behaviour are just as guilty of denying free
will as biological determinists. According to Church doctrine, both sides of
the nature versus nurture debate are subverting free will by ascribing behaviours to the 'uncontrollable forces of heredity and environment'. From this
perspective growing up in poverty is no excuse for engaging in criminal
behaviour, just as growing up in a wealthy family does not ensure living a
moral life. Free will means that moral behaviour emerges only through 'self-
discipline' and the 'training of conscience', which can be developed no matter in what developmental environment a person was raised. According to
Riley, biological and environmental determinists were 'blaming our parents
for our own sins or regard[ing] our environment as merely a stimulus for
impulses over which we have no voluntary control'. This stance meant that
the Catholic Church would have been equally disapproving of *The Bad Seed*
if the film had blamed her murderous personality entirely on the environment in which she was raised.

Hypnotism, brainwashing and mind control

The Catholic Church's acceptance of psychiatric practice in the 1960s
came from a growing belief that psychiatrists could do much to emancipate
patients from compulsions that took away free will such as addiction, phobias and panic disorders. But they were still worried about a few psychiatric
therapies because they seemed to operate by controlling a person's psyche.
Hypnosis produced a trance-like state that opened up the subject to suggestion and could, therefore, be used therapeutically to treat anxiety and phobias. For the Church, the therapeutic potential of hypnosis was outweighed
by the dangers of a technique where the hypnotised individual seemed to be
a powerless subject of the hypnotist's commands. It did not help hypnotism's
reputation with the Church that the technique had primarily been deployed
by charlatans and music hall entertainers.[34] Hypnotism had been a concern
for the Legion of Decency since the 1930s. For example, the Legion threatened to condemn the film *Sleep, My Love* (1948) until the studio removed
dialogue indicating that a man was using drugs to hypnotise his wife.[35]

By the late-1950s they had accepted the inclusion of hypnosis if it was
clear to audiences that the technique was dangerous in the hands of amateurs, as was the case for *The Hypnotic Eye* (1960), or that trained medical

professionals were deploying hypnotherapy as in *Freud*.[36] If a story seemed to condone amateurs practicing hypnotism, then the Legion was quick to let studios know that this was unacceptable. This was the case when they negotiated with Paramount Pictures over the production of *The Search for Bridey Murphy* (1956). The best-selling 1956 book *The Search for Bridey Murphy* created a cultural sensation with its supposedly 'true' story of an amateur hypnotist, Morey Bernstein, regressing a woman into the past where she recalled earlier lives.[37] Given the story's sensationalist nature it was not surprising that Paramount Pictures wanted to buy the book's film rights even before its publication.[38] Paramount sent an unpublished copy of the book to the Hays Office to get their opinion on the story's suitability under the Production Code. The Hays Office told the studio that the story 'would offer no basic problems under the Code'. However, they knowingly warned them that the story 'would most certainly run into the most severe difficulties with the Legion of Decency'.

To get ahead of any problems with the Legion the studio sent them the script asking for their opinion.[39] The Legion told the studio in no uncertain terms that they had two fundamental problems with the script: reincarnation and hypnotism. The story's inclusion of reincarnation perverted Catholic doctrine about the judgement of the soul after death and its placement in Heaven, Hell or Purgatory. More importantly, they believed that 'the presentation of hypnotism (granting that it has legitimate therapeutic function in society) in the mass medium of film would be an incentive to quackery and is potentially morally harmful'. From their perspective the film depicts hypnotism in such a way that even the most 'uninformed' audience member would be able to replicate the technique. Although the script included an anti-hypnotism Catholic priest character, the Legion found that character to be 'weak' and seemed to approve the hypnotic regression. Further, the Legion warned the studio that the Catholic Press has already thoroughly discussed the book and that lay Catholics 'have already been forewarned that this material is a serious danger to faith and morals'.

Producer Pat Duggan's response reflected the studio's willingness to compromise with the Legion on the issue of reincarnation. He agreed to film the hypnotised woman, Ruth Simmons, in a way that made it clear that the 'regression' is all in 'her imagination and not an objective attempt on the part of the film to recreate a realistic past life'.[40] Duggan's response to the issue of hypnotism, however, revealed his exasperation with the Church's demand that the movie reflect Catholic moral beliefs about the power of hypnotism. The studio did make some concessions by changing the script to emphasise 'Bernstein's shortcomings as a practical hypnotist'. They also 'made it abundantly clear by the final hypnotic session that hypnotism is dangerous except in the hands of a qualified medical expert'. They even added some new dialogue for Bernstein denouncing amateur hypnotism:

> The whole reason hypnotism is cold-shouldered by medicine and science is because phonies like the feller you're talking about try and turn a serious medium into a load of baloney and set hypnotism back another hundred years.

The fact that Bernstein nearly kills Ruth during the final session also showed the dangers of the technique. From Duggan's perspective, the studio had gone to great lengths to make sure that the film was not disseminating a pro-amateur hypnotist message.

Yet Duggan also made it clear that the studio considered many of the Legion's demands unreasonable. He maintained that Paramount was 'committed to portray the experiment in hypnotism as published by Morey Bernstein' in a documentary style.[41] This documentary style meant adhering to the fact that Ruth was a Protestant and not a Catholic. They were unwilling to put words in Ruth's mouth that reflected Catholic doctrine on hypnotism because the real woman was a Protestant as was her supposed earlier incarnation Bridey Murphy. Duggan testily told them that the film's depiction of hypnotism could not be 'a perversion of traditional Catholic dogmatic doctrine' because the person espousing these views is 'not within the Catholic Church, any more than are the millions of Jews, Protestants, Mohammedans, Buddhists, Brahmans or theosophists in our world audience'. Duggan's writing also clearly indicated his irritation with their complaints about the priest character as 'weak'. The studio specifically created that character to put across the Catholic point of view to non-Catholics in a sympathetic manner. If the studio changed the character as the Legion suggested, then the priest would no longer come across as thoughtful. Instead, he would come across as an unsympathetic 'scold', which would defeat the purpose of introducing the character in the first place.

Duggan argued that a moralising priest character would not be the most effective means for getting the audience to accept the Church's position. The priest character would have an obvious interest in dismissing hypnotism and would make the film feel like watered down Catholic propaganda. He wanted the Legion to instead appreciate the fact that the script included three sceptical scientist characters that audiences could take as totally objective:

> The three professors are equipped to present the arguments against hypnosis and reincarnation, dispassionately and without private axes to grind. This being, in our opinion, the most realistic and rational form of presenting arguments that we wish the audience to accept.[42]

In the end, Duggan's arguments failed to sway the Legion as to what would make the script acceptable. The Legion still wanted a religious figure to be the centre of the anti-hypnotism argument. They suggested that a Protestant priest character could serve that role, an idea that the studio loved.[43] The studio also tried to stave off further criticism by consulting with Catholic and Protestant priests, psychologists and hypnosis experts.[44]

Ultimately, nothing the studio did to accommodate the Legion's critiques made any difference. Perhaps the studio's modifications and arguments prevented a C (condemned) classification. But the film still received a dreaded B classification for its 'undue emphasis on the power and effect of hypnotism, as presented in this picture, without clearly establishing the necessary moral precautions can lead to serious misinterpretation.'[45] No matter how many sceptical priest or scientist characters the studio added, they could not overcome the fact that audiences would have witnessed Ruth's hypnosis, her discussions of past lives, and flashbacks of her life as Bridey Murphy. The Church's distaste for hypnotism was far too great for the Legion to sanction a film that clearly demonstrated how dangerous a psychological tool the method could be.

For the Catholic Church an even more frightening use of hypnotism emerged in the 1950s. The idea of 'psychological warfare' gained traction in the mid-1950s with fears in the West about communist governments brainwashing American and British POWs in the Korean War.[46] For Catholics brainwashing was a nightmare moral scenario. The Catholic Church had a long history of anti-communist rhetoric.[47] The idea of communists using drugs, hypnosis, sensory deprivation and other psychological techniques to completely remove a person's free will and turn them into Soviet agents invoked the same level of dread as demonic possession. Hollywood movies became the central cultural outlet for the West's fears of communist brainwashing in the late 1950s.[48] The Legion's response to these films reveals a conflict that pitted the Legion's hostility towards brainwashing against their desire to see movies warn Americans about communists' use of these techniques.

The Manchurian Candidate (1962) was the most well-known brainwashing film of the era. The plot involves a captured American soldier who was brainwashed during the Korean War with orders to assassinate a US presidential candidate. All the Legion's reviewers were horrified at the thought of communist brainwashing. A few reviewers wanted to give the film a B classification because they found the communist brainwashing plot to be irresponsible. One reviewer even wanted the film condemned because he believed it was 'politically and culturally dangerous.'[49] Most other reviewers believed that the film was not morally problematic for American audiences because, in their opinion, the Soviets were employing these insidious techniques in the real world. Rather than condemning the film, they wanted it to serve as a warning about the type of psychological warfare that the Soviets were willing to employ. One reviewer, for example, found the brainwashing plot to be revolting. However, she was willing to overlook her concerns because she had spent time in Korea before the war and was 'all too familiar with the lengths to which the Russians went to further their diabolical ends.'[50]

Disagreement amongst the Legion's reviewers about the suitability of brainwashing for the popular medium of cinema was just as pronounced when the brainwashing was undertaken by scientists from Western countries. The 1963 British drama *The Mind Benders* involves a brainwashing plot in which a scientist attempts to prove the efficacy of sensory deprivation by brainwashing himself so that he stops loving his wife. Some reviewers were in favour of condemning the film because they felt that it conveyed a false impression that scientists could completely remove the freedom of choice given to us by God.[51] Other reviewers, however, felt that the story was a powerful rebuttal to the notion that scientists could control the human will using psychological techniques. They took this position because at the end of the film the scientist's brainwashing is undone by the birth of his child. One reviewer, Father Sal Miragliotta, felt very strongly that the movie was a 'cogent psychological study' whose ending provided a strong spiritual counterpoint to the potency of brainwashing.[52] According to Miragliotta, 'the intrinsic good in birth and motherhood is, in itself, a powerful enough antidote to remove any destructive thoughts rightfully induced in man'. Miragliotta argued that the 'forceful, spiritual value' of a birth would cause a person's subconscious to wrest control away from the 'conscious evil' of brainwashing. Ultimately, Miragliotta's argument convinced the Legion to classify the film as A-3 (adults only) rather than denounce the film with a B or C classification. The Church understood that psychological mind control techniques might exert a powerful effect on the human will. But they wanted the public to know that there were even stronger spiritual forces that could break these brainwashing effects.

The dangers of real-world psy science in fictional narratives

The use of obviously fictionalised psy science was certainly an issue since such overt fictionalisation could distort psychiatric ideas in dangerous ways. However, as the 'golden age of psychiatry films'[53] continued into the 1960s the Legion became more disturbed by fictional narratives deploying real-world psy science to validate problematic concepts. They felt that exposure to legitimate psychiatric ideas was only safe when they were conveyed by trained experts in a professional setting. From the Legion of Decency's perspective, the simplistic nature of movie narratives meant that the medium was incapable of providing this expert support. In their opinion the inclusion of psychiatric and psychoanalytic themes in films required expert intercession by real-life psychiatrists. Otherwise, these themes became dangerous because audiences would inevitably misunderstand the psychiatry. In fact, they thought that the more realistic the science was the more dangerous these misunderstandings would be because the science in the film would seem more legitimate.

The Legion's concern about realistic psy science in cinema grew as movie psychiatry became more accurate in the early 1960s, driven by the increased use of psychiatric consultants discussed across this book. Given science's general complexity, it has historically been useful for filmmakers to bring in science consultants to help them seamlessly integrate science into fictional stories.[54] As will be seen throughout this book, filmmakers were attempting to create more sophisticated cinematic stories at this time by utilising modern psychiatric theories and techniques that were nuanced and often controversial. Therefore, it made sense for filmmakers in the early 1960s to consult with psychiatric experts during production. Some censorship groups actively encouraged the use of psychiatric consultants during this period. Starting in the 1940s the Hays Office frequently recommended that studios with psychiatric themed films consult with working psychiatrists.[55]

The Legion's response to the classic 1965 psychological horror film *Repulsion* illustrates their concerns about films supported by authentic psychiatric theories. Since it was a British production, the British Board of Film Censors (BBFC) vetted the film before, during and after production to make sure it met with their standards (see Chapter 2). The film was meant to visualise the psychological deterioration of its female protagonist as she struggled with the repression and misogyny of the early 1960s. For the BBFC, the consultation with and resultant endorsement by their 'psychiatrist friend', Dr Stephen Black, was enough for them to pass the film uncut with an 'X' certificate, but for the American-based Legion of Decency, the film's scientifically authentic portrayal of a woman's psychological breakdown was exactly why the film was not suitable for any audience. The Legion 'condemned' *Repulsion* not because of its horrific elements but because the film's horror was based on underlying psychological theories that were dangerous unless the viewer was trained in psychiatry like Dr Black. The film's goal was to use ideas from the psy sciences to externally visualise a woman's inner mental deterioration. In doing so, the film allowed audiences to virtually experience her psychological breakdown.

Unlike the BBFC, the Legion felt that a movie was not the appropriate place to lay bare a woman's psychiatric wounds. They believed that most people in the audience would be harmed by such unadulterated access to a diseased mind. Several of the Legion's reviewers found the film to be excellent from an artistic standpoint. Miragliotta felt that Polanski's 'study of a mind sinking into madness, is cogently sustained in impeccable psychiatric exposition.'[56] While Father Stanley Grabowski believed that 'the artistry the director has fashioned [is] a tense visual interpretation of a mentally and emotionally disturbed girl.'[57] Despite *Repulsion*'s 'technical brilliance' the Legion concluded that the film's 'viewing can be a dangerously dehumanizing experience for anyone who is not a professional clinical psychologist.'[58] Although the main character's actions would have been disturbing on their own, the film would not have warranted any more concern from the Legion than any other horror film. But the suggestion that the film's imagery and mental health depictions were grounded in real-life psychiatric science turned the story from scary to truly horrifying in their minds. Despite reviewers praising the film's artistic merits, the Legion gave it the dreaded C classification. From the Legion's perspective psychiatric authenticity was the real horror.

The Legion felt that any inclusion of psychiatric or psychoanalytic themes in films required expert intercession by real-life experts or these themes became dangerous. The Legion's handling of the 1962 'biopic' *Freud* provides another example of how censors worried about the inclusion of real-world psy science in fictional narratives without appropriate expert guidance for the audience. More importantly, it also demonstrates their own deference to the psychiatric community. It is clear from the archival material that the production studio, Universal-International Pictures, was very concerned about negative responses to the film from religious communities (see Chapter 3). Attempting to ward off potential censorship issues or religious protests they consulted with psychiatrists and theologians during early scriptwriting. Their primary science adviser was Dr Earl Loomis, a psychiatrist and theologian from Union Theological Seminary.

In his review of the initial script Loomis addressed the accuracy of the science, the characterisation of the scientists, the ethical and religious implications of Freud's psychiatric theories, and the potential emotional impact of the story on audiences.[59] He found the scientific accuracy of the film to be excellent, especially in terms of the mechanisms of the mind. He also thought that the script was morally sound and that it underplayed Freud's issues with religion. He concluded that there was nothing offensive for religious people and that the story conveyed good moral messages (such as, try to understand yourself and your faults; do not give up in the face of adversity; do not settle for half-truths, and so on). Overall, he believed that the filmmakers did a great job portraying 'the birth of a science'.

Despite this extensive preparation, the studio still worried there might be censorship problems because in the public's mind Freud's scientific theories were synonymous with sex. The film's producer William Gordon understood that manoeuvring the studio's proposed Freud biopic past the censors was going to be difficult and that the 'subject matter requires very special, delicate treatment and handling from its inception'.[60] Therefore, Gordon sent the initial script to the Legion as a way to pre-empt any censorship problems before the studio began production. The Legion then asked several priests to review the script and offer their opinions on its suitability for the screen.[61] The priests who reviewed the script agreed that the narrative was not sensationalised. They also felt that the story treated Freud's development of his theories about human sexuality in a restrained and sensitive fashion. They decided that any reasonably intelligent person watching the film would be able to understand these scientific theories without concluding that they were all about sex.

The priests' problem with the script, however, was the fact that they did not believe that most moviegoers were reasonably intelligent people. Father James Ray's sentiments were typical of their attitude towards public audiences, '[The script] is suitable for a specialised audience but hardly for unlettered adults, who would tend to dwell on the more sensational aspects of the exposition.'[62] From the priests' perspective, the average viewer would not be able to comprehend Freud's complex scientific ideas and, thus, they would misinterpret the narrative and the moral implications of his science. The Legion made it clear that such misunderstandings would be 'dangerous.'[63]

The Legion's priests did not think that the public would be able to understand Freud's theories and their moral implications without the assistance of an expert guide like a psychiatrist or a priest. Catholic theologian and literary critic Reverend William F. Lynch made it clear in his review of the script that these ideas required extensive consultation with a trained psychiatrist, not 2 hours in a movie theatre:

> These materials are usually explored under the protection and safeguards of the professional analytic situation, and they take a long, careful time to explore. Doing the same thing in a brief powerful movie is open to the same charge that Dr Freud brings against Dr Breuer in the text of the ms. (sic): the truth is powerfully given without sufficient help.[64]

In fact, Lynch conceded that even priests might not possess enough expertise to determine the suitability of the science in the script by claiming, 'I do not believe it is a question to be resolved by the clergy.' Instead, he recommended that the Legion endorse the script only if they had assurances from the American Psychiatric Society and the American Psychiatric Association (APA) that the science in the script was safe for presentation in the powerfully persuasive medium of cinema. Unlike in earlier time periods, the Legion did not confidently pass judgement on the appropriateness of a film's depiction of the psy sciences. By deferring this decision to these psychiatric societies, they allowed a scientific community to determine the most appropriate messages about Freudian psychiatry.

Hitchcock's pop psychology and 'psychiatric science fiction'

While the Legion deferred to professional psychiatrists when the depiction of real-world psy science was involved, there was often the question of which cinematic depictions counted as genuine psy science and which depictions were merely 'pop psychology'. The Legion assumed that if their reviewers could not tell whether the psychology was real or not, then surely audiences would not be able to tell the difference between real and pop psychology. Their concern over the moral danger of cinematic psychology meant that they did not want filmmakers engaging in pop psychology that explained away their characters sinful behaviour. Popular psychiatric explanations for madness and psychopathic behaviours were frequent themes in the films of Alfred Hitchcock.[65] Hitchcock's celebratory treatment of psychoanalysis in *Spellbound* played a significant role in creating the boom in psychoanalytically driven movies in the 1940s.[66] Two of Hitchcock's films in the early 1960s, *Psycho* (1960) and *Marnie* (1964), caused the Legion difficulties because they believed that the psychological explanations that each film put forward to explain characters' immoral behaviours were nothing more than what one Legion reviewer called 'psychiatric science fiction'.[67]

There was plenty in *Psycho* for the Legion to hate that had nothing to do with its pop psychology. The story involved a sexually active unmarried woman stealing money who is violently murdered by a sexually deviant motel owner. But overt violence and sexual activity were not the only reasons the Legion gave for their threat to condemn the film. The Legion also objected to the idea that multiple personality disorder explained Norman Bates' actions. They considered the notion that there were two unique people inside Norman's head to be pop psychology rather than based on sound science. One reviewer's labelling of the film as unconvincing 'psychiatric mumbo-jumbo' sums up the general opinion of the Legion's reviewers.[68] The reviewers were concerned with the film's psychiatric explanation because the notion of two distinct personalities within a single person's mind conflicted with established Catholic doctrine on the nature of the soul.

Although several reviewers raised this issue, Father Daniel J. O'Donnell provided a detailed explanation for why the film's pop psychology interpretation of multiple personality disorder was theologically problematic.[69] According to O'Donnell, the film's explanation was conflating two different mental disorders – disassociation through multiple personalities and transference of personality. A patient exhibiting multiple personality disorder has a primary personality and a secondary personality, which is repressed and competes with the primary personality for dominance. O'Donnell explains that the secondary personality is derived from the subconscious material of the primary personality. This secondary personality does not represent an entirely separate person as the film implies. That would be the phenomenon of transformation of personality which entails the person believing that they are a completely different person (for example, Jesus or Napoleon). O'Donnell understood why Hitchcock combined the two disorders for dramatic reasons. But from a Catholic perspective the conflation of these two disorders indicated that Norman's mother has replaced Norman and, thus, the mother's soul had co-existed with Norman's soul in his body.

For Catholics the idea of two souls in one body had disturbing theological implications. Several films in the 1940s had run into problems with the Hays Office over this same issue when it was run by the staunch Catholic Joseph Breen, as was the case for *Bewitched* (1945).[70] On its own this theological issue would not have been enough for the Legion to threaten condemning the film at this point in their operation. But the issue added some more weight to their argument for condemnation when they confronted Paramount Pictures about their concerns.[71] Ultimately, they were most concerned about the scene of Norman spying on a woman undressing and the extreme violence when Norman, dressed as his mother, stabs a private investigator. In their negotiations with Paramount their complaint about the theological implications of the psychiatrist's explanation could easily be bargained away so that they could get what they really wanted, which was the shortening of those two scenes.[72]

With Hitchcock's movie *Marnie* the Legion was not worried about the theological issues surrounding the film's pop psychology. Rather, they were concerned that Hitchcock was using pop psychology to excuse Marnie's immoral behaviours. Most of the Legion's reviewers appreciated that the film did not glamorise Marnie's thievery or her aversion to men. But they wanted the film to punish her in some way for these actions. Instead, the film provided a psychological rationalisation for these behaviours. Marnie's husband Mark conducts some 'armchair psychology' and traces her obsessions back to repressed memories of a traumatic childhood experience. This revelation cures her mental illness and, since Mark paid off her former robbery victims, she faced no punishment. For the Legion's reviewers this ending was problematic.

According to one reviewer the filmmakers were essentially using pop psychology to excuse her crimes, calling it 'a rather far-fetched attempt to explain her compulsion to steal'.[73] For another reviewer, Hitchcock's film was just the latest example of what he saw as a growing trend amongst filmmakers using pop psychology to explain the neuroses of individual characters.[74] He not only considered pop psychological rationales for characters problematic from a moral perspective, he also believed that it wasted the medium's potential for exploring broader ideas. He complained that rather than aiming to reveal essential truths, these stories merely explained unusual individual behaviours by using implausible psychological solutions. He concluded that for 'some, the investigation of individual psychoses may qualify as entertainment but without the universality of Dreiser or Dostoyevsky it palls as dry as a psychiatrist's notebook'. The Legion believed that filmmakers in the 1960s were beginning to use legitimate psychology in intellectually and morally useful ways. But they were disappointed when filmmakers like Hitchcock instead chose to use pop psychology to excuse immoral behaviours.

Serious psychiatry versus sensationalism

Because the Legion of Decency did not trust the public to understand the complexities of psychiatric theories, they also worried that filmmakers were using the psy sciences to make sensationalistic films under the guise of scientific verisimilitude. The Hays Office and the Legion had consistently prevented filmmakers from including sexual content on the grounds that these depictions were merely gratuitous and did not fulfil any roles in most stories. But with the growing acceptance of psychological themes in films, filmmakers could use psychiatric explanations as the reason for including not only sexual content but what at the time was considered 'deviant' sexual content like lesbianism and nymphomania. If they were challenged by the Hays Office or the Legion, the studios could claim that there were legitimate storytelling reasons for the inclusion. If they were going to properly tell a story involving psychiatry, the studios argued, then this surely required them to depict the manifestations of legitimate psychiatric disorders no matter how immoral they were believed to be. The reviewers at the Legion were sceptical about many of these claims. They believed that filmmakers were often including scientific explanations just to have an excuse to include sensational content.

The plot of *Shock Corridor* (1963) involved a journalist getting himself committed into a psychiatric hospital asylum to investigate an unsolved murder. He then wrote an award-winning exposé about the mistreatment of inmates by the asylum's doctors and staff. Samuel Fuller wrote, produced and directed the film. Fuller claimed that he was making a socially conscious film that equated the societal 'madness' of the time (that is, nuclear proliferation and race relations) with the notion of personal madness. He also wanted to expose what he saw as the deplorable conditions of mental hospitals at the time.[75] Several reviewers at the Legion approved of the film's messages.[76] But many of the reviewers wanted the film to be given a B or C classification because they believed that Fuller incorporated specific psychiatric disorders just so that he could include sensationalistic sexual elements.[77] The Legion's assistant executive secretary, Patrick J. Sullivan, also found Fuller's claims to be dubious and threatened to condemn the film: 'Samuel Fuller may claim to be concerned with a social message of contemporary urgency, but the treatment he has given to the film is rank sensationalism for its own sake.'[78]

Sullivan and the Legion's reviewers complained that the film contained psychiatric disorders that did not seem crucial to its social message. From their perspective, several scenes were essentially just hyper-sexualised caricatures of Freudian psychiatry. This included a scene in which the male journalist is nearly raped by a group of women suffering from 'nymphomania' (see Figure 1.1).[79] One scene the Legion's reviewers found particularly problematic involved the head psychiatrist's assessment interview with the protagonist near the start of the film. As part of his plan to infiltrate the hospital, the journalist pretends that he has an 'incest fetish'. During the interview the psychiatrist asks him questions related to his supposed disorder such as,

Figure 1.1 A scene from *Shock Corridor* (1963) condemned by the Legion of Decency as being included in the film only for sensationalistic reasons

'Did you want to have your mother?' and 'Did you want your sister?' From the Legion's perspective this scene was unnecessary and only included for its salacious content.

The Legion's executive secretary Monsignor Thomas F. Little's letter to the studio, Allied Artist, asked them to explain the point of including an incest element if the only goal of that scene is for the journalist to convince the psychiatrist that he is insane and admit him to the asylum.[80] Little told them that were numerous other possibilities that could establish the journalist as insane that did not rely on an incest fetish or anything of a sexual nature. If the studio would not consider an alternative non-sexual disorder, then Little wanted them to explain how this specific disorder furthered the film's message. To avoid a C classification the studio compromised with the Legion. They were unwilling to remove the induction scene but they would edit it and a few other scenes to remove their most sensationalised aspects.[81] Instead of condemning the edited film, the Legion gave it a B classification. But in their justification for this classification, they made sure to note that the presence of these unnecessarily lurid elements robbed the film of its social message: 'Sensational subject matter and treatment so predominate in this film that any purported social message is completely lost.'[82] They wanted studios to know that despite their recent acceptance of psychiatric themes in cinema, the studios should not take their open-mindedness as an excuse to incorporate sexual material.

From the perspective of the Legion, which had been re-named the National Catholic Office of Motion Pictures (NCOMP) in 1966,[83] the psy sciences and mental health were serious subjects that were not meant to be portrayed in a frivolous manner. It was not acceptable to use real-world psychiatric ideas or techniques as an excuse to introduce sexual subjects. It was also not appropriate to include psychiatry for comedic purposes. The farce *A Fine Madness* (1966), for example, focused on an over-the-top hedonistic Greenwich Village poet, Samson, who engaged in problematic behaviours including drinking and promiscuity. Several of NCOMP's reviewers noted that while these behaviours were indicative of a 'moral anarchy' it was 'offensive to Christian standards of judgement and taste', nothing in Samson's behaviour warranted any more than an A-3 (adults only) classification.[84] But around half-way through the story Samson is placed into the Para Park psychiatric sanatorium. The story then turns into a dark comedic satire on psychiatry. The film treats Samson's psychological issues lightly and depicts psychiatrists as self-serving, deceitful and callous. For many reviewers such a farcical depiction of psychiatry and mental illness was unacceptable. One reviewer's comments sum up the attitude of most of them, 'Mental hospitals and their inmates are not material for comedy, much less caricature.'[85]

One storyline was considered particularly problematic because it involved a controversial psychiatric procedure. The first lobotomy took place in the United States in 1936. The procedure is an invasive form of neurosurgery that involves severing neurological connections in the brain's frontal lobes. Lobotomies were controversial from the outset given the destructive nature of the surgery and the uncertainty about long-term effects. Use of the technique increased dramatically in the 1940s and early 1950s, but it had largely disappeared from American medicine by the late 1950s.[86] In *A Fine Madness* one of the sanatorium's psychiatrists insists that his experimental form of lobotomy could control Samson's violent tendencies. Several other psychiatrists, including the sanatorium's director Dr West, oppose the experimental lobotomy on ethical grounds. After West catches Samson and his wife in bed together, however, West decides to throw away his ethical objection and allow his colleague to conduct the experiment.

Most Legion reviewers were angry that the film treated such a controversial and disturbing psychiatric procedure as a joke.[87] They were concerned that the film downplayed the potential harm of the psychosurgery by depicting it as having no effect on Samson. The fact that West was willing to abandon his moral position for selfish reasons was also problematic. NCOMP's response to the film's frivolous treatment of lobotomy is best summed up within Phil Hartung's extended review for the Catholic magazine *Commonweal*:

> One of the doctors at Para Park insists on performing a prefrontal lobotomy, his own version of this frowned-upon operation, on Samson. And from that point on, the fun and games in 'A Fine Madness' are over ... The blackness has set in and we find ourselves embarrassed at laughing at any events connected with this deadly serious subject.[88]

Ultimately, NCOMP assigned the film a B classification. Their justification was that the film's 'flippant approach to the serious ethical implications of psychiatric procedures becomes offensive.'[89] The Legion had become accepting of psychiatric themes in films, but they expected these films to treat the issue seriously. As the next section shows, they hoped that filmmakers would use the psy sciences to explore universal themes of human suffering and human dignity. However, if filmmakers insisted on deploying the psy sciences merely for showing sexual deviance or for low humour then NCOMP was prepared to keep Catholics away from their films.

The Legion certainly did not endorse filmmakers using legitimate psychiatry as an excuse for sensationalism. Yet the line between sensationalism and legitimate depiction was often unclear. If the Legion appreciated a film's artistic value and if the psychiatry was morally and scientifically sound, then they were willing to excuse behaviours that might otherwise have led to them condemning a film as sensationalistic. The Legion's response to Ingmar Bergman's *Through a Glass Darkly* (1961) shows how artistry plus sound psychiatry justified behaviours that would otherwise have been condemned as sensationalised. The film focuses on a woman, Karin, who learns that her schizophrenia may be incurable and the responses to this knowledge from her father, husband and younger brother. Karin has withdrawn sexually from her husband and there are some frank discussions of sexual themes. But for the Legion a scene strongly implying that she engaged in an incestuous relationship with her brother was the most problematic (see Figure 1.2).

The Legion's reviewers asked themselves the same questions that they asked about disturbing scenes in *Shock Corridor* and *A Fine Madness*: is this scene necessary? Does it serve a legitimate story function? Is the psychiatric explanation for the scene justified? Or is the psychiatric explanation merely an excuse for sensationalism? One reviewer felt that there were no story reasons that could justify including such a repugnant scene. From their perspective the audience just needed to know that the character was insane, they did not need to see her insanity displayed on the screen:

Figure 1.2 The Legion of Decency's concerns regarding this scene from *Through a Glass Darkly* (1961) was outweighed by their trust in filmmaker Ingmar Bergman

It isn't necessary, in the illustration of the battle of Good and Evil, to go into lewd details of how the Devil might manifest himself especially to a tormented mind. A person in that condition has no responsibility for his actions and cannot be judged, but what is gained by the rest of us getting a closeup on these sordid delusions?[90]

Most reviewers, however, recognised that Bergman considered the scene significant in representing the overlap between psychosis and sexuality for Karin. Yet the reviewers still struggled with whether they should allow such a scene. They understood that Bergman believed the scene was essential, but they had to determine for themselves if they believed his artistic reasoning justified it.

In the end the Legion decided to defer to Bergman's filmmaking expertise. They decided that if Bergman judged the scene to be essential then that must be the case. One reviewer's comments are representative of the Legion's decision to trust Bergman's judgement, 'Because it's Bergman, one has the tendency to go along with his presentation even without fully understanding his entire point of view.'[91] If it were a less respected filmmaker or if the psychiatry in the film had been shaky, then it is likely that they would have asked the studio to remove the scene or they would have condemned the film. But they trusted that Bergman's skill and the film's psychiatric underpinnings. In fact, the Legion was so taken with his handling of Karin's mental illness and the film's overall 'artistic quality' that they awarded the film their top prize as part of the 1962 Berlin Film Festival.[92] Ultimately, the Legion concluded that the line between sensationalised psychiatry and legitimate psychiatry was determined by expert filmmaking and sound science.

Moral psychiatry and elevating the dignity of human beings

The Legion of Decency's classification system was not just a warning to Catholic viewers about films that were morally problematic. Their classifications were also meant to provide guidance about which movies contained themes that were appropriate to their faith. For the psy sciences this meant that the Legion used their classifications and film reviews to highlight stories they found inspirational or which they believed reflected Catholic value systems. One type of story they appreciated were films that treated mentally ill characters like human beings that were suffering, rather than as side show freaks who were on display. For example, the film *David and Lisa* (1962) focused on two emotionally disturbed adolescents who were being treated at a home for mentally ill children. One character, David, did not want to be touched. The other character, Lisa, displayed multiple personalities. As 'Muriel' she was completely mute, while as Lisa she talked only in rhyme. The Legion's reviewers singled the film out for treating its characters compassionately. One reviewer felt that the film's 'sensitive and sympathetic portrayal' of these mentally ill characters merited an award.[93] Reviewers also appreciated how the film conveyed the complicated topic of psychiatry through its characters' actions rather than by overwhelming the audience with scientific jargon.

In his extended review for *Commonweal*, Philip Hartung applauded the film for its 'sound psychology'.[94] He endorsed the film's portrayal of psychiatry because the teenagers' road to recovery was not solely reliant on psychotherapy. The developing relationship between David and Lisa played a significant role in their path towards becoming healthy. For Hartung, and other Legion reviewers, this story element demonstrated the healing power of love and community for mental illness. He compared the film's message with that from *Freud* which was also in production in 1962, 'While *Freud* is coolly emphasising Know Thyself, *David and Lisa* is warmly teaching us to love and understand our neighbour.' This comment captures the Catholic Church's key hope for psychiatric treatment. They believed that while Freudian psychoanalysis might be useful in identifying potential causes for psychological problems, it is too inward looking and too focused on sex to be truly therapeutic. *David and Lisa* showed audiences that psychiatric techniques could be most useful when they also asked patients to look outside themselves for salvation. The Legion found this message to be so refreshing that they nominated the film for their highest honour at the International Catholic Office of the Film awards in 1965.[95]

The Legion liked the 1963 film *A Child is Waiting* so much they gave it a special recommendation encouraging Catholic audiences to see the film.[96] They understood that the film was not great cinema. But they admired the way it handled the subject of mentally disabled children so much that it overcame any issues reviewers had with it is as a piece of entertainment. They appreciated the film's realism in its depictions of mentally ill children at a psychiatric hospital. The film's depictions of children with severe mental disabilities were not over-sentimentalised. It did not treat these children as naive little angels. Instead, it portrayed them as real people with problems and needs.

The film's message is that these children should not be ignored just because they are different. The film addressed the question, 'why bother with these children when there is so little hope of improvement?' For the Legion, the film's answer mirrored what they believed was at the heart of Catholic values; we try to improve these children's lives because they are human beings.[97] This is why they felt, as one reviewer wrote, that everyone should see the film because it treated its subject 'with such great compassion and understanding that it adds one stature to the dignity of the human being'.[98] For the Catholic Church this was an important point, especially given that a major political issue in 1962 concerned funding for mental illness treatments. President John F. Kennedy had made funding a National Program for Mental Health one of his priorities for 1963.[99]

Several Legion reviewers felt that the film was an answer to Congressional critics of Kennedy's proposal. These critics claimed that resources would be wasted on children who, at best, would be able to work at menial jobs. They argued that these resources would be better spent on bettering children with the potential to become exceptional who could improve the country by becoming scientists or surgeons.[100] One reviewer summed up the Legion's belief that the film's message countered this line of reasoning in his extended review for *Catholic World* magazine. He contended that *A Child is Waiting* refuted critics' argument against Kennedy's proposal by showing audiences that every life has meaning and purpose even if that purpose is mundane. For him the film beautifully illustrated the notion that in God's eyes these mentally ill children were equal to any other person on earth. He finishes his review by asserting that because *A Child is Waiting* shows such respect for human dignity 'it is truly a significant motion picture'.

The Legion's decision to give the film a special recommendation turned out to be controversial within the broader Catholic Church because the film showed real mentally ill patients (see Figure 1.3). The filmmakers had chosen to include actual mentally impaired children in the production to add authenticity.[101] For the American Legion of Decency this was a powerful way to show audiences that these mentally ill individuals were still human beings. But the Legion's French equivalent, Office Catholique International du Cinéma, considered the inclusion of these children to be problematic because they felt that many audience members would be repulsed by visibly ill children.[102] The French organisation chided the Legion for giving the film a special recommendation and refused to recommend the film to French Catholics. The Legion's assistant executive secretary Sullivan responded to the French organisation defending their decision to give the film the recommendation, but they told them that each national organisation could decide for themselves whether they wanted to pass it on to their congregations.[103] Sullivan then made it clear that the Legion considered this concern to be unreasonable and should not prevent people from seeing a film with such an important message.

A review in the Protestant magazine *The Christian Science Monitor* had a different take on the film's merits than the Catholic Legion of Decency.[104] They were also impressed that it did not sensationalise the mentally ill children and treated them as equal human beings. But they had two complaints

Figure 1.3 Scenes involving real patients in *A Child is Waiting* (1963) caused disagreement between the Legion of Decency and the Legion's French equivalent, Office Catholique International du Cinéma

that conflicted with the Legion's opinions. Unlike the Legion they believed the film made a mistake in using real disabled people. They felt that audiences would be repulsed by these real patients and, thus, would not be able to empathise with them enough to buy into their plight. In addition, they were disappointed with the film's lack of a 'spiritual means of solution' to the children's illnesses. They wanted some acknowledgement that Christian spirituality and prayer were required for the alleviation of mental illnesses. Prior to 1953, the Legion would have agreed with that assessment. They would have insisted that the film acknowledge God's role in the treatment of mental disorders in *A Child is Waiting* and other films. But the Catholic Church's growing acceptance of psychotherapy and psychiatric interventions had changed the Legion's perspective on what constituted God's intervention in these treatments. In contrast to this Protestant film reviewer, the Legion was confident that God was playing a role in the psychiatric treatment of the children in the film. From the Legion's perspective God was there working through the medical professionals.

Praising the limitations and failure of psychoanalysis in *The Pumpkin Eater*

Occasionally the Legion endorsed a film not because they approved of its psy science content, but, rather, because the film criticised what Catholics considered the dangerous practice of psychoanalysis. For example, from a moral perspective *The Pumpkin Eater* (1964) presented obvious problems for the Legion. The movie contained an abundance of topics that on their own had resulted in B or C classifications for earlier films. The plot featured a twice divorced woman, Jo, whose third husband, Jake, engages in several extramarital affairs. Jo has at least eight children from her two previous marriages.[105] Jake does not want more children and believes that their marital difficulties stem from her being trapped in her domestic situation. When she becomes pregnant again Jake does not want her to have the baby. Following the advice of Jake and her psychiatrist, she gets an abortion and agrees to be sterilised. Divorce and infidelity were already problematic from a Catholic perspective, but the inclusion of abortion and sterilisation meant an automatic B or C classification for some reviewers. One reviewer felt that 'the abortion episode would be enough, in my opinion, to put it in the B classification.'[106] While another reviewer insisted they give it a 'B classification for the sterilisation episode.'[107]

Most reviewers, however, wanted the Legion to overlook these significant moral issues and to encourage Catholic viewers to see the film. One reason they gave for appreciating the film was that it showed average people facing marital problems and mental illness, not just 'ogres, moral degenerates [and] stereotypes of evil'.[108] But the primary reason so many Legion reviewers approved of the film had to do with how it depicts the failure and damaging effects of psychoanalysis. Jo is being treated for depression by a psychiatrist who considers her constant childbearing to be pathological. During a psychoanalytic session he concludes that she enjoys sex, but that she finds the act 'obscene' and 'messy'. He tells her that she needs to justify her sexual activity to herself, saying that 'sex is something you feel you must sanctify, as it were, by incessant reproduction'. He suggests that if she were to have another child this would be devastating for her mental health by exacerbating her depression. When Jo becomes pregnant again Jake convinces her to get an abortion for the sake of her health and their marriage. Based on the advice of her psychiatrist a judge agrees that an abortion is justified for health reasons and that she should be sterilised to prevent being put in this position again.

The psychiatrist's suggestion to separate sex from procreation was concerning to the Legion for several reasons. For one, Catholic theology held that the primary goal of marriage was procreation and the education of children.[109] But it also reinforced their opinion that psychoanalytic therapy always reduced psychological problems to sex. Even more disturbing for Catholics was the psychiatrist's encouragement of abortion and sterilisation as a solution to Jo's mental health issues. If the movie had stopped right after the surgeries or if the surgeries solved the couple's marital problems, then the Legion would have undoubtedly condemned the film. Instead, the abortion and sterilisation take place about halfway through the film. The second half of the film then demonstrated how little these surgeries did to cure Jo's mental health issues or solve the couple's marital problems. The film ultimately showed that the psychiatrist's advice about the therapeutic value of abortion and sterilisation turned out to be detrimental to Jo and her family.

The Legion's reviewers were almost gleeful in their discussion of how less happy Jo's life became after her abortion and sterilisation. According to one reviewer, 'Abortion is shown to be a cold and brutal operation that proves to be no solution at all for the woman's problems.'[110] For another reviewer, 'The abortion and sterilization were not portrayed as the key to any real, lasting happiness . . . The continued frustration felt by Jo after her sterilization obviates much of its supposed psychological benefits.'[111] These comments were typical of most reviewers and reflected their gratification at seeing the failure of these procedures to cure Jo's psychological problems.

But the Legion did not endorse *The Pumpkin Eater* just because the psychiatrist suggested abortion and sterilisation. It was also the fact that his psychoanalytic approach *did not* help her address her primary psychological problem. Early in the film we learn that Jo began visiting a psychiatrist because she felt her life was in 'an empty place'. By following the psychiatrist's advice she became more comfortable with sex, but that did not fill this 'empty place'. The Legion's reviewers believed that the film made it clear that no amount of psychoanalysis would have filled that space because her ultimate problem was not in her head but in her soul. As one reviewer said, '*The Pumpkin Eater* is a pretty accurate account of the kind of spiritual malaise and emptiness that is one of the dominant moods of modern urban society.'[112] Another reviewer acknowledged that the psychoanalysis and abortion/sterilisation may have solved her sexual issues, but it did nothing to ameliorate her feelings of emptiness: 'So she submits to sterilization. Freer now for physical openness, she finds herself in fact less able to cope with her own affluent emptiness.'[113] According to another reviewer the only thing that would have helped her was 'the guidance given by Divine Revelation about the nature and meaning of marriage'.[114] Of course, there is no explicit discussion of religion or spirituality in the movie. The Legion's reviewers, however, were just happy to have a cinematic story that pointed out the limitations of secular approaches to mental illness when that illness is rooted in the search for meaning in life. That was a story about psychiatry that they could get behind.

Regulating cinematic narratives of the psy sciences

The Catholic Church's begrudging acknowledgement of the psy sciences in the 1960s did not mean that they accepted everything associated with psychology and psychiatry. Catholics could gain the benefits of psychiatric treatment. Yet the Church was still concerned about the moral dangers they believed were inherent in the psy sciences. Catholic leaders published policy statements, magazine articles and theological tracts clarifying the Church's stand on psy science topics, including psychotherapy, hypnosis and free will. But they realised that popular culture narratives, including movies, had much more influence on the cultural meanings of the psy sciences than any piece of literature that they could publish. Using the Legion of Decency, they tried to modify cinematic narratives in order to tell what they considered more appropriate stories about the psy sciences as a social, cultural and moral force. They hoped that by controlling the stories told about psychology, psychiatry and psychotherapy in cinema, that they could regulate the broader cultural meanings of psy science itself.

The Legion's classification system worked by convening a diverse group of Catholics to watch and report on films each week, including ordained priests, professional film reviewers, Jesuit scholars, university professors, retired businessmen and stay-at-home mothers. This meant that there were always differences of opinion amongst reviewers about the appropriateness of a film's content for Catholic viewers. It is not surprising, then, that there were disagreements throughout the 1960s about how to handle the inclusion of the psy sciences in cinema. Some reviewers remained cynical about the suitability of exposing movie audiences to any aspects of the psy sciences. Some acknowledged in their reviews that they may be 'behind the times', but they still remembered why the Church considered the psy sciences suspect in the first place. Other reviewers were more progressive and wanted the Legion to take a more lenient approach to cinematic depictions of the psy sciences. This was often the case when the Legion brought in Catholic psychiatrists and psychologists to weigh in about films that heavily featured the psy sciences such as *Freud* and *Psycho*.

In spite of this range of opinion, there were some elements of the psy sciences that reviewers collectively agreed were problematic. For one, they all believed that the medium of cinema was not well suited to conveying the complexity and seriousness of psychiatry and allied disciplines. They felt that the medium's simplicity made dangerous misinterpretations likely. For the Legion, movies were an especially problematic medium because (most) filmmakers were more interested in sensationalising the sexual aspects of the psy sciences then they were in handling it with the gravitas it deserved. They were also wary of movies depicting psychotherapy being performed by amateurs. They considered psychotherapeutic techniques to be far too powerful to be used for pop psychology or in the hands of amateur hypnotists. For the Church, psychotherapy was only 'safe' when it was deployed by highly trained experts (unless the psychotherapist was utilising psychoanalysis). In addition, the relationship between the psy sciences, mental health and free will remained an issue throughout the 1960s for the Church and the Legion. Cinematic depictions implying an overly deterministic model for human behaviour were always inappropriate in film narratives, whether this determinism emerged from inherited behaviours, the environment or general psychiatric essentialism.

One of the primary reasons for the Church's shifting attitude towards the psy sciences in the 1960s was that they were proving to be effective in helping people with their mental health issues. The Church's new approach to psychotherapy required a re-framing of the psy sciences for their congregation. Before Pope Pius XII's 1953 speech, the Church framed psychiatry as another incursion by secular science into realms that were better addressed by the spiritual. After the pope's address the Church wanted Catholics to feel comfortable with psychiatric care, so they began re-framing the psy sciences as God working through psychiatrists and other psy practitioners. For the Legion this meant approving film narratives in which the psy sciences emphasised human dignity or that indicated how all human lives have value. They were fond of films where psychiatric professionals unselfishly strove to cure people of their mental illnesses. They believed the goal of psychiatric care should be to help people find contentment with their lives, since the Legion believed that what constituted our 'contentment' was defined by the Catholic Church. They wanted film narratives to acknowledge that these best lives were not attainable through the psy sciences on their own. True mental well-being was only achieved when psychiatry was supplemented by spiritual assistance from a priest.

Conclusion

In 1966, the Legion of Decency changed its name to NCOMP. With that name change the organisation also began to adjust its mode of operation. Catholic demographics changed and the threat of a Catholic boycott did not pose the same economic threat as it once did. They still published their classifications in the hopes of influencing Catholic consumption of movies. But by the end of the 1960s, they were no longer focused on efforts to coerce studios into changing their films to suit Catholic viewers. Instead, NCOMP began to publish film awards in the hopes of encouraging studios to make more Catholic-friendly films.[115] The Legion had not only changed their name, they had also changed their approach to the psy sciences in movies. The Catholic Church became even more accepting of the psy sciences after the Second Vatican Council (1962–1965) where the human sciences, including psychology and sociology, had become important tools for understanding the dynamics of social change in the secular world.[116] In 1973, Pope Paul VI even recognised the value of psychoanalysis for mental health.

These changes did not mean that the Church fully accepted every aspect of the psy sciences. They also remained concerned about the potential moral impacts of movies. The Catholic News Service (CNS) still publishes classifications for movies that are basically the same as they were in the 1960s with the replacement of B by L (limited, films whose problematic content many adults would find troubling) and C with O (morally offensive). This means that they are still vigilant about movie narratives that depict the psy sciences in what they see as problematic ways. For example, the CNS classified *Joker* (2019) as L because the character's homicidal actions are blamed on his mental illness rather than his choices.[117] Even if the Church cannot control how stories based on psychiatric themes are told in movies, they still want to determine what constitutes a morally acceptable story about the psy sciences.

2

The BBFC's 'psychiatrist friends': psychiatric consultation and the British censors

This chapter will demonstrate the significant influence that psychiatric consultants exerted on British Board of Film Censors' (BBFC) policy and, as a result, cinematic representations of mental illness and psychiatric practices during the long 1960s. John Trevelyan, appointed as Secretary of the BBFC in 1958, is frequently described as a liberalising force in film censorship who 'repeatedly defended the independence of the Board's decision making'.[1] This chapter will not seek to discredit this liberalisation narrative, but to highlight a concurrent one of increasing deferral to psychiatric expertise outside the BBFC to make decisions about film censorship and certification, and even, in some instances, scriptwriting and editing. Whilst media scholars have acknowledged this process of psychiatric consultation in relation to Roman Polanski's *Repulsion* (1965), this has been understood in isolation, necessitated by the unique nature of that film, rather than representative of a wider shift in BBFC practice and policy.[2] A proliferation of American and, later, British films dealing with mental health issues caused BBFC examiners to lose confidence in their ability to make censorship decisions in the mid-1960s. This necessitated initial unsuccessful consultation with the government affiliated and funded organisation the National Association of Mental Health (NAMH) and, subsequently, a small group of Trevelyan's 'psychiatrist friends' affiliated with Guy's Hospital and the Tavistock Clinic who played a key role in deciding cuts and certification of films, including *The Caretakers* (1963), *Repulsion*, *The Collector* (1965) and *The Boston Strangler* (1968). Throughout the long 1960s, the BBFC moved from a default position of prohibition to one of enabling 'serious' films dealing with mental health issues to be made. This was achieved by brokering collaboration between filmmakers and specially selected psy professionals who were trusted by Trevelyan and employed on an ad hoc basis as paid consultants across the production and censorship process.

Academic studies of the BBFC have understood the 'BBFC's adoption of the language of psychology and psychiatry' to have been a 'new rationale' introduced during the tenure of James Ferman (secretary from 1975 to 1999), and particularly in relation to waves of moral panic surrounding the so-called 'video nasties' from the mid-1980s.[3] Furthermore, these narratives of British censorship have conceptualised this deployment of psychiatric expertise in relation to a wider neoliberalist project of governmentality emerging from Thatcherite Conservative politics of the late twentieth century. As film scholar Julian Petley explains:

> But whereas once the BBFC consulted (and indeed employed) specialists in political propaganda and countersubversion, it now turns to psychologists, psychiatrists, paediatricians, and other such 'engineers of the human soul'. And its main function is no longer trying to ensure ideological conformity but engaging in a form of moral regulation. But in this endeavour it is, of course, hardly alone in Britain where, since the Thatcher era, questions of social order and control have been framed in ever more explicitly moral – and moralising – terms.[4]

However, the consultative processes identified in this research not only date this shift in priorities and policy almost twenty years earlier, but also reveal the BBFC's deployment of a select group of trusted psychiatrists, partly as a strategy to maintain autonomy from the state rather than reproduce it. As it gained confidence in the authority and advice of these psy professionals, the BBFC sought to give expression to the contention within the mental health fields – including critiques by radical psychiatrists who challenged the tenets of mainstream psychiatry and its unwavering advocacy of biomedical treatments and institutional care – rather than promote the moral and political consensus.

The analysis in this chapter will focus on case studies of three films that were submitted to the BBFC from late 1963 to mid-1964 which raised issues for the Board's reviewers, largely due to the frank treatment of characters with serious mental health disorders and the portrayal of mental health institutions on screen. These were the Hollywood production *The Caretakers*, finally released as *Borderlines* in Britain in 1965; the Anglo-American co-production *The Collector*; and the British production *Repulsion*. *The Caretakers* was submitted to the BBFC as a completed film in April 1963, but was not released in Britain until late 1965, due to its protracted journey through the BBFC following consultation with the NAMH. *The Collector* and *Repulsion* were submitted for approval at draft script stage in August

1963 and June 1964, respectively, and were subject to confidential consultation with Trevelyan's 'psychiatrist friend' Dr Stephen Black. *The Collector*
passed through the BBFC with only minor recommended changes on 'points
of detail' at script stage, while for *Repulsion*, although requiring a longer process of consultation with Black across production and post-production, this
was described as a productive even creative collaborative process by all parties. This chapter will conclude by briefly discussing *The Boston Strangler* to
highlight Trevelyan's widening of his circle of psychiatric consultants in the
second half of the decade, bringing in requisite clinical expertise such that
the Board could make increasingly bold decisions.

The treatment of these three films highlights the BBFC's emerging policy of in-house consultation and collaboration with a select group of liberal
(rather than radical) mental health professionals as it shifted discursive terrain from one of protecting the supposedly naive (or, at best, ill-informed)
public to one of mental health awareness. Drawing upon Annette Kuhn and
Nick Crossley's ground-breaking research on contention within the fields
of film censorship and mental health, this chapter will highlight the BBFC's
productive engagement with psychiatrists as a form of resistance to institutional power and control as well as an exertion of it.[5] As a result, it will offer
new insight into the policies, processes and practices of the BBFC during
this significant period of transition; introduce key issues of film censorship
and classification into recent historical debates about mental health representation; and highlight the mutually productive interactions between the
fields of mental health and cinema.

Censorship as productive

Drawing upon Michel Foucault's assertions that power is exercised rather
than possessed, Kuhn's study of early British censorship eschews the dominant 'institution–repression' model in arguing that film censorship and
regulation is productive as well as repressive. She explains her method as
'direct[ing] itself not at texts or contexts, nor at organisations and rules of
exclusion, but at the nature of the practices, relations and powers involved
in film censorship, and at what these produce – their effectivity – at particular moments in history.'[6] As a result, she defines censorship 'as something
that emerges from the interactions of certain processes and practices', rather
than something possessed by organisations such as the BBFC.[7] Borrowing
Crossley's term, film censorship could be seen as part of a field of cinematic
contention that, during the long 1960s period, productively converged
and interacted with the fields of mental health (primarily associated with
psychiatric orthodoxy at the time) and an escalating 'field of psychiatric

contention',[8] associated with the ideas of progressive psychiatrists such as Ronald D. Laing (UK) and Thomas Szasz (US) and later described as the 'anti-psychiatry' movement.[9]

Crossley's study is particularly useful for mapping the interactions of competing mental health organisations and advocacy groups, 'who converge around common areas of concern (whether in agreement or disagreement)' and the diffuse currents of discourse and demands they circulated during the post-war period in Britain.[10] At the centre of this field of contention in the long 1960s is the struggle between psychiatric orthodoxy, which favoured biomedical models of understanding and treating mental illness, and the emergent anti-psychiatry movement, associated with progressive psychiatrists such as Laing, which advocated for psychotherapeutic 'talking cures' and de-institutionalisation of treatment. The anti-psychiatry movement originated in the late 1950s as a series of challenges to dangerous and coercive physical treatments such as electroconvulsive therapy (ECT) and psychosurgery (for example, lobotomies), but by the early 1960s sought to challenge the 'very basis of psychiatry itself; its purpose, its foundational concept of mental illness and the very distinction between madness and sanity'.[11] From the mid-1960s, Laing became the go-to media spokesperson for these contentious ideas, gaining him a significant counterculture following and a level of public awareness.[12] The key organisation seeking to maintain the status quo in advocating for orthodox psychiatry was the NAMH. Although the NAMH was formed in the immediate post-war era with the reformist agenda of thinking about mental health more holistically (as an issue that affected all and that should be addressed through social policy and education as well as medicine), when the psychiatric establishment came under attack in the 1960s, the NAMH adopted the role of defenders of both orthodox psychiatric methods and government policy.[13]

The fundamental clash in understanding and treating mental 'illness' played out not only in professional journals and conferences, but increasingly within the wider political and public sphere. As Crossley highlights, overlapping fields, such as the media, also contribute to the psychiatric field of contention through their converging discourses and demands.[14] As *Demons of the Mind* and Michael DeAngelis' 2018 book *Rx Hollywood* highlight, in the 1960s cinema and television became significant 'actors' in the mental health field through a succession of narratives addressing contemporary developments in therapeutic and psychiatric practice and research.[15] However, as our project research has highlighted, the liberalisation of the media/cinematic field necessitated an expansion of the media field to include psy expertise in the areas of film production, censorship and reception. As the following sections will highlight, a cycle of Hollywood films emerging from America's de-institutionalisation context made the BBFC secretary and examiners realise that they did not have the expertise and therefore authority to make decisions on the classification and censorship of these films whose perceived accuracy and authenticity (often due to their resemblance to actual people diagnosed as psychotic and real-life events such as investigations of violent crime), rather than sensationalism, was the key concern for the Board.

The BBFC's policy on mental health

Films representing mental illness and institutions had always been a sensitive subject for the BBFC, but became a near 'no go' subject once the 'moral and political censorship came into force in the 1930s'.[16] In the 1930s, the Board was closely tied to government through its membership and policies.[17] The Board's conservative priorities in protecting the medical profession (alongside politicians, soldiers, the police) from criticism,[18] and avoiding controversial political and social subjects that could inadvertently evoke public anxiety and unrest, meant that films dealing with mental illness and its treatment were likely to be banned, irrespective of whether they were British or American. During and immediately following the Second World War, censorship switched more to representations of patients suffering from mental illness, undoubtedly due to the return of servicemen, many of whom were both physically and psychologically scarred by the war.[19] As a result, a short-lived post-war cycle of Hollywood films set in mental institutions created significant concern for BBFC's new secretary Arthur Watkins (1948–1958), who, on banning the mental hospital set crime film *Behind Locked Doors* (1948), explained that only films presenting 'an authenticated aspect of an important social problem' of mental illness would be considered for classification.[20] The BBFC's handling of this late 1940s cycle and in particular its extended deliberations over *The Snake Pit* (1948) is a useful comparative case study – both in its convergences and divergences – to the mid-1960s.

Prior to Watkins' arrival, a screenplay based on the 1946 novel *The Snake Pit*, a semi-autobiographical account by Mary Jane Ward, had been tentatively submitted to the BBFC for consideration by Alexander Korda's London Films, but they had been told that any film adaption would be 'quite unsuitable for public exhibition' given its setting within and depiction of a mental institution (the titular 'snake pit').[21] In the novel and film a woman is institutionalised following a nervous breakdown and responds extremely negatively to a range of biomedical treatments at the state hospital (including ECT, insulin shock therapy and hydrotherapy) until she begins the slow process of recovery through a programme of psychotherapeutic treatment.

Ultimately produced across the Atlantic by 29th Century Fox, *The Snake Pit* was released in the United States in November 1948 to huge critical and commercial success, as well as being screened in the White House.[22] This promoted much speculation in the middle-brow press regarding whether the BBFC would and should revise their policy of prohibition to accommodate this high-profile film.[23]

When the completed film was submitted to the Board on 18 February 1949, Watkins restated the Board's default prohibition position to the distributor, but asked them to arrange a preview screening for 'leading psychoanalysts and superintendents of mental institutions'. He then viewed the film with the director, Anatole Litvak, stating that scenes featuring patients and ECT would need to be cut and a foreword 'disassociating the mental institution scenes in the film from conditions in English mental institutions' would be required.[24] Even with these heavy edits and disclaimer, the film would receive an 'H' certificate – the much-derided classification reserved for horror films. The subsequent cut version was screened for the Board of Control (the government body responsible for mental hospitals in England and Wales and the well-being of patients detained in these hospitals) and the Minister of Health, who stated that no amount of cuts would make the film suitable for release and put pressure on the BBFC to ban it outright.

Watkins defended the BBFC's deferral to 'expert opinion' to the disgruntled distributor, but simultaneously warned the Ministry of Health that there would be a media backlash if the film was banned. He subsequently attended a meeting of the film industry's Trade Representative Committee where he was presented with supportive letters from doctors and psychiatrists that 'materially affected' the Board's decision.[25] Disregarding the demands of the Ministry of Health and Board of Control, in April 1949 the BBFC passed the film with an 'A' certificate, subject to the agreed cuts and foreword. This reversal prompted by joint pressure from the film industry, independent medical experts and the media, asserted the BBFC's independence from governmental control. The case of *The Snake Pit* set an important precedent not just in this landmark decision to revise its approach to mental health representation and to 'adult films' more generally, but also in regard to reorienting wider process and practices away from state and press scrutiny. The contention between media, political and medical fields over the censorship and classification of *The Snake Pit* involved important interaction with mental health professionals, but unlike the later period we are analysing this external consultation was heavily mediated and debated within the public sphere.

A more productive and pre-emptive use of psy consultants was established by John Trevelyan who was appointed as BBFC secretary in 1958, asserting that under his direction the Board 'cannot accept responsibility for guardianship of British morality' any longer. Trevelyan's reputation for liberalisation was established by his passing of a number of 'British New Wave' films such as *Room at the Top* (1959), *Look Back in Anger* (1959) and *Saturday Night, Sunday Morning* (1960), which featured much more frank depictions of sex, issues such as abortion and swearing. To date, scholarship on Trevelyan's reign as secretary has focused excessively on this period and on these films in order to lend weight to the arguments regarding the BBFC's increasing liberalisation and autonomy from external influence.[26] These accounts do not analyse any of the concurrent films and cycles dealing with mental health discussed in this chapter. However, Trevelyan does so in his book.

In his 1973 biographical account of the inner workings of the BBFC, *What the Censor Saw*, Trevelyan highlights that mental illness is 'a subject that has produced censorship problems', but he does not acknowledge the role of psychiatric expertise in solving these problems. Instead, he suggests that the Board's policy during his tenure was that: 'It is only the irresponsible use of mental illness for sensationalism that becomes censorable.'[27] He suggests that this policy led the examiners to pass films that 'treated [mental illness] seriously' and to reject those in which the depiction of mental hospitals and illness were 'unjustified and alarmist'.[28] Trevelyan highlights *Family Life* (1971), on which R. D. Laing was employed as 'technical adviser', as an exemplar of the former stating: 'If mental illness is treated seriously, as in *Family Life* made in 1971 by Ken Loach from a script by David Mercer, it can be entirely acceptable as material for a film, but if treated sensationally I would find it totally unacceptable' (169). He then goes on to highlight the 'American films' *Shock Corridor* (1963) and *Shock Treatment* (1964) as exemplars of the latter.[29]

Trevelyan's account suggests that the examiners were attuned to making distinctions between a 'serious' and 'sensational' depiction of mental illness and were autonomous in their decision-making. However, from our research in the BBFC archives, we discovered a number of examiners' reports and Trevelyan's correspondence with and between a range of psy professionals and filmmakers that suggest otherwise. Across this period, the BBFC employed psychiatrists to make key decisions about whether and which British audiences would see films dealing with psychiatric themes and medical practices associated with the experience and treatment of people diagnosed with a mental illness. The following section will highlight the increasing deferral to psychiatric experts to make final decisions about films dealing with mental health, with those depicting mental institutions initially remaining, if not a 'no go' area, most certainly a 'touch and go' one.

Formal consultation with 'the Association'

The cycle of American films emerging from the late 1950s/early 1960s de-institutionalisation context discussed in Chapter 1, including *The Caretakers, Shock Corridor, David and Lisa* (1962), *Shock Treatment* and *Lilith* (1964), provided a significant test for the BBFC. These films were influenced by and emerged in the context of high-profile media exposés of conditions in mental institutions and bestselling books in the early 1960s by the likes of Erving Goffman and Thomas Szasz that questioned the efficacy of mental health practices and diagnosis.[30] There has been some academic work on the banning of *Shock Corridor*, typically cited as evidence of the Board's ongoing problem and prohibition of films dealing with mental illness and institutions.[31] However, the films that were passed by the Board following considerable psychiatric consultation, offer deeper insight into the complex considerations and contentions within and between the cinematic and mental health fields. The BBFC's evolving priorities and processes can be usefully explored through the prolonged passage of United Artists' *The Caretakers* (released in the UK as *Borderlines*) through the BBFC, which was initially submitted for consideration as a completed film in April 1963 but was not released until November 1965.[32]

The Caretakers/Borderlines was the first in this cycle of de-institutionalisation–context films to be submitted to the BBFC and the one that caused the most difficulty for all concerned. Pressure to consider revising its policy for *The Caretakers* was not so much due to the critical and commercial success of the film in America, as with *The Snake Pit*, but rather its perceived political influence in 'affecting national legislation' on mental health. The film was previewed for the US Senate in spring 1963, and, according to Lister Hill, chairman of the Senate Committee on Labor and Welfare Policy, 'contributed to creating the very favorable climate and presenting the challenge that brought the victory of the Mental Health and Mental Retardation Act (1963) by an overwhelming vote'.[33] This legislation led to considerable de-institutionalisation and a shift towards community-based care in America.[34]

The film, based on a 1959 novel by Dariel Telfer, tells the story of Lorna Melford (Polly Bergen) who is committed to a mental institution following a psychotic episode in a cinema. She is initially placed in the care of a progressive psychiatrist, Dr MacLeod (Robert Stack), who is struggling with the hospital's administrative authorities to run an experimental group therapy ward for borderline patients whom he believes can be re-socialised and cured. Across the film, MacLeod's progressive psychotherapeutic methods – particularly an out-patient programme of group therapy for Lorna and other women under his care – are juxtaposed to the conventional biomedical approaches favoured by orthodox psychiatry, such as ECT. These conventional treatments are represented in a negative and at times horrific way, in part through their association with the harsh disciplinary approach of head nurse Lucretia Terry (played with relish by Joan Crawford). The film positions the protagonists at the centre of the emergent struggles between the traditional mental health field and the field of psychiatric contention in the form of group therapy sessions with a clear argument for the more compassionate and effective approach of the latter.

The initial BBFC Examiners Report on *Borderlines* expressed reluctance at making a decision on whether to reject or pass the film subject to cuts, explaining that 'whilst we don't doubt that some of the theories about the care of the mentally ill are quite right, the story is . . . conducive to alarm and despondency in the mentally ill and their relatives'.[35] As a result, Trevelyan decided to 'consult the National Association for Mental Health to give their view as to whether the good points in this film are so outweighed by the bad that we should reject it'.[36] In a subsequent letter thanking United Artists (UA) for conceding to a special screening for members of NAMH's Public Information Committee at UA's viewing theatre, Trevelyan explained:

> This association [NAMH] does first rate work in educating the public to a more rational approach to mental illness and educating some of the mental hospitals to a more humane treatment of their patients. I would not want to put out a film of this kind in a form that would do harm to their work; indeed it would be anti-social to do such a thing. They are most reasonable people and I would like to obtain their views on the film before we make a decision on it.[37]

Trevelyan, therefore, saw the film as encroaching upon the mental health field – perhaps negatively in its potential to 'do harm' to NAMH's work – taking the film outside the expertise of the BBFC and necessitating a delegation of decision-making to an outside body specialising in mental health issues and the welfare of patients.

In brokering this consultation with NAMH, known as 'the Association' within the mental health field, Trevelyan tapped into the heart of psychiatric orthodoxy and officialdom in Britain in the 1960s. NAMH was formed in 1946 out of a merger of three interwar voluntary groups that, while having different focuses, were influenced by the 'mental hygiene movement' which advocated for a medical understanding of mental illness and the promotion of mental health at the level of the individual, family and society as a whole. This formalisation was very much influenced by the early development of the welfare state with mental health and parliamentary fields converging through their complementary interests and concerns.[38] By the start of the 1960s, NAMH had become, in many respects, the voice of orthodox psychiatry, working closely with and being part-funded by government to advocate for and advise upon medical practices and policies on mental health, including the 1959 Mental Health Act.[39] In this capacity, NAMH adopted a paternalistic and censorial approach to educating the public (particularly the working classes) about mental health, and saw cinema as the most important medium for disseminating information and, if handled irresponsibly by filmmakers, misinformation about psychiatric practices.

NAMH had always been interested (and worried) about the persuasive power of film. In 1947, they formed the 'Film Visiting Committee' (FVC) with the purpose of protecting against misrepresentation of the psychiatric professions and practices, and in 1963 formalised its ongoing collaboration with members of the British Film Academy to form the Mental Health Film Council (MHFC). In forming this new organisation, which sat within and shared membership with the Association's Public Information Committee, NAMH expanded its remit to include film production as well as reviewing them. From 1963, MHFC organised courses to train members to make films to counter what it saw as potentially harmful misinformation spread within mainstream cinema. Some NAMH films on mental health were screened for the public in cinemas as supporting features.[40] With this shift into production NAMH became direct social actors within the cinematic field rather than just converging with it through reviews and recommendations. It is within this context that Trevelyan approached NAMH to consult on the censorship and classification of *Borderlines*, triggering an extended contestation between the BBFC, NAMH and the film's producers that lasted more than two years and resulted, it would seem, in the BBFC moving away from this type of official consultation.

NAMH's Public Information Committee thanked Trevelyan for making the decision to consult them, but General Secretary Mary Appleby reported that the members of the Committee considered *Borderlines* 'a bad film from almost every point of view' and 'should be sorry to see it shown in this country'. They felt that the film would 'mislead, and quite unjustifiably dismay and alarm, the British audience, who will undoubtedly assume conditions in our own mental hospitals to be similar, whereas in fact they are much better'. In particular, they deplored the inaccurate ('at least as far as the British scene is concerned') portrayal of biomedical treatments such as ECT which would 'confirm quite groundless fears of patients and their relatives'. NAMH demanded that scenes featuring ECT and others showing harsh disciplinary methods within the hospital should be cut if an 'X' certificate was to be seriously considered (see Figure 2.1). She continued: 'The impression is given by this film that only group therapy will have any effect

Figure 2.1 The NAMH called on the BBFC to cut scenes from *Borderlines* (1963) showing the disciplinary use of psychiatric restraints and treatments

on disturbed patients, where as the overwhelming change in mental hospital treatment in this country is drug therapy.'[41] NAMH was clearly paternalistic and censorial in its approach – protecting an uninformed and easily alarmed audience from conflating the two national contexts – but also objected to the film's supposed bias against biomedical approaches that were standard British psychiatric practice, even though these practices were coming under increasing criticism from the field of psychiatric contention. NAMH, therefore, sought to bring the film in line with psychiatric orthodoxy in Britain, and attenuate the polemics that played into the hands of progressive psychiatrists like Laing who were beginning to become recognised public figures and outspoken critics of conventional psychiatry.

Trevelyan responded by explaining that the Board mostly concurred with the Public Information Committee's recommended cuts, and went further in proposing to ask the producers to add a 'written foreword stating that mental hospital treatment in this country is very different in many ways from that shown in this film'. However, Trevelyan's letter takes a different tone in subtly, but firmly, chastising the Committee, or at least one of its members, for disregarding the confidential nature of the Board's work, and specifically for sharing information with government officials. He stated:

On my return yesterday I heard that the Ministry of Health had received a report from someone, presumably a member of their medical staff, who saw the film with your committee, and were concerned about it. They asked if we can arrange a viewing for them. I stated that to propose this to the company would present difficulties, but that I might be able to make some arrangements on a private basis when we saw the film again, on the understanding that the decision about the film rested with this Board.'[42]

Trevelyan's response can be understood in the context of both the BBFC's long-standing struggle to maintain independence from government control and intervention, and NAMH's reliance on its close association with the government for political capital to gain leverage and visibility.[43]

NAMH ignored Trevelyan's concerns regarding their sharing of information with government and, instead, upped the stakes by pushing him further on the idea of a written foreword, demanding a one-minute filmed prologue featuring a publicly recognised British psychiatrist. The Committee specified that 'they had reason to believe' that Dr David Stafford-Clark or Dr William Sargant – known to the public as broadcasters on BBC television programmes such as *Lifeline* (1957–1962) and *The Hurt Mind* (1957) – 'would be willing to appear' and would serve as 'an authoritative figure' to not only distance the film from British psychiatric practice but also to advocate for it.[44] At the time, both Stafford-Clark and Sargant were key establishment figures (and high-profile members of NAMH) who advocated for biomedical approaches, with Sargant in particular being a staunch public defender and ardent practitioner of 'physical therapies' such as ECT and psychosurgery.[45] NAMH's unusual request for a filmed prologue to an American film featuring a British psychiatrist both reflects and belies their increasing confidence in intervening in the cinematic field through production as well as comment. Furthermore, the choice of a celebrity psychiatrist on the side of medical orthodoxy – not the progressive group psychotherapies advocated within the film – was an overt attempt to hijack the film to advocate for the physical approaches that *Borderlines* exposed as harmful but, following the Committee's recommendations, most of which were to be cut from the film.

Trevelyan acceded and contacted United Artists (UA) to explain NAMH's proposed cuts – which he suggested 'were much in line with our own, but in some respects would probably want to go further than we would' – and put forward their suggestion of a filmed prologue by a well-known psychiatrist which 'clearly established with British audiences that what they were to see would not be a true picture of mental hospitals, and mental treatment, in this country.'[46] The suggestions of the extensive cuts and the filmed foreword prompted UA to contact the director, Hall Bartlett, who then responded directly to the BBFC/ NAMH's joint suggestions. Bartlett sought to defend (whilst grudgingly accepting) some of scenes to be cut, including the ECT scene which, invoking his own social capital and backing of esteemed medical experts in the United States, he countered 'has been called accurate and justified by such people as Dr Robert Felix, Director of National Association of Mental Health of Washington D.C.' Bartlett declined the suggestion of an expensive filmed foreword, but conceded to 'an inexpensive printed foreword on the picture, for release in Britain, giving specific credit, from an inspirational point of view, to the leaders of mental health in England'. He continued 'the stress on group treatment, even for very difficult cases, began in Britain'.[47]

Bartlett, therefore, conceded to a foreword that retained the film's (and his personal) preference for the psychotherapeutic approaches favoured by progressive British psychiatrists and psychoanalysts like Laing and David Cooper.[48] This triggered several months of 'seemingly endless correspondence' between UA, NAMH and the BBFC, regarding the exact wording and ownership of the foreword.[49] Rather than a pedantic exercise, this struggle is significant in framing the ideological positioning of the film in respect to the ongoing struggle within and between the fields of orthodox mental health and the field of psychiatric contention in both Britain and America.

NAMH stated that they were 'naturally disappointed' that UA refused to 'go to the expense of shooting the foreword spoken by someone like Dr Stafford-Clark', but conceded to a written foreword dictated by themselves, and signed on screen by NAMH, stating that: 'The conditions portrayed in this American film should not be taken as representative of psychiatric hospitals in Britain today. Recent advances in the treatment of mental illness have reduced violence among patients to a minimum and removed the need for forcible restraint.'[50] The NAMH statement highlights innovation in British psychiatric practice – presumably the development and use of antipsychotic drugs – as the solution to an inherent problem of violent mental patients. Bartlett responded personally, again, stating 'I do not care for the foreword for *Borderlines* proposed by the National Association of Mental Health' and proposed his own wording and his own signature:

> This is an American film about a mental hospital in the United States.
> The progressive concept of the day hospital for which the doctor of our pictures struggles against archaic ideas and practices, is a major contribution by Britain to the whole world of mental health.
> It is the aim of all leading mental health authorities in America to follow Britain's leadership so that there will be no need for forcible restraint or violence in the handling of mental patients.
> This enlightened goal has already been admirably achieved in Britain.
>
> Hall Bartlett.[51]

Bartlett, therefore, endeavoured to anchor the meaning of the film in his original intention, rather than hand over power to NAMH to reframe and take ownership of its portrayal of mental health and related issues.

NAMH crafted a patronising response to Bartlett's 'delicious' 'little encomium of the British services', but rejected it as uninformed and inaccurate. They stated that we 'should not agree that the day hospital is our greatest contribution to the field' of 'which, incidentally, we have only a handful' in Britain. NAMH sought to amend Bartlett's statement to make it more generalisable to the wider British mental health field, reading: 'Leading mental health authorities in America acknowledge Britain's leadership in this field and, as this film suggests, struggle against the archaic ideas and practices which Britain has discarded.'[52] The foreword brings innovations in physical approaches – like drug therapies and ECT administered with muscle relaxants – into the realm of progressive mental health care. UA conceded that 'the Producer was agreeable to the Foreword', but required a minor change to the final paragraph that in fact presents a significant shift in inflection. It read: 'The progressive concept of the day hospital which the doctor of our picture struggles against archaic ideas and practices, is a major contribution by Britain to the whole world of mental health.'[53] The BBFC and NAMH agreed to the new paragraph and, finally, the film was cleared for an 'X' certificate.[54]

Following almost a year passing through the BBFC, the edits and addition of the foreword held up the film's British release for a further eighteen months. Once it was released, its poor reception highlighted that the film showed the marks of its convoluted and contested journey through the BBFC. As *The Times'* film review highlighted: 'Long delayed, this American melodrama about life in a mental hospital turns out a curious hodge-podge. The narrative progresses in such shuddering fits and starts one wonders if it has been brutally shortened at some stage.'[55] Likewise, *The Daily Telegraph* review identified a discord between the foreword and the film, highlighting that *Borderlines* 'appears to have serious intentions, opening with a tribute to the advanced state of the treatment in British mental hospitals compared with American. Then the deluge.'[56] BBFC's consultation with NAMH, therefore, can be seen as a failure on a number of accounts: in failing to represent and retain the artistic and ideological intentions of the filmmakers; in keeping their processes confidential and free from government influence; and in maintaining the authority of BBFC's decision-making. It is clear to see why Trevelyan chose not to involve the organisation in reviewing or censoring films again.

Whilst Trevelyan did not consult NAMH following the *Borderlines* debacle, minutes of the Public Information Committee from 15 June 1966 highlight NAMH's continued pressure on the BBFC to have a say in censorship decisions. Trevelyan responded by making a conciliatory offer that 'he would be prepared to put on a special showing, for NAMH members, of mental health films which the Board had rejected'. They declined his offer saying 'there wasn't much purpose seeing films that had been already rejected' by the Board and intended to go back to Trevelyan asking instead to see films 'on which no decisions had been taken so that our views and suggestions could be put forward, as had been done in the "Borderlines Case"'.[57] NAMH clearly saw their consultative role on *Borderlines* to be productive in a way that the BBFC (and the wider cinematic field of filmmakers and critics) did not. However, Trevelyan's concurrent experiment of confidential in-house consultation with a trusted 'psychiatrist friend' would pave the way for the Board's strategy of psychiatric consultation for the rest of the decade and beyond.

In-house conversations with 'psychiatrist friends'

Submitted just one month after *Borderlines*, *The Collector* was a very different case cinematically – an Anglo-American co-production based on a critically acclaimed 1963 novel by John Fowles, which was brought to the BBFC's attention at script stage. It also raised different issues relating to mental health and human psychology: it depicts a male case of psychopathy rather than a female case of psychosis, is set in a domestic space as opposed to the more familiar setting of a mental institution, and does not depict any mental health professionals or practices. Directed by multiple Oscar-winning classical Hollywood director, William Wyler, *The Collector* tells the story of a young, solitary psychopath with a penchant for collecting butterflies, Freddie Clegg (Terence Stamp), who uses his betting pools winnings to buy a mansion in the English countryside with the intention of imprisoning a young woman, Miranda Grey (Samantha Eggar), with whom he has become infatuated and stalks. At the conclusion of the film Miranda has been kidnapped by Freddie and despite repeated attempts to escape she dies in captivity. The film ends with a scene of Freddie, showing no signs of remorse while driving through the streets of London looking for a new female captive. Despite these significantly different narrative and psychiatric concerns, the film raised similar issues for the BBFC as *Borderlines* with regard to the Board's perceived lack of expertise to examine, censor and classify the film.

The Examiner's Report from 1 August 1963 responding to the first draft screenplay concluded almost apologetically: 'I am not an expert on this field of psychology and I am not sure how much value I can contribute to the discussion of this script.' Furthermore, the examiner was particularly concerned that the film's 'strongly perverted sex-element of tying and shutting up the girl' had a real-world resemblance to a recent 'case in the papers about two years ago of a young man who kept a girl locked up in a room for a long time'.[58] Likewise, Trevelyan concurred with the examiner, explaining to Columbia's head of production, Mike Frankovich:

> I am a little uneasy about the subject, because it seems to be a very accurate analysis of mentally disturbed young man . . . [T]he nearer it is to reality the greater danger there is it may produce problems. This takes me into the fields of psychiatry that are beyond my experience.[59]

This correspondence explicitly states the BBFC's realisation of a lack of medical or psy expertise and therefore authority in making decisions on the censorship and classification of new films engaging with psychiatric themes. Furthermore, it is precisely their accuracy and authenticity – their basis in or proximity to real 'mentally disturbed' people and contemporary news reports of violent or sexual crimes – that is seen as the issue. Trevelyan therefore sought permission from screenwriter John Kohn in 'taking some expert advice on it'.[60]

In a subsequent letter Trevelyan explained that he had passed on the script 'to a psychiatrist friend of mine who has a good deal of direct experience on cases of this kind'. The 'psychiatrist friend' was Dr Stephen Black, a doctor and psychologist at Guy's Hospital, London. Black had previous experience as a documentary filmmaker and more recently as a medical consultant on film and television. Black began his career as a journalist before moving into filmmaking, producing documentaries with his brother Jay for television broadcasters and for the UK government's Central Office of Information; this included a documentary on the state of mental health care in Britain, intended as a riposte to *The Snake Pit*'s depiction of the 'dreadful conditions of some American asylums' in an effort to reassure British audiences 'that it is not like that here'.[61] Black subsequently studied medicine at King's College and Westminster hospital, and at the time of acting as a BBFC adviser, split his time between clinical work at Guy's Hospital York Clinic and conducting research for the Medical Research Council. He had a particular interest in psychosomatic medicine and hypnosis, compiling some of this research in his 1969 book *Mind and Body*. During the 1960s, Black regularly presented and appeared on BBC television programmes focusing on psychiatry and other medical topics, notably *Men at the Heart of the Matter* (1963), *A Matter of Mind* (1965) and *Hypnosis and Mind* (1969). With his extensive experience and expertise across medical and media fields, it is understandable that Trevelyan should see Black as an ideal consultant for films such as *The Collector*. Black's work in the media is likely where he and Trevelyan struck up the friendship that appears, from the tone of their letters, to have predated this professional association.

In his letter to Kohn, Trevelyan directly quoted the whole of Black's letter: 'There have indeed been such cases – ending in tragedy. However I do not think there is any danger of this unreal story setting off a psychopath on such a course; if he wasn't already set on it. In other words this is a highly organised form of erotic stimulation and does not come to an individual out of the blue.' Black concluded: 'My verdict: harmless in principle. Direction will be important, however.' Trevelyan explained to Frankovich that Black's opinion had 'naturally reassured us' and the BBFC was now in a position to discuss 'points of detail' regarding the treatment.[62] The subsequent list of recommendations, around two pages, are fairly minor and mostly suggest avoiding lingering too long on shots of Freddie's 'sadistic' enjoyment or on his 'imitable technique' such as the use of chloroform to render his victim unconscious. There is also a clearer request to cut a line of dialogue that directly references English serial killer John Christie (who used domestic gas to subdue and asphyxiate his victims). *The Collector* was offered a provisional 'X' certificate based on these recommendations.[63]

On the same day the film was classified, Trevelyan sent a cordial thank you letter to Black, acknowledging that 'this kind of advice is most helpful to me, and I value it enormously', enclosing a cheque for 3 guineas as payment and an invitation that 'we must meet again soon'.[64] Remarkably, the entire process of psychiatric consultation and reporting back the Board's decision took less than two weeks. Black's consultation on *The Collector* demonstrated the value of in-house consultation with Trevelyan's psychiatrist friend, not in banning or censoring difficult material but in facilitating the film's production. Most reviews of the film praised the producers for embarking on such a difficult and potentially controversial project of adapting, what Dilys Powell of *The Times* referred to as, 'the novel nobody in this country [was] ready to risk making' into a film.[65]

Trevelyan and Black's next major test came in the form of Roman Polanski's *Repulsion*, which, perhaps more than *The Collector*, could be seen as a case of productive consultation and, moreover, creative collaboration between the cinematic and psychiatric fields. The plot of *Repulsion* focuses on the psychological experience of a young Belgian woman, Carole Ledoux (Catherine Deneuve), living in a flat in London with her older sister Helene (Yvonne Furneaux) and, intermittently, her sister's married boyfriend Michael (Ian Hendry). Carole, a manicurist, is extremely detached and struggles with social interactions and personal relationships. Distressed by Michael's relationship with her sister and his visits to their apartment and the uninvited attention of men, particularly a young suitor Colin (John Fraser), Carole descends further into despair and eventually when her sister and Michael leave for a holiday, she experiences a psychotic episode. The spectator is encouraged to share Carole's aural and visual hallucinations, as well as her

Figure 2.2 The spectator is encouraged to experience Carole's psychotic episode in *Repulsion* (1965)

delusions through a range of formal techniques and perceptual experiments (see Figure 2.2). Carole murders her suitor Colin when he breaks into the flat to declare his love for her, and subsequently kills her landlord when he tries to sexually assault her. Helene and Michael return from holiday to discover the catatonic Carole and the bodies of the two men.

Submitted on 23 July 1964, the initial Examiners Report on the draft script for *Repulsion* (under the original title *Lovelihead*) recommended that the Board would not be able to give the film a classification, and therefore it would not be distributed in mainstream British cinemas. The examiner explained: 'Any film which came out of this project would be essentially a cinema club piece, not for general distribution.' He condescended: 'We have got standards to maintain ... not perhaps to the welfare of the intelligentsia who make up the greater part of the club audiences, but certainly to the average "X" cinema audience with its high proportion of older adolescents.' While the examiner stated that he would feel 'very uneasy about any proposal to get together with the makers to secure a watered-down version', he also conceded that:

> If the Board feels differently, I would most strongly urge that our friend Dr Black be asked – by *someone*, not necessarily us – how the piece strikes him. I should have thought here is a strong possibility of it sending some carefully poised personality right round the bend.[66]

The examiner's comments reveal his explicit politics of taste regarding the intellectual capacity of different audiences and, therefore, their vulnerability to cinematic suggestion (and, perhaps, susceptibility to mental health issues). For the purpose of this chapter, however, what is most significant is the examiner's practical suggestion – subsequently taken up by Trevelyan – that the BBFC adopt a position of brokering, at-a-distance, a productive collaboration between filmmakers and the Board's trusted psychiatric expert.

Trevelyan telephoned Black to ask him to act as a confidential script consultant for the filmmakers, and sent him a copy of the draft screenplay with the note: 'Let me emphasise again that the director is one of the few really great directors in the world . . . I should want you to meet Polanski, who is an interesting young man, and discuss it with him.' He continued that for Polanski 'it is very important that the mental disintegration is one which is true to fact, and he was pleased that I should put it to an expert'.[67] Black and Trevelyan met with Polanski and the film's producer Gene Gutowski on the 22 July 1964 and had a 'most tiring' but 'interesting and fruitful discussion' about the script.[68] The following day, Trevelyan wrote to executive producer Michael Klinger:

> My psychiatrist friend said he considered it a great script and one that was very accurate in psychiatric terms. It was largely for this reason that he was concerned with the possibility of the film having a dangerous effect on some psychotics; it's very accuracy might encourage them to seek relief from their tortures in dangerous ways such as are shown on screen.

Trevelyan explained that their long discussion resulted in two key recommendations by Black to alleviate the concerns quoted above. First, that 'the girl should not be shown to get happiness and peace as a result of the killings'; and, secondly, that 'it would be advisable to emphasise that the girl could have been saved if she had had expert help at the right time'. Trevelyan mentioned that Polanski had taken note of the first general point and agreed to add a line of dialogue in which Michael suggests that 'Carole is behaving rather oddly and should see a psychiatrist'.[69] A version of this line was added to the shooting script and appears in the finished film.

A follow-up letter to Gutwoski on 27 July reiterated and elaborated on these points, but also highlighted that Black had identified a scene that was 'out of character' with a clinical diagnosis of schizophrenia. The scene involved a third murder, Michael's wife, using vitriol sulphuric acid when she visits the flat unannounced, mistakes Carole for Helene, and discovers the bodies of the two men murdered previously. Black suggested that the calculated on-screen murder was inconsistent with the behaviour of a person diagnosed with schizophrenia and Carole's delusions relating to men. The scene was subsequently cut from the script as a result of Black's recommendations regarding diagnostic accuracy. Polanski's autobiography backs up the claim, though he mistakenly refers to the medical consultant as 'Dr Stephen Blake'.[70] While Black's other recommendations serve more conventional concerns of protecting vulnerable audiences and advocating for the psychiatric profession, the cutting of the third murder scene is another instance of productive censorship and creative collaboration. In the same letter Trevelyan chastises the producer for not keeping their consultation confidential, stating: 'I was somewhat surprised to read a comment in the *Sunday Telegraph* to the fact that I was consulting a psychiatrist about this production. I would prefer all negotiations to be kept confidential.'[71] The producers, as well as the BBFC, clearly saw consultation with Black as lending authenticity and authority to their project.

Following filming, Black was taken by Trevelyan to Twickenham Studios to view a rough cut of the final film so he could contribute to editing decisions and advise the BBFC on the classification of the film and on whether it 'presented any danger from his professional point of view'. On 4 December 1964, Trevelyan reported to the producers that Black was 'immensely impressed with the picture' and its 'portrayal of mental illness was remarkably accurate, and that the compassion of the picture justified its portrayal'. Black's only suggestion on viewing the rough cut was that in the final edit it should be clearer in the rape scenes that the hallucinations are happening in the 'girl's imagination as a fantasy, and is not a reality'. With his concerns about the film now 'entirely alleviated', Black completely reversed the BBFC examiner's earlier position, recommending that he 'saw no reason why from this point of view the picture should not be passed if it was satisfactory to the board in normal censorship terms' to be shown to a general audience.[72] Informed by Black's recommendations, the Board passed the film without a single cut – much to the surprise of Polanski – giving it an 'X' certificate so it could be viewed by anyone over sixteen in regular venues rather than being restricted to the small cinema club audience.[73]

The psychiatric consultation process on *Repulsion* exemplifies the shift in the BBFC's policy from a default position of prohibition to one of productive enabling of what Trevelyan and his colleagues considered to be worthwhile films – especially when created by 'really great directors'. While medical accuracy was clearly a key concern for all involved, the role of the BBFC's 'psychiatrist friend' went beyond merely fact-checking to involve productive and creative consultation that had a marked influence on the film's storyline, narrative, character development, editing and distribution. This chapter's aim to identify a shift in BBFC policy from a position of prohibition to productive collaboration, for all parties involved, is also supported by a letter from executive producer Klinger to Trevelyan following the film's release and reception. Klinger clearly states that *Repulsion* 'could not have been possible without your help and guidance and enlightened point of view. We were pleased to see that all the serious critics praised you for your approach to this particular film.' He concluded: 'Maybe everyone is growing up just a little which will make our job, and I'm sure yours, much easier in the future.'[74]

As the representations of mental illness and their proximity to real people and news events became more explicit (as discussed in Chapter 6), Trevelyan extended his network of psychiatrist friends to include professionals who possessed what he believed was the requisite expertise to serve as consultants with the BBFC and filmmakers. From 1967 onwards, Dr Derek Miller, medical director of the Adolescent Department at the Tavistock Clinic, took up Black's role as Trevelyan's principal 'psychiatrist friend', passing judgement on a number of films, including the ongoing banning of *The Trip* (1967), a 'psychedelic film' made by Roger Corman for American International Pictures (AIP). While the BBFC files for the film are lost, contemporary newspaper reports and Trevelyan's book explain that three psychiatrists – which included Miller, and likely Black – were shown the film and warned that 'there was a danger of it stimulating young people to try LSD'. Trevelyan went on to explain that the BBFC's policy on banning such content was 'whether a drug-scene or film was "stimulative in form"'. He clarified, 'if a "stimulative" scene occurred in a distinguished work of art' – which clearly he felt *The Trip* was not – then the filmmaker would be offered the opportunity to cut or re-edit the scene.[75] It is interesting that, as with some of the films discussed above, it was a fear of the accuracy and authenticity of the film's simulation of a psychotropic experience that was seen as problematic rather than its inaccuracy or sensationalism. Trevelyan explained, in *What the Censor Saw*, that one of AIP's representatives tried to challenge the decision in 1971 by bringing 'his own psychiatrist to see me and one of my advisers [Miller], only to find that his psychiatrist agreed that it was a dangerous film'.[76]

While by the late 1960s Miller had taken up the role of the BBFC's go-to psychiatric adviser, he also recommended other psychological experts for specific or contentious cases.[77] For example, for the Hollywood police procedural film *The Boston Strangler* – directed by Richard Fleischer and loosely based on a true crime book by Gerold Frank about a series of recent murders and ongoing legal case – Trevelyan consulted with three psychiatrists. In addition to Black and Miller, the BBFC was advised by Dr Arthur Hyatt Williams, a psychiatrist in the prison service and the Tavistock Clinic specialising in violent crime, who Miller introduced as 'the leading expert on murder'.[78] When the rough cut of the film was submitted, Trevelyan put on a screening for Black, Miller and Hyatt Williams, reporting back to producer Stephen Lions that: 'All three of the psychiatrists said that this was a brilliant film in many ways. They were, however, unanimous in their view that we would be advised to remove as far as possible certain sections of the film which dealt with sexual perversions, and especially those involving sadism.' The psychiatrists called for the editing or cutting of a number of scenes of sexual violence from the first two-thirds of the film but, as Trevelyan explained: 'None of the psychiatrists considered the acting out of the strangling in the final scene was dangerous on the grounds that this was in the hospital situation which thus provided a secure background.'[79] In this extended final scene set in the secure mental health unit, Albert DeSalvo (Tony Curtis) experiences a harrowing flashback in which he realises both his mental health condition and his violent crimes.

It is interesting, given the BBFC's earlier position on representing mental institutions, that *The Boston Strangler*'s clinical setting is seen to neutralise the potential harm of the scene and the film rather than cause it. The setting of the mental institution is not seen as a red flag for potential prohibition – the BBFC's default position up until 1963 – but rather as the solution to portraying contentious psychiatric material. While the BBFC was, on the whole, praised by critics for being bold in certifying *Repulsion*, newspapers and trade presses were extremely disapproving of the BBFC, and Trevelyan in particular, for passing this controversial and potentially libellous film.[80] As one critic pondered: 'Are human tragedies recently retailed in the quiet of a courtroom – and still sounding harmonics of horror – quite the right material to exploit for presentation to a mass audience?'[81] From *Borderlines* to *The Boston Strangler* in just five years, the increasingly sophisticated deployment of psychiatric expertise within the BBFC allowed censors to move from a conservative default position of panicked prohibition to one of enabling challenging depictions of mental disturbances that provoked questions and opened debate about the limits of mainstream cinema and its audiences.

Conclusion

As demonstrated in Chapter 1, in the early 1960s conditions become conducive for converging and co-producing fields of psychiatric and cinematic contention, with Hollywood filmmakers collaborating with psychiatrists and other mental health professionals to produce films that not only depicted, but also questioned the diagnosis and treatment of people diagnosed with mental illness. Feeling that they no longer had the expertise and therefore authority to pass judgement on these increasingly complex and contentious depictions, the BBFC responded, initially, by reproducing the unsuccessful consultative model of *The Snake Pit*. As early as the immediate post-war period it was felt that this response compromised the BBFC's ongoing struggle for independence from government control and its role of representing the industry's creative interests. Consultation for *Borderlines* with NAMH failed not only because it compromised the Board's independence, but also because the Association's paternalistic opinion of cinema audiences did not cohere with the BBFC's shifting position.

This was a significant paradigm shift for the BBFC, from a default position of protecting a supposedly naive or ill-informed public to one of promoting mental health awareness partly through acknowledging recent approaches to the diagnosis and treatment of serious mental disorders. The Board's move towards this more enabling position (for producers and audiences) was facilitated instead by brokering creative collaboration between psy experts and film practitioners that went well beyond mere fact-checking, and shaped filmmakers' narrative and editing decisions, as well as the Board's judgements on how films were distributed and seen. As *Repulsion* and *The Boston Strangler* highlight, in a relatively short period of time the Board's processes of consultation with psychiatrists allowed them to move from a position of excluding to one of advocating for and enabling challenging and controversial films. Furthermore, the BBFC files for *Twisted Nerve* (1969) and *Family Life* – the latter discussed in Chapter 5 – highlight that by the late 1960s, the Board felt confident enough in their position on mental health to trust filmmakers to negotiate their own psychiatric consultation in order to guard against external criticism of the cinematic field. The use of psychiatric expertise was not solely to enable creativity, however. The deployment of BBFC's psychiatrist friends was also a strategy to maintain a degree of autonomy from state intervention, not reproduce it, as had been the case in the United Kingdom during the Thatcherite era and beyond.

3

Freud goes to Hollywood: translating psychoanalysis to cinema

This chapter uses a case study of John Huston's Sigmund Freud 'biopic' *Freud* (1962) – in which a number of his case histories are conflated in a single character/patient, Cecily, and mapped onto biographical details from Freud's early professional and personal life – to consider different types of conscious and converging interactions between cinematic and psychiatric genres, ideas, technologies and expertise. The chapter will also use this multifaceted film to highlight ongoing historical contention within the psy sciences about both traditional Freudian psychoanalysis and pseudo-Freudianism, as popularised through mass media and pop culture. Drawing upon research on the files from the John Huston papers and Production Code Administrations papers (both Margaret Herrick library), the chapter will detail the complex and contested production and censorship processes involved in making the film, involving legal battles with the Freud family, lengthy deliberations with the Hays Office and Legion of Decency (as discussed in Chapter 1), and extensive consultation with a wealth of psychiatrists, psychoanalysts and theologians. It will contextualise these contestations and consultations in relation to the 'paradoxical fate of Freudianism [in America] in the 1960s – mass diffusion and precipitous decline'.[1] Zaretsky claims that in the 1960s when Freudian psychoanalysis came under attack, both within and outside the psy sciences, there was a spilt in the 'the psychoanalytic church' between the defenders of the orthodox Freud (aligned, he suggests, with a patriarchal American Cold War politics) and those reformers who were willing to embrace and meld a 'second, demonic Freud, [for whom] personal life served as point of critique and transcendence' more amenable to the shifting cultural and political climate of the 1960s.[2] Huston's *Freud* is interesting in how it tries (and in some respects fails) to placate both sides, and how the production history and reception of the film reflects these schisms.

Academic writing on *Freud* typically reduces the film to one failed creative interaction with existentialist philosopher John Paul Sartre, who was courted by Huston to be the film's screenwriter, but abandoned the project – and was uncredited – after ongoing contention with Huston over his unwieldy and un-filmable script.[3] Reflecting this academic miasma, Gabbard and Gabbard state, 'The film is interesting if only for the role played by John Paul Sartre in the genesis of the script.'[4] The released film (rather than the much-discussed Sartre script) is usually disregarded as a vestige of the fading classical Hollywood era, both in its debt to the 'Great Man' biopics of the 1930s and 1940s and in its adoption of classical Hollywood's hegemonic narrative structure for psychiatric dramas of an omniscient psychoanalyst's investigation and revelation of a patient's trauma and resultant 'cathartic cure' as popularised in 1940s films.[5] This chapter highlights that the film was far more than an anachronistic restaging of the 'Golden Ages' of psychoanalysis and Hollywood, representing rather more complex interactions between psychiatric and cinematic forms and expertise, and between the psychiatric, cinematic and societal contexts that it represents (the late 1800s) and those in which it was produced (the long 1960s). As a result, the film transformed the American cinematic field, creating a favourable production and censorship environment for a range of new psychiatric films that challenged as much as celebrated scientific knowledge.

Adapting the father of psychoanalysis

The production history of *Freud* is itself a multi-act drama featuring an international cast of actors. It demonstrates the complex interactions and, importantly, contentions between ideas, genres, expertise and techniques from the fields of cinema and the psy sciences identified within *Demons of the Mind*. These contentions start with the father of psychoanalysis himself. Sigmund Freud was famously resistant to the idea of film being an appropriate medium with which to engage and communicate psychoanalytic ideas. In 1925, MGM studio mogul Samuel Goldwyn travelled to Vienna to meet Freud, to make him an offer of $100,000 to consult on a silent epic exploring history's great love stories, from Anthony and Cleopatra onwards. Freud refused to see him responding, 'I do not intend to see Mr Goldwyn.'[6] Freud was famously critical of American consumerist culture, and Goldwyn and Hollywood seemed to embody its flaws for him. However, he also declined a contemporary request from a respected Austrian filmmaker, G. W. Pabst, to make a truly 'psychoanalytic film' based on Freudian ideas. Freud's close associates Karl Abraham and Hans Sach's acted as consultants on the project instead, becoming the German silent drama *Secrets of a Soul* (1926), in which a professor consults a renowned psychoanalyst after experiencing nightmares and paranoia that he will murder his wife. The film's experimental dream sequences combine elements of German expressionism with innovative multiple exposure and stop-motion animation techniques. This film and Pabst's subsequent *The Diary of a Lost Girl* (1929), based on a book for which Freud wrote a foreword, were both investigated by Huston's researchers to establish if Freud had any direct participation in them, including trying to visit Pabst in Italy to discuss the elderly director's claims that Freud had directly participated in the film.[7]

Despite Freud's distaste for cinema – and Hollywood cinema particularly – psychoanalytic themes, theories and practitioners became staples of popular film, particularly as the sound-era took hold. Within Hollywood, psychoanalytic ideas and principles were incorporated across a range of genres and narrative forms, but in the 1930s and 1940s two genres were prominent in explicitly depicting psychoanalytic practitioners and treatments: the psychological melodrama (sometimes critically described, often critically derided, as the 'women's film') and psychological thrillers (often subsumed into 'horror'). These (sub)genres typically, though not exclusively, depicted character types as either the benevolent 'godlike' psychotherapists of melodramas such as *Now Voyager* (1942) or *The Snake Pit* (1948),[8] or the deranged, villainous clinicians of *Captive Wild Woman* (1943) or *Shock* (1945). The latter trend – often based on a psychological-reorientation of the classic horror 'mad scientist' trope – provoked backlashes from critics and clinicians regarding their potential damage to the reputation of and trust in the psy professions.[9] The representation and reception of *Freud* must be understood in relation to these opposing genre film traditions (though sometimes converging in films such as Hitchcock's *Spellbound* (1945)), but also in relation to the character and narrative tropes of the 'Great Man' (occasionally 'Great Woman') biopics of the 1930s and 1940s, such as *The Story of Louis Pasteur* (1936), *The Life of Emile Zola* (1937), *Edison, the Man* (1940) and *Madame Currie* (1943).

In his autobiography, 'maverick' director John Huston states that he had been considering making a film about Freud since the late 1930s while working with Wolfgang Reinhardt on the script for *Dr Ehrlich's Magic Bullet* (1940), a biopic of German scientist Dr Paul Ehrlich.[10] A Huston-directed Freud 'biopic' was prematurely announced in April 1956, which was to be based on Freud's close friend Hans Sach's *Freud, Master and Friend* (1945).[11] However, it was a publication by another of Freud's 'inner circle', Ernest Jones' three-volume Freud biography, *Freud: His Life and Work* (1953, 1955, 1957), that was the catalyst and basis for Huston's pet project to move forward. Echoing the title of Jones' lengthy account of Freud's life and works, Huston sought to integrate biography and theory in melding stylistic and narrative tropes of the classical Hollywood biopic with narrational elements of the psychiatric case history. Specifically, the film was at least in part an adaption of the five case studies from *Studies in Hysteria* (1895), Freud's first book, co-authored with his mentor Josef Breuer. This generic interaction – and tension – between Hollywood biopic and adaptation of a ground-breaking science work, is central to the ensuing contentions and confusions during the stages of conceptualisation, production, censorship, mediation and reception. Huston maintained a stance throughout production and release that he 'did not want to make a biography of Sigmund Freud, but a motion picture which would dramatize the experiments that led to his discoveries',[12] and, he claimed, made the decision to remove co-screenwriter Charlie Kaufman from the project because 'he was intent on following the pattern of the biographical pictures Warners had done before the war', such as *Zola* and *Pasteur*, in which 'the protagonist is inevitably a hero'.[13]

Huston's Freud film does indeed resist some of the narrative tropes of the 1930s and 1940s 'Great Man' biopics. First, the film does not tell the story of Freud's life or career, but focuses on just a key ten-year period when he developed key tenets of psychoanalytic technique and theory: moving from hypnosis to free association, developing his understanding of transference, developing and then abandoning the seduction theory, and resultantly discovering key ideas of infantile sexuality and the Oedipus' complex. This tighter focus is not unique to *Freud*, but many of the earlier biopics are more synoptic in their 'life of' or 'story of' approaches. There is also a degree of innovation in the typical 'Great Man' characterisation. As Huston stated, the film also balances his 'greatness' with a greater sense of vulnerability and fallibility, aligning his own mental trauma and development with that of his patients. Most importantly, the film is very limited in biographical detail relating to Freud's personal life, especially the removal of his role and experience of fatherhood at the time the film is set, though this choice appears as much an issue of potential litigation as generic innovation.

The announcement of the revitalised 'Freud' project in March 1958 prompted a twin legal challenge by his daughter Anna Freud – a leading British psychoanalyst who was in the process of setting up her Hampstead Child Therapy Course and Clinic (1959) – and the late Ernest Jones' estate to block the production of the film. The lawyers acting for Jones claimed they could invoke copyright law if 'matters included in the book' were explicitly used,[14] while the solicitors acting for Anna Freud, who had 'refused to give her consent' to previous films, stated that she would 'use all legal methods to oppose it' and 'make it publicly known by all means available, in all countries where the film is likely to be shown' that Huston's film had been made in opposition to her and the Freud family's express wishes.[15] Subsequent correspondence between Edward Bernays, self-introduced 'double nephew of Professor Freud',[16] and Huston (though carefully crafted by Universal International's (UI) lawyers) explains that the producers had made a number of attempts to engage with Anna Freud and other members of the Freud family, including asking them to read draft scripts. Bernays' own offer to cooperate on the script was politely turned down.[17] Marilyn Monroe stated – in a personal letter to Huston on Beverly Hills Hotel letterhead – that the Freud family's ongoing disapproval was her reason for turning down 'the part of Annie O' [sic] despite, or perhaps, in spite of her 'personal regard' for Freud's work.[18]

Huston was set on another *star* name for the project. In 1958 he approached Jean-Paul Sartre, whose existentialist play *No Exit* Huston had directed in 1946, to write the screenplay, thinking him 'the ideal man' as he assumed Sartre 'knew Freud's work intimately and would have an objective and logical approach'.[19] Huston overestimated Sartre's knowledge of Freud. The director was pleased with Sartre's initial ninety-five-page synopsis, delivered in December 1958, but the creative collaboration started to unravel during and after Sartre's visit to Ireland to work with Huston on the script in October 1959, as the already unwieldy draft script had 'actually expanded to sixteen hundred pages' which would have necessitated a running time of, it was estimated, between 5 and 8 hours.[20] Huston handed over script editing and revision to trusted collaborators Wolfgang Reinhardt and Charlie Kaufman, who started to cut the film down to 3 hours. On 24 August 1961, Sartre said he wanted to 'withdraw my name since I recognise nothing of the initial project'. In 1960, Universal bought the property from Huston, though with him still attached to the project as director, but were concerned about the film's reception by the Production Code Administration (PCA) and, as discussed in the previous chapter, the Catholic Legion of Decency (the Legion). Universal were right to be concerned.

Although it is rarely highlighted as such, *Freud* is very significant in censorship terms, with its 'specialised nature' necessitating changes to the Code and its application, and, arguably, contributing to its subsequent suspension and demise. The PCA were presented with Sartre's script in mid-1960. Subsequently, the PCA's Geoffrey Shurlock and Jack Vizzard met with Reindhardt, and explained 'that because of the highly clinical nature of the script, dealing as it does with all sorts of incestuous relations and other sexual aberrations, we would not feel justified in taking on ourselves the responsibility of issuing a Code Seal for it'. They continued that the film 'did not fall into the normal category of entertainment films' and therefore 'in view of the very specialized nature of this material, we felt that, if the producer wished for a Code Seal, it would be granted by the Review Board'.[21] When the second draft script revised by Reinhardt and Kaufmann was submitted, the PCA reiterated to Huston and UI that the script triggered the 'same Code problems',[22] namely, the film was 'in violation of the sex perversion prohibition of the code' because it 'deals with such sexual aberrations such as infant sexuality and incestuous attraction between children and their parents'.[23]

Therefore, the nature of Freud's ideas regarding infantile sexuality and the Oedipus complex introduced in the late 1800s were, by their nature, in violation of the Code's 'sex perversion prohibition'. Rather than an issue of representation, the film's well-established and widely accepted scientific basis itself was the problem: this clearly raised an awkward issue for the PCA and highlighted the Code as antiquated. This prompted the PCA to do two things. First, to revisit the Code itself to assess whether it was still fit for purpose, and, secondly, to acknowledge the limits of its expertise and concede, like the Legion, to the opinion of psychiatric experts on whether this 'specialised film' was legitimate and suitable for general audiences. Shurlock suggested to Huston's publicist and 'fixer' William Gordon that 'the Production Code will be modified to the extent that the Production Code Administration will be allowed discretion to approve films which are now in violation of Section 3.6 (forbidding any inference of sex perversion)'.[24] The MPA Board of Directors met on 18 August 1961 to consider the Code change. Following this meeting, the nature of the correspondence on *Freud* shifts to suggest that the script now 'meet[s] the requirements of the Production Code', with Shurlock now flagging up mostly minor issues with script changed pages such as reducing the number of uses of terms such as 'sexual' and 'sexuality'.[25]

The investment in additional psychiatric expertise was, at least initially, motivated more by placating censors, the Catholic Church and wider public relations concerns. However, the intervention of key Freudian and wider psychiatric experts had a significant impact in reorienting, redressing flaws and updating the script for a 1960's psychiatric culture and audiences. Following initial consultation with the PCA, publicist William Gordon was brought in with a specific remit to 'create the climate requisite for general acceptance of the finished picture of Freud' through ongoing consultation with a variety of clinicians and clerics.[26] As discussed in Chapter 1, his initial consultation with the Legion raised their alarm that the film would perpetuate a public perception that Freud's ideas (and indeed 'the root of all mankind's problems') were all about sex, and encourage audiences to engage in dangerous self-analysis. However, they recognised that they did not have the requisite expertise to decide ultimately if the film propagated a positive or negative depiction of psychoanalytic history and technique, and therefore called on the filmmakers to 'obtain the advice and support of responsible mental health auspices', chiefly the American Psychoanalytic Association (APsA) and APA.[27] As a resultant, Gordon consulted a range of leading American and European psy experts, including prominent developmental psychologist and psychoanalyst Dr Erik Erikson, who underwent training analysis with Anna Freud, and American psychoanalyst and psychiatrist and co-founder of the American Foundation of Religion and Psychiatry Dr Smiley Blanton, who was in analysis with Sigmund Freud from 1929 to 1938. These consultations resulted in varied responses that can be understood in relation to shifting dynamics within the field of psychoanalysis and allied disciplines.

While popular culture was saturated with pseudo-Freudianism – from laymen's versions of his ideas in mass-market paperbacks like Rachel Baker's *Sigmund Freud for Everyone* (1955) to EC Comics 1955 'Psychoanalysis' comic book series – orthodox Freudian psychoanalysis as a science was in decline, with this mass cultural assimilation a simultaneous sign and cause of a perceived increasing scientific irrelevancy. Zaretsky explains that by 1960, applications for membership to the APsA were dwindling, the 'average age of members was rising sharply, and the number of patients was dwindling.'[28] He continues, 'Poised yet again between absorption into a therapeutic "feel-good" culture and relegation to its margins as its carping critic, the analytic church underwent one last convulsive schism.' Zaretsky explains that proponents of internal reform willing to 'adapt analysis to the needs of the age' stood on one side. While on the other side stood 'defenders of orthodoxy.'[29] In shifting from an intra-psychic idea of ego to the inter-subjective 'self', following the psychosocial thinking of ego psychologists like Erik Eriksen (who responded positively to the idea of the film), psychoanalytic 'reformers' were able to align more with youth cultural and, later, countercultural ideas of identity, lifestyle and liberation. This didactic division of the psychoanalytic community into two factions – the orthodox defenders of classical theory, and reformists sympathetic to aligning Freudian ideas with the 1960's shifting psychological and cultural landscapes – is useful in understanding the psy sciences' divergent responses to *Freud*.

Uniting the psychoanalytic church

The schism between defenders and reformers can be appreciated in the responses of the psychoanalytic community consulted on *Freud*. From the outset, many of the psychiatrists and psychoanalysts were critical of a film about Freud and his ideas – particularly given the Freud family's opposition. Even those who read the script and saw merit in it were sceptical that a popular film about Freud should be and could be made. As prominent German-born psychoanalyst Dr Martin Grotjahn explained, 'No matter what you people do, the family and most analysts will be critical.'[30] While

Grotjahn saw the script as a 'masterpiece', he did not wish to be involved or be seen to publicly endorse it. Similarly, the National Assortation for Mental Health (US) expressed that they were 'happy to give informal consultation', but stated categorically that they could not be seen to give 'formal endorsement' for it.[31] Others were more explicit about their position with regard to the factions of defenders or reformers. Dr Charles Curran of the Menninger Clinic, stated categorically that Freud could not be portrayed safely for the public, the profession or political status quo, 'in a popular movie even if it has an elite audience appeal'. He explained:

> Freud misunderstood, leads to a very shallow concept of public and private morality and to a general confirmation of the Communist propaganda view of the decadence of capitalist society. We already have too much of this in the film portrayals of ourselves that are seen at home and abroad. I feel that a popular but serious film on Freud will only add to this and therefore ignominy to our self-portrait.[32]

Curran makes explicit here, therefore, a link between the protection of the orthodox Freud and a protection of 'American world hegemony' in the context of Cold War international relations.[33]

However, one of the psy professionals Gordon consulted, Dr Earl Loomis, was surprisingly positive, detailed and measured in his response to the proposition and the draft script, and was happy to go on record stating so. As a result, he was appointed and credited as the film's technical adviser, for which he was paid a fee of $4,000. Loomis was a Professor of Psychiatry and Religion at the Union Theological Seminary in New York, the oldest independent seminary in the United States which was known for its progressive Christian scholarship. Loomis was in an ideal strategic position to bridge the fields of the psychiatry and religion as required by the PCA and Legion (as well as being open to a more reformist approach to foregrounding the more 'charismatic' Freud for 1960's sensibilities). As Gordon explained later to Huston while the film was in production in Vienna and Munich, 'I want to commend to you that which you are fully cognizant of – Earl's great value to us as the bridge and catalyst between his professional and/or religious colleagues in his chosen field – particularly when the picture will first get over here.' He continued, 'I want to reiterate that I think it is absolutely essential that before the picture is finally cut you give him an opportunity to look at it and perhaps show it to some key people . . . in order that the film received a vital support which will mark the difference between approval and rejection by the Legion of Decency.'[34]

As this above quote suggests, Loomis' role developed beyond brokering the 'support of the organised psychiatric fraternity', which was an 'essential element' of his contribution, to become a key creative influence in script development, even production and post-production decisions such as editing. As Gordon reiterated regarding the final edit stage, 'you value Earl's judgement and will want his advice'.[35] In June 1961, Loomis supplied an initial four-page response to Sartre's screenplay that was based on three script readings, cross-referencing 'for accuracy' with Freud's letters and *Studies in Hysteria*, and comparison with the concurrent 1961 Broadway play about Freud's life, *A Far Country*. Loomis' conclusion was that the film's screenplay was 'a work of essential fidelity and fact'.[36] His report comments on key aspects of accuracy, characterisation, insight, emotional impact, aesthetic value, and ethical and religious implications. Loomis was positive on all of these aspects, commending the manuscript's demonstration of 'remarkable aesthetic sensitivity' in balancing narrativising 'a life drama and the birth of a science', and suggested on the final aspect of religious implications that, '[t]he story is basically one of high ethical standards and, if anything, underplays Freud's impatience with both religion and the pseudo-morality of conventional society'. Despite these significant 'virtues', he foresaw problems that more orthodox Freudians may have with the necessary simplification of theory and condensation of history, the characterisation of a 'fallible' Freud ('Some are unwilling to see him taken off his pedestal') and the revelation of the science's 'inner secrets'. He explained, 'Some analysts will object to their patients knowing in this way, and some non-analysts may object to the picture, seeing it as propaganda for analysts.'[37]

Despite his significant praise for the screenplay, Loomis made some directed suggestions for changes and additions. He advised caution in handling the dream scenes 'with a view to keeping them sufficiently "unreal" or "bizarre" to avoid their confusion with reality' for audiences. Despite 'these cautions' he also warned of the 'opposite possibility' of losing the 'impact of sexuality and the depth of emotion attendant thereto', so this aesthetic distinction was recommended as a mechanism to defend against losing the power of these important scenes and ideas. As discussed in the following section, devising distinct visual styles to differentiate between reality, dreams and reminiscence within the therapeutic setting were central to the film's art direction and were foregrounded as a mechanism to counter the Legion and PCA's moral concerns about the film. Whether Loomis was a key influence on these later stylistic decisions is unsure, but certainly psychiatric and cinematic thinking aligned here.

One important area in which we can be sure that Loomis was influential is in regard to gendered representation of patients. Loomis posed the question, 'Do you need more male cases?' In particular he explained, 'As I said during our luncheon, the "hysteria" case might be a male, the better to bring out the point that up until Freud's time hysteria was felt to be exclusively a

Figure 3.1 *A Clinical Lesson at the Salpêtrière,* 1887, by André Brouillet. André Brouillet, Public domain, via Wikimedia Commons. Wellcome Collection CC-BY

female condition.'[38] The scene to which Loomis is referring is the Charcot scene, from which the inspiration and mise en scène was directly taken from André Brouillet's 1887 painting *A Clinical Lesson at the Salpêtrière* (a lithograph of which hung above Freud's couch) (see Figure 3.1).[39] The painting features a female hysteria patient being presented to a group of postgraduate students by French neurologist Jean-Martin Charcot, who, as the film shows, Freud studied with in Paris.

In Sartre's script, which was sent to Loomis, two female hysteria patients (Jeanne and Paulette) are presented and hypnotised in front to the students. In the final film, the first patient closely resembles the woman in Brouillet's painting, but the second hysteria patient is changed to an adult male, Servais, who is subsequently placed in a somnambulic trance (see Figure 3.2). Mark Micale's revisionist history, *Hysterical Men*, highlights the significance of this scene in countering the ingrained image of hysteria as a purely female malady: 'What on earth is a male patient doing on stage as a chosen clinical subject of the most renowned hysteria doctor in history?'[40] But Micale attributes the film's important gender reorientation to Huston, rather than its technical adviser Loomis. Loomis was at pains to stress that many of Freud's patients – and case history subjects – were male, and to caution against perpetuating an over-emphasis on his female patients and underplaying his significant role in revealing that 'hysteria', and other contemporary diagnoses, were equally 'male maladies'. This undersold both

Figure 3.2 John Huston restaged and updated Brouillet's painting to include a male patient for *Freud* (1962)

Freud's historical resonance and contemporary relevance to 1960's analysts, analysands and audiences. Loomis did suggest the focus on 'Freud's own problems', and resultant self-analysis, as an important compensation for the 'minor' nature of the male cases.

It was reported during production, in both trade and news presses, that the actors portraying the hysteria patients in the Charcot scenes were real psychiatric patients undergoing hypnosis on the studio set. *Variety* reported on the authentic hypnosis scenes currently being filmed in Germany, which were flagged up as a marker of both the film's 'documentary' realism and its ethical treatment of its subject. *Variety* reported that having completed location shooting in Munich and Vienna, filming for these scenes had been moved to a studio in Bavaria where, 'Shooting takes place behind locked doors with such secrecy as though stage two were actually a treatment room. At times it is.' The article explained that leading US psychotherapists and their patients had been flown in to perform treatment 'in front of the Huston camera'. The article stressed the producers' concerns regarding objections by the American Medical Association stating, 'For fear of infractions of ethics of the profession, the whole procedure was handled with documentary type clinical approach.'[41] The *Los Angeles Times* also reported that Huston had used 'a real patient and had her hypnotised on screen', identifying her, through the accompanying image, as the woman in the Charcot scene who, 'because of her high susceptibility to hypnosis, is often a subject in research'. Huston claimed 'no actress could convincingly portray someone under deep hypnosis.'[42] On release, *Life* magazine focused on this scene in its promotion of the film, using images of the original painting and a still of the films' Charcot hypnosis scene to indicate their visual comparability and Huston's 'insistence on authenticity'. The article explained, 'The reconstructed event makes cinema history: the patient in the movie was actually put in a hypnotic trance before the scenes was filmed.'[43]

One of the other aspects raised by a number of the other psy consultants was the demand for a more wide-ranging depiction of other psychoanalytic, psychological and psychiatric approaches, and an explication of how Freudian ideas and techniques had developed since within these fields. For example, one psychology professor stressed that it was 'very important' that an epilogue be added to explain 'rival theories', including Jung and Alfred Adler's (founder of school of individual psychology), both of whom 'opposed and left' Freud due to his pan-sexualism'.[44] Loomis contested these demands, going further in calling to further de-complexify related elements of Sartre's script, 'I suggest avoiding any attempt to present comparative schools of psychoanalysis as a backdrop to this play', stating that 'the Breuer–Freud differences are sufficiently elucidated to indicate one major variation in emphasis. This is enough for the public to digest.' He defended:

> This is the most compelling presentation of the insight of the early stages of psychoanalysis that I have ever encountered. It is authentic and convincing, and it leaves one with a flavour the truth is just beginning. This flavour should not be destroyed by preambles, prologue, epilogues. This is a work of art and should be presented as such.[45]

Huston and Gordon held comparable esteem and respect for Loomis' expertise, as expressed in a memo between the two men that stated, 'Your original estimate of this fine gentleman is certainly fully justified.'[46]

In addition to his ongoing role in script development – including one-to-one meetings with Huston to go 'deeply into the implication and details of the Sartre script' – Loomis' role involved instigating and overseeing the process of consultation with a number of other psy experts. In August 1961, Loomis consulted with well-respected and connected New York physician and psychiatrist Dr Harvey Tompkins (soon-to-be president of the APA, 1966–1967) and his assistant Dr Campbell, as well as Reverend William C. Bier (co-founder of the American Catholic Psychological Association and a professor of psychology at Fordham University). Tompkins expressed concern that the plan was for an 'entertainment' film rather than a documentary, and, perhaps as a resultant, felt that it would do 'harm to Freud's image and that of psychiatry in the eyes of the public'. In particular, 'He was troubled by the amount of lineage given to dream sequences and by the extent to which they disclose personal aspects of Freud.' This criticism corresponds with Loomis' prediction that some psychiatrists would oppose the idea of exposing Freud's vulnerability and fallibility – which Loomis welcomed – and the disclosure of the profession's inner secrets, particularly through the interpretation of Freud's own dreams.[47] The 'dream themes' were also a key issue for cleric-clinician Bier, who wished to see them 'de-sexualised'. While he commended that the screenplay 'corrects continually the false impression about sex, he feels that the general audience is going to miss these aspects and see only the general aspects'. Like Tompkins, Bier makes a clear distinction between 'sophisticated persons' and general audiences, stating 'Since the plot is admittedly sexual, this feature will confirm the public in their belief about Freud.'

Loomis' response to these criticisms was to go back to Freud's original texts. To even more explicitly 'draw parallels between the sequences of experiences in the development of Cecily's neurosis and Freud's', and in addressing the misconceptions that 'repression is the cause of neurosis, that repression is always bad, that sex is the only thing that is repressed'. Addressing Freud's first major speech on repression, Loomis stated, 'There is even a chance here to begin to show society's function as being a little more complex than simply forcing the repression of sex. To be specific, Freud learned that sexuality was divided into pre-genital and post-genital sexuality. Society's denial of the existence of the first is what delayed the discovery of infantile sexuality.' He continued, 'Both neuroses and perversions are as much due, Freud learned, to the *unsuccessful* functioning of the mechanism of repression (and the consequent return of the repressed) as to the existence of repression.' Therefore, rather than simplify what the critics perceived as being the 'too technical' nature of the material for general audiences, Loomis advised adding more complexity and nuance in discussing the concept of repression, while foregrounding the continued relevance of Freud's ideas to understanding the operation of power through societies, structures and ideologies.[48]

Concurrently, Loomis sought approval of a number of religious representatives ('two priests, six ministers, and a rabbi approve of the play'),[49] including Rabbi Hollander of the New York Board of Rabbis who also provided some technical advice. In September 1961, Loomis visited the (Oska) Pfister archives in Zurich, Switzerland – Pfister being a close friend and correspondent of Freud who resisted the city's Jungian turn – undertaking further research for the film, and consulting with a number of renowned Swiss psychoanalysts who expressed 'unanimous concern about the [Freud] family's objections to the film'. This realisation of 'active objection' by the psychoanalytic establishment triggered a momentary bout of 'soul searching' for Loomis regarding his role, but this was allayed by meeting Huston, his family and scriptwriter Reinhardt on production in Vienna and Munich. Being on-set reinstalled his commitment to 'work toward making this the best possible film of its kind'.[50] Loomis continued to advise on script changes both on location and from New York throughout the 118-day filming schedule,[51] focusing particularly on the authenticity of the dream sequences and the quality of the dialogue when Freud and Breuer interpret and discuss them.[52] British physician and 'celebrity psychiatrist' Dr David Stafford-Clark, then head of psychiatry at Guy's Hospital and regular presenter for BBC medical programming, was brought in as an additional adviser during the shooting phase in Europe.[53] Correspondence in the Huston archives suggests that his role on-set was, whether intended or not, more acting as a personal physician to the troubled Clift (struggling with impacting mental health and alcohol issues) and to a lesser extent, Huston himself, than offering advice on the film, although there are examples of his input here too.[54] He was accordingly credited with the suitably equivocal title of 'Medical Adviser' in the film's credits.

In May and June 1962, Loomis hosted a series of preview screenings in New York for influential psychiatric and religious groups. First, Loomis screened the film to two influential figures in the APsA, chairman of the local public relations committee Dr Lyman Harrison, and Dr Rudolf Eckstein, a Viennese analyst who was 'one of the select five or six non-medical men who have been accepted as members of the American Psychoanalytic Association'. While both initially expressed 'horror' at his involvement in the film and were concerned he would 'be ruined professionally', both did a 'complete switch' following the screening, congratulating him on his involvement and offering their help in advocating for the film and recruiting key figures to attend the New York screenings.[55] Loomis reported to Gordon that a 'more favourable general impression that has begun to circulate' in the American psychoanalytic community, and while the APsA refused to change their 'hands-off' position on endorsing the film, key members had expressed a wish to 'help in every way possible', including '"getting their licks in" for the picture' at the forthcoming annual convention of the APsA in Toronto.[56] In a letter from Gordon to Production Chief Muhl, he expressed that through Loomis, 'This is all according to the plan as originally evolved' when the Legion 'asked us to obtain support' from the main psy science bodies.[57] Loomis' expertise and advocacy were clearly pivotal in establishing a clinical context and climate in which Freud's work could be translated to the screen; it then fell to Huston and his creative team to marshal their expertise in visualising Freud's 'complex psychiatric language' for both an informed and lay audience.

Translating psychiatric language into visual images

In his *New York Times*' article examining 'his own motivations' for making *Freud*, Huston explained 'We have attempted to accomplish something new in storytelling on the screen – to penetrate through to the unconscious of the audience . . . to shock and move the spectator into at least a subliminal recognition or awareness of his own hidden psychic motivations.'[58] Stopping just short of positioning the film *as* therapy, Huston's lofty ambitions were to innovate a new mode of 'storytelling' that, challenging Freud's own scepticism about the medium, would work psychoanalytically in penetrating through spectators' defences and bringing unconscious material, at least subliminally, into their conscious minds. In concluding on the film's intervention, Huston grounded his strategy within a more familiar and popular storytelling mode, stating, 'I believe our film is a species of thriller – a mystery of a very special sort in which it is demonstrated through the people on the screen that the assassin which Freud sought and captured lies hidden deep within each of them . . . within each of us.'[59]

Huston's characterisation of this 'psychiatric biography' as actually 'a mystery of a very special sort', aligns with rather than opposes academic understandings of the Freudian case histories on which it is based. As Carol Berkenkotter explains, 'in Freud's hands, the case history takes on a number of attributes of literary narratives; these include a plot, characters, temporal movement (past–present–future), dialogue in the form of reported speech, and, finally, a climactic peripeteia, not unlike a Sherlock Holmes mystery novel.'[60] The use of such literary stylistic devices and longer narrative forms to capture the complex 'double narrative', of the verbatim exposition of the analysand's reported speech and the analyst's evolving interpretations and techniques, distinguished the Freudian long case history from earlier psychiatric case histories.[61] Before Freud, psychiatric case histories were modelled on the reporting style of established medical case histories as they assumed that mental illness was a 'physical problem that could be approached through physical treatments and understood with reference to hereditary degeneration and lesions that ideally could be discovered on autopsy.'[62]

As Sealey demonstrates, the 'Freudian long case history' was distinguished not only in terms of its detail, but also in terms of narrative structure, eschewing chronology for a narrative of treatment and diagnosis that may jump around historically. Sealey explains, 'Freud thought that case histories should reflect the disjointed narratives offered by patients.'[63] It also differed in terms of the psychiatrists' diegetic positioning as 'character' with 'Freud's case histories impl[ying] a different doctor–patient relationship. Freud was both author and character in his texts.'[64] Therefore, the film's complex narrative structure and use of Freud as a character in the story of his discoveries – a double detection narrative interweaving his and his patients' revelations – speaks of fidelity to its source text, *Studies in Hysteria*, rather than a Hollywoodisation. Through its narrative structure and formal innovations, Huston's *Freud* seeks to capture this sense of simultaneity in the birth of a scientific method and the birth of narrative form, what Forrester calls 'thinking in cases'.[65]

Freud begins with a spoken prologue, voiced by Huston who also pro-vides commentary throughout, that compares Freud's discoveries to those of Copernicus and Darwin. An establishing shot of the Vienna skyline is superimposed with the title 'Vienna 1885' as the camera pans down to show a large hospital. Inside Vienna General Hospital, thirty-year-old neurolo-gist Freud (Montgomery Clift) argues with his superior, Professor Theo-dore Meynert (Eric Portman), over the nature of hysteria and takes a leave of absence from the hospital. In Paris, he studies under Professor Charcot (Fernand Ledoux), a pioneer in the use of hypnosis to demonstrate that dis-ease can be mentally induced. On his return, Freud presents on his fellow-ship and initial findings with Charcot at the Vienna Society of Physicians, receiving a critical response. Following his marriage to Martha Bernays (Susan Kohner), Freud becomes the protégé of Dr Joseph Breuer (Larry Parks), another advocate of hypnotism, and together they treat Cecily Koertner (Susannah York), a semi-paralysed young woman who also suffers from insomnia and impaired vision. Cecily is based on Anna O (and named as such in Sartre's original December 1958 synopsis), who is considered the 'ur-patient of psychoanalysis'[66] and was actually Breuer's patient (in the film Freud subsequently takes her on). The Cecily character incorporates elements of other Freud's cases in *Studies in Hysteria* (particularly Emmy von N.), though not Cäcille M. after whom she is named (as Cäcille in Sartre's original script).

As a result of his sessions with both Cecily and Carl von Schlosser (David McCallum), a young man who assaulted his father because of an incestuous love for his mother, Freud determines that all neuroses stem from repressed sexuality. Cecily and Carl are 'vehicles through which to show the develop-ment of Freud's thinking, and thus the development of the psychoanalytic apparatus'[67]; his discovery of Carl's death in an asylum drives him on to his discovery of a 'general theory of neurosis' based on sexual repression. His revolutionary theory, partially based upon his own childhood recollections and analysis of his dreams, offends the entire medical profession, including Breuer. Nevertheless, Freud continues experimenting with Cecily and even-tually drops hypnosis in favour of the new technique of 'free association', in which he is able to analyse her dreams and interpret the meaning of chance remarks she makes during their conversations. As Cecily's mental health gradually improves, Freud develops his theory of the Oedipus complex and delivers a lecture on the subject; his colleagues react with derisive shouts, but psychoanalysis is born. The film concludes with a poetic spoken epilogue, again voiced by Huston, superimposed over Freud visiting his father's grave.

The film's prologue and epilogue were the subject of much discussion and debate and, as explained above, were seen by clinicians and clerics as key to framing the film's positing of Freudian psychoanalysis as a science, and its connections to other approaches to understanding psychology and human nature.[68] The prologue in the film maps the 'three great changes in man's idea of himself' through Copernicus, Darwin and then Freud's discovery of 'the existence of another part of our mind, which functions in darkest secrecy and can even rule our lives'. The prologue concludes, 'This is the story of Freud's descent into a region almost as black as hell itself: Man's unconscious, and how he let in the light.' As discussed in Chapter 1, the wording of the prologue was seen as central to the Legion and their psy/religious advisers, and it remained contested beyond the premiere of the film . The wording stating that the unconscious 'requires our blind obedience' was softened to 'can even rule our lives' for the subsequent theatrical release.[69]

Huston was concerned that the competing clinical, clerical and creative requirements had necessitated 'quite a long forward' and that as a result, 'animated abstractions' rather than a static background was required, one 'that would move and change according to the text' as it shift its reference to Copernicus, Darwin and Freud.[70] He consulted trusted art director Stephen Grimes, who suggested that rather than traditional animation, they could use 'static abstracts' painted on photographic glass plates that, through oscillating back lighting and 'in-and-out vaseline glass', create 'a mysterious sort of burgeoning of shapes and shadows. This would foretaste and lead-into the "Dream Technique".'[71] Huston followed Grimes' advice, with the technique allowing the abstracted image, through manipulation and inference, to take on shifting connotations of the cosmos, a primordial organism, the unconscious, even a Rorschach inkblot (a widely used and recognised psychiatric symbol in Hollywood films) (see Figure 3.3).

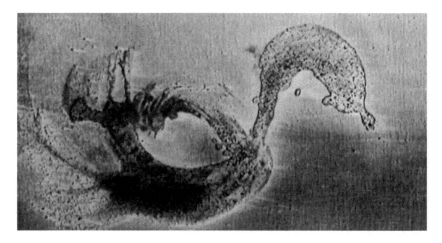

Figure 3.3 The ambiguous, abstracted background for *Freud's* foreword

To highlight the innovations of *Freud*'s staging of its therapy scenes and dream sequences, an interesting contrast is the psychological drama *Pressure Point* (1962). The film was released at the same time as *Freud* and stars Sidney Poitier as a psychiatrist, simply named Doctor, assigned to treat a racist prisoner, called Patient, who is played by Bobby Darin. The film was based on the wartime experience of Jewish-American psychoanalyst Dr Robert M. Lindner (whose 1944 book *Rebel Without a Cause: The Hypnoanalysis of a Criminal Psychopath* had already been adapted as successful 1955 film), who, while working at a prison in 1942, treated an American fascist. The story of his analysis with the Nazi sympathiser was published, alongside four of Lindner's other case histories, in his best-selling book *The Fifty Minute Hour: A Collection of True Psychoanalytic Tales* (1954). For the psychotherapy scenes, director Hubert Cornfield chose a more theatrical technique, using temporal overlaying of voiceover of the therapy session in the present and visual 'flashback' to the Patient's recollections of childhood, but also, at times, visually overlaying these two moments within same mise en scène. For example, when the Patient acquiesces to treatment, the Doctor explains, 'After several extremely slow and difficult months of analysis there came a knowledge, a beginning.' The rear view of a child (the adolescent Patient) on a black background slowly appears as the Doctor's voiceover continues explaining his traumatic childhood as a result of an angry, alcoholic father and the 'vengeful resentment he felt towards his son'. The father, framed in the foreground now, turns and chases the son. As he goes to strike the child, the lights go on and the altercation between father and son plays out within the same compositional space as the therapy session in which these memories are being recounted (see Figure 3.4).

The camera pans across to the adult Patient as he mimes, in the child's voice, 'I wouldn't cry. I promised myself I wouldn't cry.' We hear the Doctor's voice ask, 'why not?' To which the Patient, still in his younger voice responds, 'Because then I'd be like her.' The camera pans left, moving from the Patient on the therapist's couch in the present, to his infirm mother in bed in his past. She calls over the child Patient, who, the Doctor's voiceover explains, has 'reluctantly been the sole object of her affection'. The boy then hesitantly joins her on the bed. There is an abrupt cut back to the therapy session in the present, where the agitated Patient sits up and says, 'How long is this gonna take anyway?' In employing a minimalist mise en scène and dramatic device of composing two planes of action on-screen, Director Cornfield heralded this 'style as entirely new, a fusion of stage technique and cinematic art' that would have the 'the eye of the spectator glued on the screen'.[72] While some critics appreciated the staging of the analysis scenes, the *New York Times* reviewer complained that these 'gooey, surrealist montages are pretentious, even absurd', making the film 'blunted with too many

Figure 3.4 The theatrical staging of the therapy scenes in *Pressure Point* (1962)

theatrical contrivances'.[73] For *Freud*, the filmmakers sought to avoid precisely these sort of stagy or surrealist cliches, driving them to innovate a cinematic approach grounded in the material cultures of film's past and present.

Freud's innovations in the use of cinematic techniques and technologies for representing dreams and regression, Grime's 'Dream Technique', were motivated by simultaneous creative ambitions and classification concerns. In a 1961 memo to Huston titled 'Freud – Dream Sequences', Art Director Grimes communicated his lofty ambition that with *Freud*, 'we might possibly evolve a whole new movie language, for dream sequences at least'. He suggested being mindful of precursory innovations, particularly the work of Bergman and Bunuel, but stressed the need to '[a]void the usual cliches of the dream sequence, the watery dissolves, fuzzed-out edges of frame, stagy fantastic sets, characters wading around in knee-deep dry ice mists, outer-space choirs, echo-chamber commentators, melting watches and cracked swans'. For dreams, Grimes wished to counter these 'stagy' cliches with location filming and 'a quite hard realism; but with distortions, distortions however that don't attract attention to themselves as tricks of mechanics, whether of camerawork, sets, sound or cutting'. To achieve this, Grimes was looking to recreate the 'grainy and Orthochromatic' look of films created in the 'silent film era' (orthochromatic film stock was used from the cinema of attractions era of the 1990s to the mid-1920s). He explains, 'For my money, the closest photographic approach to a dream mood is seen in early movies, and as this opinion seems to be fairly general, I think we should go out to recreate this affect . . .' Grimes explains that this effect could be created by 'shooting on Eastmancolor negative and printing in black and white', but also using some of the techniques employed during the silent period to counter some of the 'limitations' of the film stock, such as 'building interior scenes out-doors as was done in the early years'. Grimes also suggested considering other effects that could be achieved on-set (rather than in post-production), such as shooting interior scenes from a distance with a telephoto lens to create perceptual tricks: 'The distortion would be confined to the characters – whose movements get them nowhere.'[74] Grimes, therefore, suggested avoiding (the perception at least) of modern technologies and scientific techniques (including the use of colour for the dream sequences which was 'thrown out' very early) in favour of creating a more materially grounded aesthetic that was contemporary with the late nineteenth-century period depicted in the film.

The aesthetic of aligning the authentically-staged turn-of-the-century setting (filmed both on location and in studio settings in Austria and Germany) with use of techniques and technologies from the same period, was shared by the film's cinematographer Douglas Slocombe. This was achieved not just through the recreation of the grainy orthochromatic effect of silent cinema for the dream sequences, but also in innovating a technique using manipulated glass photographic plates from the period of early photography as a mechanism to create a distinct aesthetic for the scenes of regression in therapy (see Figure 3.5). Slocombe spent a month testing out these different techniques on-set prior to shooting. He explained:

> What John Huston wanted here was an overall style, and within that two separate styles, one for the dreams and one for the flashbacks, which would be so different that the audience always knew where they were. I used very sharp photography for the main part of the film, to give the clarity of steel etchings and help the period feeling. For flashbacks I shot through a glass plate, treated to fuzz out all details except those most clearly recalled by the patient. For the dream sequences I aimed for a very contrasting, grainy affect and extreme black-and-white, in which chalky faces and relevant details would stand out like luminous figures in a tunnel of blackness.[75]

Slocombe states that his experimentation with selection, exposure and development of different film stock began on *Freud* (working contrary to the Kodak instructions on the film), but was then adopted and adapted for other projects after 1962 including British psychodrama *The Servant* (1963).[76]

As discussed in Chapter 1, the Legion and their psychiatric experts were concerned about an unsophisticated general audience's perception that Freud's ideas were all about sex, and about their inability to understand the

Figure 3.5 Douglas Slocombe's innovative technique for therapy scenes, shot through a manipulated glass photographic plate

narrative and moral implications of his 'dangerous' science. This patronising and paternalistic opinion of the public led to a particular concern about depictions of prostitution in the brothel scenes. Producer William Gordon sought to address these concerns not by countering these opinions with the sophistication of cinema audiences, but by stressing that cinematographic mechanisms had been marshalled by expert filmmakers to redress these misunderstandings. He explained, 'As you will recall, all of these scenes are played during visualized dreams and I am confident that all of the phantasy segments will communicate a bizarre, unreal, never-never land atmosphere which should do much to ameliorate and mitigate the adverse effect which you anticipate.'[77] The sound design for the film also sought to enhance the distinction between material reality and interiority by contrasting its more traditional score, by renowned Hollywood composer and conductor Jerry Goldsmith, to 'special electronic musical compositions composed and recorded by [experimental Indo-Dutch composer] Henk Badings for the dream sequences, marking the first use in an American film of this unusual type of music'.[78] These dream and regression sequences represent more than a device to placate censorship concerns, however, forming a central structuring principle of the film's core aim to demonstrate the creation, even co-creation, of a science.

Through visual parallels and temporal overlaps and confusions, the film stresses the importance of the dialogues between Freud and Cecily's dreams and reminiscences, in the co-creation and abandonment of seduction theory and its replacement with infantile sexuality and the Oedipus complex. Loomis discussed with Huston the efficacy and accuracy of the 'parallels of the Egyptian women in both Freud and Cecily's dreams'

Figure 3.6 *Freud*'s orthochromatic dream sequence draws links between Freud and Cecily's dreams and reminiscences

(see Figure 3.6). While he warned that some might question its credulity, he explained, 'In my own experience patients and I have dreamed similar dreams and used similar images in striking proximity of time.'[79] Therefore, the Egyptian dream motif introduced by Cecily in a therapy session halfway through the film represents both a flashback and foreshadowing of Freud's own dreams featuring his mother in Egyptian dress. The significance of the dreams and regression scenes – and their dialogue – has been foregrounded by Sigler. Although the film eschews details of individual case histories, in 'teach[ing] us to read hysteria through flashbacks, free association, and parallel asynchronous story lines', the film, Sigler argues, becomes a 'very subtle and sophisticated adaptation of *Studies on Hysteria*'. He explains that 'The film is literally hysterical: Huston seems to have taken to heart Freud and Breuer's warning that the act of telling a nonfictional story is inevitably so, in that "*hysterics suffer mainly from reminiscences*" [author's emphasis].'[80] While some critics would identify this narrative complexity and formal innovation as a form of fidelity to Freud's theories and texts, others experienced it as either failed storytelling or failed art, or both.

Identifying the audience for *Freud*

A three-hour version of *Freud* was premiered on 12 November 1962 at Ivy League university Dartmouth College's new Hopkins Arts Centre. The choice of venue and programming with a semi-academic panel discussion on 'the motion picture as an art form' – with Huston, veteran *New York Times* film critic Bosley Crowther, and film academic and former executive Arthur Mayer – sought to further legitimise and distinguish it from other Hollywood entertainment films. A *New York Times'* article on the 'prevue' explained that Huston's pre-screening framing of the film was 'sufficiently technical and knowing to satisfy the students of psychology who may have suspected him of being one of the "Hollywood commercialists" who came in for much implied criticism from the student questioners.'[81] The film, now edited down to 2 hours 20 minutes, was subsequently show on an exclusive run in December 1962 in a couple of prestigious first-run cinemas in New York (new art cinema Cinema I and Cinema II) and in Los Angeles (Beverly Hills Music Hall) ahead of an unspecified 1963 nationwide release. These screenings allowed the film to qualify for Academy Award nominations, while also, hopefully, generating positive reviews and word-of-mouth. These strategies did not translate into huge success in regard to critical acclaim – *Freud* was nominated for only two Oscars, for its script and score, and won none. Though it did initially receive positive critical and audience reception in New York and Los Angeles, where the film was hailed as a 'traumatic cinema experience', 'a masterpiece, very probably one of the great motion pictures',[82] this did not really translate nationally or internationally.

The film was released in other metropolitan areas including Chicago and Boston in late February 1963,[83] moving slowly around the country until it reached some of the neighbourhood theatres in America's small towns in the autumn. While the film held over in some of the major cities (it was still playing in New York and Los Angeles after twelve and nine weeks, respectively), when it received the wider national release, it struggled to attract audiences outside these metropolitan areas. As *Variety* reported on the 'let-down' of the film in Minneapolis where bookings were cancelled, 'too many of their potential patrons were unacquainted with the discovery of psychoanalysis and the title was detrimental to business'. The distributor responded by changing the title to *Secret Passion* – an abridged version of the European release title, *Freud: The Secret Passion* – which was reported to have 'considerably boosted bookings and audiences.'[84] Despite such innovations, across the film's theatrical run it took only $2.9 million at the domestic box office, failing to recoup the $4 million it cost to make (the original budget was $2 million).

The film's retitling for European release raised some confusion and contention from critics and censors with regard to the distributor playing on public perceptions of Freud being synonymous with sex. When asked by distributor Rank to provide a new certification for the film under the new title *Freud: The Secret Passion*, BBFC Secretary John Trevelyan expressed his dismay at the sexualisation of this 'film of delicacy and quality'. He explained:

> The ordinary cinema public will know very little about Freud – although I hope that the film will educate them – but I think that if they know anything about him it will probably be the last to mistaken idea that people's actions are highly motivated by sexual urges. To introduce sex into the title would seem to me to aim at attracting people on an utterly wrong basis.[85]

While the filmmakers had sought to placate the censors, clerics and clinicians' concerns regarding the sexual connotations of Freud and *Freud*, the film's domestic and overseas distributors sought to maximise their sexual connotations, even for those who may have little or no knowledge of him. While initial trade adverts for the metropolitan release sought to reproduce the dark and serious aesthetic and tone of the film (a *New York Times* advert featured a monochrome image of Cecily's shadowed face and read, 'Few of man's great adventures can challenge a journey into the uncharted depths of the human mind'), for the film's national release campaign, more sexually suggestive imagery and taglines populate the posters and pressbook (one tagline read, 'A girl barely out of her teens . . . yet obsessed by strange desires and forbidden dreams'). These angles were further foregrounded for the retitled film's domestic and overseas markets, operating almost entirely within the realm of the double entendre.

In terms of its critical reception, after initial high praise in the *New York Times* and *Los Angeles Times*, the film received mixed reviews on its wider release. Irrespective of whether critics liked it or not, they focused on similar areas, but judged them divergently depending on their and their readership's perceived priorities. Three key areas of concern were: what genre it was; whether it was authentic; and who its audiences would or should be? A primary point of contention within the reception of the film is its generic status – whether biography or theory are dominant, or indeed are balanced in an effective fashion – and whether these choices are appropriate for imparting Freudian ideas (chiefly a concern for the middle-brow press's film critics), or appealing for mainstream audiences (the chief concern for the trade presses). On the whole, middle-brow critics who disliked the film dismissed it as a biopic or film biography in the classical Hollywood tradition, while those who liked it aligned it with other more literary and artistic traditions. For example, the *Listener* highlighted the 'insoluble problem' of the film biography, juxtaposing the notable exceptions of Orson Welles' *Citizen Kane* (1942) and Max Ophuls' *Lola Montes* (1955) – 'only biographies in the loosest sense of the word' – to 'those Hollywood life stories' of the 1930s and 1940s 'which were usually about scientists, and which pur-ported to "tell all", with solemn and apparently scientific truth'. The critic laments, 'John Huston's *The Secret Passion*, though much superior in quality, is of this genre.' He wonders whether a 'more fanciful director', like Fellini, might have 'given us a more imaginative perhaps more dishonest study'.[86] Following Huston's lead (and the film's PR), *Time* characterised the film as a 'taut intellectual thriller'; 'a vastly exciting drama of detection, in which the audience simultaneously sees a lurid mystery and unfold and a momentous theory develop'.[87]

Conversely, the *Hollywood Reporter* is positive about the film precisely as it is seen to follow 'the tradition of the great film biographies of the 1930s' while being 'scrupulous in in scientific detail'.[88] This successful meld-ing is referred to as 'objective biography' by the *Reporter*. *Variety*, on the other hand, bemoans that this balance is not achieved in this 'psychological drama', with theory winning out:

> ... not even the keen and fruitful imagination of John Huston, its director and prime creative force, can quite isolate the stirring per-sonal drama of the man and his story from the dry, impersonal, somewhat stuffy and pretentious characteristics of a text, the aca-demic shell from which the dramatic scenes never quite escapes.

Although *Freud*'s 'integrity and artistic merit' is commended, the reviewer concludes that the film – more akin to 'educational television' than enter-tainment – will have 'limited appeal and acceptance'.[89] The 'electrifying and chilling' dream and regression sequences – attributed creatively to Slo-combe as well as Huston – are highlighted for pumping 'visual vigour into a screen story basically static and clinical in nature'. For *Variety* the clinical and cinematic are in opposition.

A number of critics praised the mise en scène for its historical authen-ticity in its settings – the Charcot scene being a key benchmark of this – as well as its casting. As veteran critic for the *Los Angeles Times*, Philp Scheuer commended, 'it takes on the very distillation of the time and place'. He also praised the 'nightmare' dream sequences and their effect– crediting both Slocombe and Goldsmith and Henk's soundscape – which he saw as 'so real that one is tempted to shield one's eyes against them'. However, invoking a derisory politics of tastes, Scheuer reserved this affective engagement with *Freud* to elite audiences, commending 'its very ability of getting inside the mind, the body, the heart, too, for those with the intelligence to absorb it'.[90] Scheuer was very positive about the casting and performances of Clift as Freud and York as Cecily, as were most critics, but others questioned these casting decisions with relation to authenticity. This included a troubling review, from the British lifestyle magazine *The Talter and Bystander*, that derided York's casting as she 'look[s] too knowing by half'. It continues, 'Miss York gives me the impression that she is just playing-up to attract people's attention – I felt a brisk spanking would do this girl a power of good – but maybe a desire to be the focus of attention is a form of mental sickness.'[91]

The film received limited discussion in medical or religious publications, but, where they did, they tended to question its generic status, authenticity and fidelity to its source texts. Christian weekly *America* magazine offered a bad review of this 'pedestrian' 'film biography', which failed to instil 'a sense of intellectual and dramatic excitement' and presented universally 'inadequate performances'.[92] Writing in *American Psychologist*, the American Psychological Association's journal, renowned psychologist and psychotherapist Saul Rosenzweig, warned that 'the much-heralded motion picture *Freud*, which is currently attracting large audiences, is an enticement to delusion'. He continued that the film failed both to inform and entertain, alerting his peers to 'caution the unwary that the picture is historically inaccurate; that it gives an utterly distorted conception of psychoanalysis; and that, as cinematic drama, it is third rate'. Expressing a clear distain for popular Hollywood forms he warned that '[t]he case histories are needlessly concocted in the fashion of science fiction' and that even the 'dream sequences, which one would expect to have been prepared with a particular sense of psychological and artistic acumen, are a caricature; the figures in them resemble those of some antiquated wax works. Better presentations of the Freudian dream have found their way into animated cartoons'.[93] Rosenzweig, who had corresponded with Freud about his laboratory experiments on repression, was most known within psychology for his work on aggression, which led to the Rosenzweig Picture-Frustration Study. The projective technique was adopted in Europe but, perhaps ironically, it is mostly remembered now for its use in Stanley Kubrick's *A Clockwork Orange* (1971).

A number of newspapers and magazines raised the question of who the film was for and whether it was good for them. As the *Saturday Review* complained, 'All too rarely can one raise the charges of over-intellectualization in the movies but that certainly seems the case here.' It continued, 'For confirmed Freudians, it must inevitably appear an oversimplification, albeit sincere and essentially honest. And for the rest, it is as remote as pure science has always been. Huston has insisted on holding Freud at arm's length, and showing us the mind instead of the man.'[94] *Variety* worried that '... many may respond to that name [Freud] for its associated sexual connotations. And come expecting to experience vicarious sexual thrills' and end up disappointed.[95] *Time* magazine was more generous in its assessment of popular audience appeal in stating that, 'Most Americans have been touched by Freud's great work – some by taking psychiatric treatment, many by observing its effects in others, many more by living in a cultural climate fraught with Freudian ideas.'[96] Reversing this sentiment more critically on both the film and Freud's more limited appeal to British audiences, the *Daily Mail* review concluded that 'it is unlikely to mean as much here as in America, where the psycho-analysts seems to be as essential as the grocer.'[97]

Freud was situated, therefore, in correspondence with Zaretsky's assessment of Freud's 'paradoxical fate' in the 1960s of 'mass diffusion and precipitous decline', with *Film Quarterly*, for example, identifying that the problem with the film 'stems precisely from the widespread diffusion of Freudian ideas and their vulgarisation.'[98] This ubiquity, both in popularisation of 'talk therapies' and in the circulation of Freudianism within popular culture manifested in a number of less sombre depictions of him. The seriousness of Huston's *Freud* can be contrasted to more comic contemporary depictions of him in 1960s popular culture, including in sketch comedy shows such as the 1969 animated spin-off *The Pink Panther Show* (in which a paranoid Inspector Clouseau consults the titular 'French Freud') and in a number of episodes of *Rowan and Martin's Laugh-In* (1968–1973). In these comedies, Freudian psychoanalysis is usually represented as a lengthy, expensive and, ultimately, unsuccessful middle-class luxury. For example, when guest Phil Silver's Doctor Siegfried Mund character diagnoses patient Dan Rowan with a 'spilt personality, the analyst reveals to his anxious analysand, 'You know what this means? I'll have to charge you double!'[99]

Freud appears directly in a 1966 episode of the fantasy sitcom *Bewitched* (1964–1972) titled 'I'd Rather Twitch Than Fight', in which suburban house-witch Samantha Stephens (Elisabeth Montgomery) and her husband Darrin (Dick York) decide to seek marriage counselling from a psychiatrist after she gives away his favourite sports-coat that she thinks is tasteless. Tabitha's sceptical witch-mother Endora (Agnes Morehead) – states, 'psychiatrists are anti-witch' – and decides that if her daughter is going to see a professional, then she might as well see 'the real McCoy', and materialises the real Sigmund Freud (Norman Fell). Initially, Freud assumes toddler granddaughter Tabitha is the analysand, prompting the quite sophisticated Freudian joke, 'For the first time, someone has called me in time', but then is introduced to his real 'patient' Samantha. Freud instigates therapy with Samantha on the Stephen's sofa, and is summarily more shocked by Darrin's tasteless sports-jacket than Samantha's revelation that she (thinks) she is a witch – 'anyone who finds that jacket attractive and alluring to anyone is showing symptoms of a severely disorganised mind'.

When Darrin arrives with his therapist, Dr Kramer (Parley Baer), Freud and Kramer begin arguing about whether the sports-coat is tasteless ('I did not suggest. I merely stated a fact. That is the ugliest sports-coat I have ever seen!'), and about their respective professional credentials ('Well, I was a psychiatrist before there even were psychiatrists'). The 'upstart' Kramer challenges Freud as representative of an outmoded professional type, with 'your beards and your old-world manners. I think you've all got father-fixations'. When Kramer and Freud square up to fight, Endora makes both therapists disappear, sending Freud 'back to the unconscious', then disappears herself when the 'nauseating' Samantha and Darrin decide to 'kiss and make up' rather than pursue further counselling. *Betwitched*'s playful characterisation of the 'old-world' Freud and his staged altercation with the unpretentious 1960s' couples-therapist Kramer can be understood in the context of Zaretsky's characterisation of the popular diffusion of (pseudo) Freudianism and the resultant schism between the orthodox Freudians and psychanalytic reformers and adaptors.

Conclusion

As this chapter has demonstrated, John Huston's *Freud* is reflective of a number of key concerns and claims of *Demons of the Mind*. It is a film that is demonstrative of a number of different types of interactions between psychiatry and cinema. In addition to its subject matter and source materials, the film demonstrates interactions between dominant generic and narrative forms from the corresponding fields; a mutually enthusiastic and creatively enriching sharing of expertise that went far beyond simple fact-checking; and convergences of cinematographic and medical material cultures to innovate new techniques. It is also demonstrable of key contentions, chiefly contestations between a perceived psychoanalytic orthodoxy (most notably the Freud family themselves) that sought to protect Freud from mass circulation and a perceived vulgarisation, and those reformists who sort to adapt and share Freud for 1960's sensibilities and audiences. The lengthy process of consultation with creatives, clinicians, clerics and censors for *Freud* reveals the complex contestations and alliances of voices – with their competing and converging demands for stasis and change –that underly the relationships between psychiatry and cinema in the long 1960s.

As the previous chapter highlighted, the consultation with converging psychiatric and religious expertise was, at least initially, motivated by a principle of limiting repressive censorship on *Freud*, while the clinical and, to some extent, clerical advisers on the film also provided positive and productive advice that allowed the film to not only be more accurate but also to align creative and clinical innovations, speaking to shifting cultural, cinematic and censorship contexts in the early to mid-1960s. The film pushed the PCA and, to some extent the Legion, to consider the question 'how can

Freud and his respected and accepted ideas be themselves objectionable?' allowing for a productive process of censorship that has parallels with the findings of the previous chapter on the BBFC. In particular, the process of productive censorship on Freud prompted a change to the Code and its application – a shift from a rigid outdated model to a more agile, flexible policy – that allowed other 'adult' films such as *David and Lisa* (1963), *The Caretakers* (1963) and *Lilith* (1964) to be made and accepted within Hollywood; this cycle of psychiatric pictures prompted the comparable policy shift at the BBFC. The production and censorship of *Freud* must also be understood within wider shift from a religious to a psychiatric basis for censorship decisions, a shift that resulted, as discussed in the conclusion, with the appointment of a New York psychiatrist as the head of the PCA's replacement organisation, the Classification & Ratings Administration (CARA), as the Motion Picture Association moved from a 'suitable for all' to age-based classification system in the mid- to late 1960s.

4

Mad housewives and women's liberation: the psychiatric reinvention of the 'woman's film'

This chapter focuses on shifting understandings and representations of gender, domesticity, mental health and their intersection within psy and cinematic discourse in the long 1960s. It will look at the production and reception of two 'women's films', as designated by a number of critics (though others use melodrama, domestic drama, etc.), and consider the (gendered) performance of mental distress therein. The main case study films are *The Three Faces of Eve* (1957) and *Diary of a Mad Housewife* (1970), which, in different ways, express the psychological ramifications of unfulfilled marriage and domesticity, and span our long 1960s periodisation, sitting either side of the emergence of the Women's Liberation Movement (WLM). The chapter will analyse these films and these issues in relationship to influential feminist works such as Betty Friedan's 1963 book *The Feminine Mystique*,[1] which challenged the myth of women's natural disposition and fulfilment in housewife–mother roles and stressed the ongoing role of Freudian psychoanalysis in stifling women's liberation.

The main case study of this chapter will be *The Three Faces of Eve*, the film that brought both actor Joanne Woodward and the diagnosis of multiple personality disorder (MPD, now dissociative identity disorder (DID)) to public and professional awareness. The film was adapted from the best-selling 'factual' case history by psychiatrists Corbett Thigpen and Hervey Cleckley, who are characterised in the film and contributed to the screenplay as expert consultants. The character of 'Eve' in the book and film were based on Christine 'Chris' Costner Sizemore (4 April 1927–24 July 2016) who Thigpen and Cleckley diagnosed with MPD in 1952. The chapter will refer to her throughout by the name she published under, Chris Costner Sizemore, though Sizemore was added when she remarried in 1953 after her diagnosis and after the period covered in most of the film. Drawing on research at the Margaret Herrick Library and on the Chris Costner Sizemore papers at the David M. Rubenstein Rare Book and Manuscript Library at Duke University, this chapter will analyse the consultation and correspondence between the filmmakers, psychiatrists and Costner Sizemore, and the power relations therein; consider the use of real film footage of 'confidential' therapy sessions within the production, and the ethics of the recording and use of this audio-visual material; and seek to address the elision of Costner Sizemore's voice within these primary sources (it is correspondence she received, not wrote) as well as within the film's production.

The chapter will address these absences, largely, by looking to the three 'multobiographies' she published in 1958, 1977 and 1989, which, according to philosopher Ian Hacking, 'these books, in retrospect, are the three faces of Eve'.[2] Her second and third books challenged the neat closure of the film (which reproduces the therapist's 'cure' from the end of the book), and her exploitation by Thigpen and Cleckley and by 20th Century Fox – in 1989 she successfully sued the studio for the rights to her story. The increasing authority and challenge of Costner Sizemore's books – the final single-authored one in particular – can be understood not only in relation to her personal psychological and professional trajectories, but also in the context of the emergence and achievements of the Women's Liberation and Psychiatric Survivors movements. The chapter will conclude by looking at of one of Hollywood's most successful female scriptwriters and 'strongest feminist voices',[3] Eleanor Perry, a former psychiatric social worker who drew on her professional experiences for her Oscar-nominated script for *David and Lisa* (1962). The focus of this section will be Perry's penultimate film, *Diary of a Mad Housewife*, which is evocative in how, paradoxically, it gives voice to silenced housewife Tina, by provoking anger in the spectator at her submission to a cacophony of humiliating and sadistic male voices. The chapter concludes by returning to the idea of 'voice' – and this question of whose are valorised and whose are silenced – often considered to be central to women's agency and power in pioneering feminist literature from this time.[4]

Wartime 'gender confusion' and post-war readjustment

In the post-war period, the expertise of social scientists and psychologists was marshalled to argue for a return to pre-war gender roles and relations. Across newspaper articles, magazines and popular books, pop-Freudian psychoanalysis was used to justify reconversion narratives. For example, in the 1947 book *Modern Woman: The Lost Sex*, Ferdinand Lundberg, a sociologist, and Marynia Farnham, a psychoanalyst, argued that, during the

Second World War, feminists had prompted women to suppress their 'true instincts' in favour of adopting flawed versions of male traits; a process that involved the repression of their nurturing roles. Lundberg and Farnham bemoaned the loss of the 'old-time concepts of the "good" and the "bad" woman', which, they suggested, 'had the merit of resting at least on generally factual physical, psychological and social differentiation of sexual function'.[5] These writers advocated a government-backed programme designed to restore prestige to the sexually ordained roles of the wife and the mother. Sections of the bestselling book were published or paraphrased in a number of American magazines and newspapers.

During the Second World War, Hollywood horror, crime films and psychological thrillers complicated the bifurcation of the 'old-time concepts of the "good" and the "bad" woman', by expressing the irreconcilable demands placed upon wartime women (to be productive war-workers and stay-at-home wives and mothers; to be the virtuous girl-waiting-back-home and the liberated 'victory girl' modelled on the pin-up). These conflicting pressures were expressed through depictions of resilient women detectives and tragic female shape-shifter characters in films like *Phantom Lady* (1944) and *Cat People* (1942), who either succeeded or tragically failed to integrate these conflicting demands.[6] After the war, some psy professionals linked these representations to a perceived post-war gender confusion, with, for example, *Variety* citing an unnamed professor of psychology who stated that a University of Chicago report offered indisputable evidence that 'American women have become more aggressive during World War II', in large part, due to the proliferation of the of 'fem heroes' and 'not-so-he-men' characters in Hollywood crime and horror films.[7] He called for a return to more traditional depictions of women and men in such films. Psy professionals and film critics also bemoaned the depiction of psychiatrists and psychologists in these wartime films – often portrayed as an updated version of the classic horror 'mad scientist' – feeling these representations were detrimental to the psychiatric profession and to America's psychological healing following the war.[8] Filmmakers responded to these twin calls for restoration of the bifurcated model of femininity and positive depictions of the psy professions – including their vital role to resolving these gender confusions. In the psychological thriller *The Dark Mirror* (1946), written and produced by Nunnally Johnson, an innovative split-screen technique is used to depict Olivia de Havilland as two identical twins – one evil (Terry) and one good (Ruth) – who can be distinguished only by an authoritative psychiatrist, Dr Elliot (Scott Ayres), via his use of a series of psychiatric methods, including Rorschach tests, a polygraph machine and free association. Psychiatry's restoration of the distinction between the good and bad woman allows Elliot to commit Terry to a mental institution and commit to a romantic relationship with Ruth.

A *Life* special issue from December 1956 devoted to the 'American Woman' marshalled the expertise of four psychiatrists on the timely issues of 'modern marriage'. Ten years on from the Chicago study, these experts perpetuated the discourse of gender confusion – 'wives are not feminine enough and husbands not truly male' – to explain the 'disturbing divorce rate', seeing women's submission to 'the delights of domesticity' and maternal instinct as the answer.[9] As New York psychoanalyst John Cotton asserts, 'the out-and-out "career woman" . . . may find satisfaction in her job, but the chances are that she, her husband and her children will suffer psychological damage, and that she will basically be an unhappy woman'. In his private practice, Cotton had identified a number of such cases, 'a pattern that might be called the New York Career woman "syndrome"'.[10]

Cotton blamed societal pressure for the 'phenomenon known as the "career woman" . . . that fatal error that feminism propagated sank deeply into the national consciousness'. He suggested that the pressures to have a career, rather than making women happy, distracted them from accepting 'their wifely functions with good humour and pleasure'.[11] While Cotton's polemic on the psychological damage caused by independent women – to themselves, their families and society – appears extreme, even for the 1950s, Herman suggest that his position is aligned with many in the psy professions, who took up the positions of 'enemies of feminism by updating the antifeminist rhetoric of earlier decades' with psychological or, in many cases, psychoanalytic inflections.[12] It is easy to see how in the following decade, as discussed later in this chapter, second-wave feminist writers such as Betty Friedan, Kate Millett and Shulamith Firestone would identify psychoanalysis – and particularly 'Freud's doctrine of penis envy' – as 'a superbly timed accusation' against first-wave feminism and, subsequently, against 'any woman unwilling to "stay in her place"'.[13]

Janet Walker analyses *The Three Faces of Eve* in this context, seeing it as responding, in complex and contradictory ways, to this moment in which 'American psychoanalytic and psychiatric practice served as agencies of women's adjustment to stereotypically conceived roles prescribed by society'.[14] Conversely, she suggests, the film prefigured a counter discourse, in employing 'psychoanalytic ideas to *resist* the totalising tendency of the adjustment impulse'.[15] While psychiatry is a masculine 'authoritarian regime' within the film, 'the symptoms of Eve's illness' – the different personalities – may be read alternatively as 'the narrative reconfiguration of ideological contradictions surfacing in the debates on women's "place"'.[16] In this way, *The Three Faces of Eve* could be seen to be looking back more to the early 1940s films discussed above that highlighted the competing ideological and bodily demands on wartime women. Justine Lloyd and Lesley Johnson explore *The Three Faces of Eve* in relation to the post-war 'tensions between discourse of modernity and femininity' and how they play out in the shifting figure of the housewife.[17] In the figure of Jane, Eve's third and 'final' identity, the film moves beyond the dichotomy of good and bad woman (played out in the neat separation of the twin narratives) to celebrate an integrated subjecthood, Jane, who 'manages these multiple conflicting pressures and finally integrates all aspects of her sexual, maternal *and* economic identities as a wife, mother and worker'.[18] Lloyd and Johnson focus on *The Three Faces of Eve* in the context of the shifting conventions of Hollywood melodrama, and, as such, see this characterisation as positive in representational terms, but do raise its resultant simplification of the case history material. Through the conventions of the Hollywood melodrama, they suggest, the 'cinematic adaption of Sizemore's story reworks an untidy and undirected sequence of events of suffering and trauma into a narrative of a woman's search for a modern self'.[19] This chapter will move on to explore the film within that context not to assess its fidelity to its scientific source material, but to explore the development and reception of the film in relation to the complicated power relations between patient and therapists as their relationships developed from couch to book to screen.

The Three Faces of Eve was based on the case history of Chris Costner Sizemore, as recounted by the two Georgian psychiatrists, Corbett Thigpen and Hervey Cleckley, who treated her and diagnosed her with multiple personality disorder (MPD), which since 1990s has been designated as dissociative identity disorder (DID). The film was based on Thigpen and Cleckley's book of the same name (published, like the film, in 1957), which detailed their two years of therapy with patient Chris Costner Sizemore (anonymised as 'Eve White' in the book and film) who, in the course of their treatment, is revealed to be 'a case of multiple personality' with 'three distinct personalities' (or alters): Eve White, Eve Black and Jane Gray. Cleckley already had a major influence on psychiatric and, resultantly, popular culture through his research on psychopathy published in 1941 as *The Mask of Sanity*,[20] which has been seen to shape post-war depiction of psychopathy in films such as *Psycho*.[21]

However, the book and film of *The Three Faces of Eve* were more directly influential on popular culture, particularly in bringing MPD to wider public and medical attention. Before the mid-1950s, MPD was a largely unknown and rarely seen diagnosis, but after Eve/Chris, and subsequent widely circulated and mediated cases (including the 1973 book and 1976 film *Sybil*), it became a much more recognised and commonly diagnosed condition.[22] It is characterised by the person having at least one alternative or 'alter' personality, typically around twenty to thirty (a subsequent psychiatrist identified that Costner Sizemore had twenty-two personalities, not three), which typically function independently of one another. There is usually a 'core' personality that 'copes with ordinary everyday life', which is usually unaware (or only indirectly aware) of the other personalities. The other alters may be aware of each other and sometimes form alliances and friendships, though many 'are not fully developed and remain fragmentary'.[23] MPD/DID was and continues to be a contested and controversial diagnosis.[24]

In 1951, Thigpen began treating a twenty-five-year-old married woman for 'blinding' headaches and blackouts.[25] From initial therapy sessions, Thigpen put these experiences of this rather 'ordinary' woman, who Thigpen and Cleckley referred to as Eve White in their book, as resulting from her 'unpleasant' marriage and unfulfilled personal life.[26] In a subsequent session, however, after Thigpen questioned Eve White about a curious letter he had received from her, which appeared to be partially written by someone else, she became agitated and then placed her head in her hands. When she looked up, according to Thigpen, in a 'bright, unfamiliar voice that sparkled, the woman said, "Hi there, Doc!"' This was the first appearance of the hedonistic 'Eve Black', an independent personality who had been present since Eve White's childhood, and who, they understood, was the result of traumatic events (witnessing accidents and death) therein. While Eve White was not aware of her, and could not remember her behaviour, Eve Black was aware of Eve White and could recollect what she had done.

In the therapy sessions, Eve Black would, as in the initial session, spontaneously 'pop out', but as the work progressed, Thigpen and Cleckley could call forth the different personalities, first only under hypnosis, and then later at any time. After several months of treatment, and perceived progress, Eve White's condition deteriorated and her severe headaches and 'blackouts' returned. It was in this period that a third personality, Jane, appeared, who offered 'the potential or the promise of something far more woman and of life than might be expected from the two Eves with their faults and weaknesses eliminated and all assets combined'.[27] However, Thigpen and Cleckley's account concludes not with the personality of Jane taking over (though they considered promoting this in the work), but with the integration of elements of the three in the 'conscious and active personality we now call Evelyn',[28] which, at the end of the book, is referred to as Evelyn Lancaster, named for her new and happy marital status. Over the fourteen months of sessions with Eve/Chris (for which they did not charge her), the psychiatrists Thigpen and Cleckley employed a range of psychiatric and psychotherapeutic tests and techniques (electroencephalography (EEG), Rorschach and other projective tests, intelligence tests, talk therapy, hypnosis, interviews with family) and recorded around a hundred hours of material, on audio tape and, importantly for our research, 16mm film.

In the post-war period, more mobile and affordable 16mm film technologies allowed psychiatrists, psychologists and other social scientists to enhance the observation, study and diagnosis of their subjects as a form of 'cinematic microanalysis'.[29] Thigpen and Cleckley used 16mm film in their 'research' with Costner, though the timing and correspondence suggests that this was as much a mechanism to corroborate and communicate their findings as part of their diagnosis and treatment. They shot some initial film of her while she was in hospital, and then undertook a professional film shoot with her on 12 October 1953 in Atlanta with a proper film crew. Thigpen's letter telling Costner to 'be sure to get each one of the personalities to read this letter and let each one suggest a dress that each feels is most typical of her personality', points more towards the former aim.[30]

However, in the book, Thigpen and Cleckley state that the films were used to introduce her alters to each other and, in theory, help to integrate the different personalities. They explain, 'By this means they were for the first time, one might say, able to see each other'; Eve Black watched 'the film with obvious amusement', mocking the propriety of her alter', Eve White, on the other hand, studied the film with solemn gravity'.[31] Thigpen contacted Costner to undertake additional filming ('another 100 or 150 feet of movie film') in mid-1956, to supplement what they had recorded three years earlier.[32] The two sets of footage were edited together for a thirty-minute educational film for psy professionals, titled *A Case Study of Multiple Personality: The Three Faces of Eve*, that was released to coincide with and promoted within Thigpen and Cleckley's *The Three Faces of Eve* book.

The colour 16mm film starts with the intertitle, 'This film is unrehearsed in its entirety', before a voiceover by Thigpen introducing the 'colourless' Eve White (in static mid-shot) while she talks to camera in mid-shot, but with the diegetic sound muted. The doctor's voiceover continues to explain Eve's case history as, following a subtle dissolve, 'the retiring and gender conventional' Eve White's demeanour changes and the voiceover explains the appearance – in the sessions and now on-screen – of the 'lovable, lying, scampish' Eve Black. He then explains the appearance, 'after eight tumultuous months', of a third alter, Jane, who, it is explained, 'impresses us as far more secure, more vivid, capable and interesting than Eve White', a 'person of merit', who is 'capable of compassion and valid love'. Following this five-minute introduction by the authors, an intertitle introduces, 'Let us hear the various personalities speak . . .' The film then alternates between lengthy interviews with Eve White, Eve Black and Jane, framed initially as a two-shot with the interviewer's back to camera, as either interviewer prompts or intertitles trigger shifts between the alters, which are perceptible to the spectator through visible shifts in accent, phrasing, diction and posture.

In a subsequent section, the framing switches to a long-shot, as Eve White, Eve Black and Jane pose in the dresses they were asked to pick out by Thigpen, and the interviewer asks them to explain why they feel the dresses represent them and how they feel about the other alters' choices. The film then returns to more detailed interviews, alternating between medium long-shot and long-shot of the subject, showing more detail of shifting posture and bodily positioning in the chair, as Costner Sizemore shifts between alters and expresses excitement, agitation or anxiety and, in one short sequence, Eve White becoming upset while under hypnosis, which, an intertitle explains, was 'rarely used' in her treatment. A final intertitle then explains that the 'case resolved itself' six weeks after the filming, and then introduces the new 'resolved personality' of Evelyn Lancaster who is 'remarried and as far as we can determine seems happy and well-adjusted'. In this additional footage, requested by Thigpen in 1956, we see but do not hear Evelyn/Chris posing in a new white dress who, the voiceover explains, 'has elements of Eve White, Eve Black and Jane, but there is more'. The voiceover identifies likely causes for her dissociations (paralleling the Hollywood film's revelation), the role of psychotherapeutic treatment in resolving her aligned mental health and domestic situations, and the fully integrated personality Evelyn Lancaster's resultant happy marital and maternal life.

In addition to its role in Costner Sizemore's treatment, study and diagnosis, and latterly, the communication of Thigpen and Cleckley's findings, the 16mm film was a key tool in the pre-production and production of the Hollywood film. In mid-1956, Nunnally Johnson screened the film to Judy Garland as a means to persuade her to take the role. Seeing the footage of the real 'Eve' successfully persuaded the previously unconvinced Garland to take the role, but later Johnson renegaded on giving her the part as, it has been alternately reported, both Johnson and Garland felt it might be hazardous to her mental health and he was concerned she might derail the film due to issues with addiction.[33]

When Woodward was subsequently cast in the role, her and Lee J. Cobb (who played Dr Luther/Thigpen) studied the film to hone their performances. Woodward chose not to imitate Costner Sizemore too closely as she felt, ironically, that it might appear inauthentic to audiences, 'They decided it was better to have Eve's personality changes manifest more gradually, especially at the beginning.' However, she followed the film more closely for the latter stages of the film, when 'the changes could be faster and that is how the device of the lowering of the head (signalling a personality change) came to be'.[34] In the late 1960s, when questions were raised again over the authenticity of Thigpen and Cleckley's research – and therefore Costner's 'performance' – new innovations in film technology allowed psychologists to revisit the 16mm film and undertake frame-by-frame analysis of Costner, which revealed 'transient asymmetries of the face, particularly a transient yet rapid and pronounced strabismus' that was 'not detectable at normal projection speed'.[35] This minute observation of the film was seen to conform the original research and diagnosis, and, therefore, the authenticity of Costner's claims.

In Costner Sizemore's 1977 autobiographical account *I'm Eve* (co-authored with her cousin Elen Sain Pittillo), she questioned the ethics of the capture, editing and distribution of the *A Case Study of Multiple Personality* film. She suggested that she acquiesced to being filmed the first time, whilst in the hospital, because she wanted to 'please the doctor', and because she was told the film was 'simply part of her medical case records' and that it would benefit her treatment.[36] Later in the book, she suggests that the second professional filming session was prompted by Thigpen's concern that time was running out to capture her alters again on film as 'some sort of resolution was impending'.[37] She suggests that the second shoot was 'less than successful' in capturing the distinct personalities as they were 'too far resolved', so Thigpen had to resort to hypnosis to invoke a stronger reaction from 'Eve White'. Secondly, she suggested that the two sets of filmed content (captured three years apart) were manipulated in the edit to tell a clearer narrative of diagnosis, treatment and resolution. Costner Sizemore also criticised Thigpen and Cleckley for distributing the film through medical rental libraries and exhibiting it in their lectures (including screening the footage in hospital at their May 1953 APA conference); she was told the films would be stored in a 'safe place' and accessed only by her psychiatrists. She protested that it was 'more than twenty years before she learned that her face, her pain, her soul, upon request for a small rental fee, had been available from Pennsylvania State University in films called *A Case Study of Multiple Personality*'.[38] As a result, she entrusted her lawyer to have the film removed from circulation.[39] These concerns over the rights to and control of Costner's narrative were central to the interactions and contentions during production, reception and, later, the legal case over *The Three Faces of Eve* as it was adapted from medical journal to bestseller to Hollywood film.

Competing expertise in *The Three Faces of Eve*

The first published account of Costner Sizemore's case history was published in 1954 by Thigpen and Cleckley as 'A Case of Multiple Personality' in the *Journal of Abnormal and Social Psychology*. This peer-reviewed article, for the pre-eminent 'psychopathology' research journal published by the APA, adopts a duly scholarly tone and structure and makes reference to a range of secondary sources. The journal article makes a case for the applicability of Morton Prince's (the founder of the journal) theories on dissociation, rather than the psychoanalytic ideas of Freud – including discounting the usefulness of the universal theory of 'castration fear' – in understanding this and other cases of MPD.[40] The article provoked stories in popular magazines, first, a rushed 1954 article in Canadian news magazine *Maclean's*, which neither Costner Sizemore nor her doctors were happy with, and then a serialised version in *The American* magazine in 1955, 'The Girl who Led Three Lives', written by Irmis Johnson with input from Costner Sizemore. Following this publication, eminent Hollywood producer, director and writer Nunnally Johnson (who wrote and produced the post-war psychological thriller *The Dark Mirror*), pursued the property and urged 20th Century Fox to buy the rights to the book ahead of its publication. The magazine articles and reporting of the imminent book and film sparked professional and public interest in MPD, as did the concurrent publication of Shirley Jackson's *The Bird's Nest* (1954) which was adapted as an MGM film, *Lizzie* (1957). *Lizzie* was released just ahead of *The Three Faces of Eve*, following pressure (a threat of legal action) on Fox to postpone their film.[41]

As part of the deal for Fox buying the rights to their book, Thigpen and Cleckley were employed as medical consultants on the film. In this capacity they supplied documents, taped recordings of sessions and the aforementioned films relating to Costner Sizemore's treatment and diagnosis from their archive.[42] They also acted as script consultants, reading and providing extensive feedback on at least two draft scripts which, although they were reported to Costner Sizemore as minor changes, constituted significant and reportedly critical contentions over cinematic as well as cinematic aspects. Costner Sizemore's co-author James Poling explained to her after the film's release, 'I saw the nine-page single spaced letter they wrote Nunnally Johnson about the movie script – or rather, the letter Cleckley wrote – and I think it was way off base.' He continued, 'It was full of legitimate criticism, but it also tried to tell Johnson how to write his movie in a few instances.'[43] A key issue throughout the production of the film was what Costner Sizemore's role would be in relation to technical advice. In Thigpen's initial announcement to her that Hollywood was interested in the book – starting the letter, 'Hold onto your hat! Twentieth-Century Fox has our manuscript. They wish to do a movie based on it' – he states that, 'They want you to go to Hollywood for technical assistance.' He suggests that she will be 'paid additional' to her rights in the movie for this role, and 'they may even find a job for Don [her husband] so he could be out here while the picture is made'. He proposes the figures of $5,000 for the rights and $50 per week for the technical role. He also assured her that she would 'remain anonymous' and that 'one thing I shall insist on is medical accuracy and to make sure that anything that they shoot that are not otherwise described in the book would be non-derogatory.'[44]

In her later account, Costner Sizemore suggests that she was initially conflicted by the offer, particularly in its potential effect on her plans 'to tell *her* story', initially in a book but, resultantly, potentially on-screen.[45] Thigpen's letter prompted Costner to seek advice from 'her only friend'[46] Irmis Johnson – who wrote *The American Weekly* article and was at the time planning to co-author Costner Sizemore's biographical account. Johnson said she was delighted for Costner Sizemore, but told her to be cautious of whether Fox was buying the rights to the book or the rights to her story, if the former she should receive $10,000 (double the proposed 'pittance' of $5,000), and, if the latter, she should receive at least $25,000. She also felt that Costner Sizemore should receive 'not less than $100 a week plus expenses' for her technical adviser role during 'the scriptwriting, or making of the movie'. She encouraged her to get an agent and graciously concluded, 'please feel sure that selling movie right now – for a good price – and deciding not to do the book, will be quite agreeable with me.'[47] A financial agreement was made, a compromise of $7,000, but the contracts were held up by the psychiatrists as, Thigpen suggested, '20th Century-Fox wanted Dr Cleckley and me to practically sign our lives away and this we refused to do'. He continued, 'Also we wished to restrict them in at the actual drama of the story so they could not go high, wide and handsome and do as they please.'[48] In a letter following their meeting to sign the contracts, Thigpen proffers the unsolicited advice, 'I hope that by the time you go to Hollywood you will have been able to lose about four or five pounds of your weight. I think you are pretty as a picture, but you're right your [sic] prettiest at just a tiny bit less weight.'[49]

During the ensuing months of the pre-production process, however, Costner's technical role was diluted and pushed back. In a letter of 3 August 1956 – which starts by explaining that his and Cleckley's script suggestions have been adopted – Thigpen explains, 'I really don't know when to say that you will go to Hollywood, but I believe it will be near the end of the shooting.'[50] In a follow-up letter in January 1957, revealing that Woodward will now play her and that Fox are 'planning big on the movie', Thigpen propounds, 'I don't want to give you another false alarm, but I think sometime in the next few weeks you should be headed for your visit to Hollywood.'[51] When the offer for Costner Sizemore's 'technical direction' does materialise, it is a very different offer. A letter in late February 1957 from Nunnally Johnson to Thigpen, asks the doctor to persuade her to appear on-screen in an interview in the film's prologue. This opening scene was conceptualised in the manner of the films Thigpen and Cleckley shot with her in 1953 but conducted by British journalist Alistair Cooke. Johnson explains:

> But I have an idea about this introduction that calls for help from you. I would like to use your patient herself in this prologue, photographed from the back. My idea is to come in and Cooke, if he should

be the one, and have him speak the foreword. Then he could move over to the table and sit down opposite the young woman and ask her a few questions, enough to establish her identity and have approval of the essential facts of the picture story to follow. Do you think she would agree to this?

He continues that it would be a closed set and they would seek to maintain her anonymity, and suggests, 'Perhaps she would be willing to do this in your company, in which case we could ask you to escort her out here.'[52] Thigpen forwarded the letter to Costner Sizemore, suggesting this might be an opportunity to move to California. Via her literary agent, Costner turned down the offer, as stated in internal Fox correspondence that reads, 'I have a letter from Eve's New York Agent, which indicates, with some finality, that she is so concerned about her identity being kept a secret that she does not feel that she can make a trip here for photography.'[53] A subsequent letter to Costner Sizemore from Nunnally Johnson, stated that he understood her 'fears of being photographed surreptitiously, but there was really no need for it'.[54] In *I'm Eve*, Costner Sizemore suggests that it was concerns over her appearance rather than concerns over her anonymity that prevented her going to Hollywood: 'She was fat and ugly; if they saw her they would choose a fat, ugly actress to play her life story.'[55] She suggests that around the time of the offer she started hearing voices again, which followed the upset and disappointed of reading Thigpen and Cleckley's book, the resultant feeling of desperation to write her own account, and emergence of self-loathing at her appearance (fuelled perhaps by Thigpen's unsolicited comments on her weight).[56] Following daily headaches and amnesia, she 'awoke' to find a note from her alter Jane, who, with this new reappearance, had adopted a far more confrontational personality, which, she suggested, included Jane encouraging Costner Sizemore to attempt suicide.

Costner Sizemore's co-author James Poling expressed relief at her decision to not go to Hollywood ('I'm happy to learn that you aren't going to Hollywood. I would really worry about that') especially given the recent 'reappearance of Jane'. In a 'P.S.', Poling states, 'You say, "you may encounter Jane". Perhaps you should prepare me for such a possibility, if it is necessary. I'm not sure I know just what the proper procedure would be.'[57] Whether or not the reappearance of Jane is related to the film's production – including the anxiety of the proposed on-screen cameo – or the publication of Thigpen and Cleckley's book, is unclear. For her literary collaborators, at least, there is certainly concern over the film's possible effect on her in light of Jane's reappearance.

In late April, Thigpen contacted her to say he'd heard from Poling that she 'had decided rather positively against going to Hollywood' and gave her an update on the film, which was 'finished other than being scored and cut'.[58] In a further update on the film and check in on her MPD, he proposes, 'It might be just as well if you and I plan to have a few private sessions and see if we cannot resolve the present "rebellion".'[59] In September 1957, Thigpen wrote directly to Costner Sizemore's husband Don following a sneak preview of the film. Although he suggests the film 'paints a very good picture of multiple personality', he warns:

> The thing I am writing you about now is that in view of some of Chris's recent difficulties I would think it advisable for her *not* to see THE THREE FACES OF EVE for the time being ... I would not want to get her stirred up. I frankly think she is doing fine and I believe her present little temporary upset will be only that.[60]

While appearing, on the whole, to be operating with good intentions, Thigpen, like other male confidants and collaborators, sought to restrict her involvement and agency in *The Three Faces of Eve* project, ultimately seeing it as detrimental to her mental health and, perhaps, the coherence of the stories within their book and films.[61] *The Three Faces of Eve* seemed to promise her the opportunity to bring her expertise to bear on the film, and on public understandings of MPD, by acting as confidential technical adviser. However, her role was reduced to an authenticating on-screen cameo that would have recreated her objectification in the 16mm medical film, which promoted a shared anxiety of compromising her anonymity – a concern both for her own mental health and for the psychiatrists who had a stake in her 'recovery'.

Like the book on which it is closely based, the film of *The Three Faces of Eve* tells a fairly neat story of diagnosis, treatment and cure, initially, at least, aligning the spectator with the perspectives of the psychiatrist(s) as they/ we discover her MPD. From the outset, the film seeks to establish its clinical authority and authenticity by marshalling the male expertise of leading figures in their fields. The film opens with a reoriented prologue shot, as an intertitle states, with 'distinguished journalist and commentator' Alistair Cooke, who speaks directly to camera from a movie theatre framed to imitate the audience's view (Figure 4.1). He states, 'This is a true story. How often have you seen that statement at the beginning of a picture?' He goes on to question the validity of such claims, but clarifies, 'Well this is a true story, about a sweet but rather baffled young housewife who, in 1951 in her hometown of Georgia, suddenly frightened her husband by behaving very unlike herself.'

Cooke moves on to explain that this was a 'case of multiple personality, something all psychiatrists have read about but very few have ever seen'. He

Figure 4.1 Journalist Alistair Cooke directly addresses the cinema audience in the introduction to *The Three Faces of Eve* (1957)

then specifically names Drs Thigpen and Cleckley, who, he says, 'one day were confronted with a woman who had one more personality more than Dr Jekyll'. He continues that the case history 'was presented to the American Psychiatric Association in 1953 and is already a classic of psychiatric literature'. He concludes by further stressing the authenticity of the events portrayed on-screen and that 'much of the dialogue was taken from the clinical record of the doctor that we call Dr Luther'. With his voiceover continuing – clarifying that 'the date is August 20, 1951' – there is a dissolve to a street scene in Augusta, Georgia, as a pickup truck pulls up, Eve White and her husband Ralph get out, and enter the office building in which psychiatrist and neurologists Drs Luther and Day (clearly, following Cooke's introduction, pseudonyms for Thigpen and Cleckley) have their practice. Cooke's voiceover returns at points in the narrative to indicate moments of progress and relapse within the course of the treatment.

In the office, Eve White is introduced to Dr Luther, played by Cobb. As Gabbard and Gabbard explain, this 'caring and effective' psychiatrist is a 'classic example' of the transcendent therapist of Hollywood's Golden Age, who through the 'de-repression of traumatic memory' (usually childhood memory) enacts a 'cathartic cure' on his grateful patient.[62] Walker highlights the gendered power relations therein, stating that, in the first half of the film, Dr Luther's 'control over the woman is that of a narrator – a narrator of personality and cure'.[63] Eve White is initially nervous and struggles to explain her symptoms, severe headaches and bouts of 'amnesia', prompting her inarticulate husband, Ralph, to intervene. Luther takes her on as a patient and, as Cooke explains in voiceover, is initially 'greatly helped by the psychiatric treatment'. However, several months on from starting therapy she has an extreme episode where she attacks her and Ralph's daughter Bonnie. In a subsequent session with Luther, she anxiously reveals that she has also been hearing a voice, telling her to 'leave Ralph, take Bonnie and run away', which she thinks is an indication she is 'losing [her] mind'. Luther responds, 'not in your case', seemingly referring both to his assessment of the symptoms and assessment of the understandable desire to leave abusive husband Ralph.

When Luther looks visibly alerted by her revelation that the voice she has been hearing 'sounds like [her] own voice', Eve White looks distressed and places her head in her hands as the sound of the vibraphone, a staple of the psychological drama, indicates something uncanny is occurring. With a shift to a sultry jazz score, Eve lifts her head and peeks through her fingers, as her expression, posture and diction (broader Southern accent) clearly changes. When Luther asks if she had another headache, Eve responds, 'No, I didn't have no headache. She did, but I didn't', continuing 'she always gets those headaches when I want to come out'. The spectator then experiences (and shares) Luther's reaction and resultant realisation as he takes in (and enjoys) Woodward's first performance of the feisty and flirtatious Eve Black (see Figure 4.2). Walker explains, 'the cutaway to Dr Luther's point of view serves as a point of identification for the spectator who sees the transition through the incredulity of the doctor's gaze'.[64] Luther calls in his older colleague Dr Day (Cleckley) – 'Have you ever seen a case of multiple personality?' – to experience the transformation of 'that dreary little woman from across the river', as Day refers to her, into Eve Black who is now smoking and listening to loud jazz music in his office.

The character/alter of Eve Black is significant in shifting the generic register of the film from melodrama to comedy, introducing not only comedic moments but also disrupting the narrative flow through her performance,

Figure 4.2 Dr Luther, and the spectator, meet Eve Black for the first time in *The Three Faces of Eve*

at a nightclub, of a song and dance number called *Rockin' and Rolling, All Night Long,* around the halfway point of the film. While Day/Cleckley is initially sceptical – 'she's faking it' – her sudden transition back to Eve White convinces him that this is a genuine case. Cooke's subsequent voiceover explains that 'On May 17, 1952, Eve White was admitted to the psychiatric section of the University hospital for observation and treatment.' While, initially, Eve White's 'behaviour is excellent', after a week Eve Black starts to emerge, propositioning a male nurse and Luther himself. This prompts Dr Luther to make a disciplinary intervention, threatening that if she does not 'behave' she'll drive Eve White 'crazy' and then they'll both be 'shut up in a place like this for life. One with bars . . . and straitjackets'. In discussion with Eve Black, he persuades her that the only way forward is to tell Eve White about the 'multiple personality' and to 'introduce [the two alters] to each other' – this amuses Eve Black who responds, 'Ha! Doc, you flip me, you really do!' Discharged after two weeks, Eve White stays in a boarding house in Augusta for further outpatient treatment with Dr Luther, promoting her initial separation from Ralph. While he initially suggests that she needs to get better from this 'multiplied personality thing', he later, on hearing about Eve Black's nightclub exploits, suggest she just needs a 'damn good whipping'. After Eve Black leads on and then misleads Ralph once again, he hits her and, subsequently, divorces her.

At this mid-point of the film, Dr Luther accedes to Dr Day, 'We're losing. This woman is in a worse condition today than when she walked into this office two years ago.' Luther rejects the idea of the divorce being an issue, acknowledging her unhappy marriage as more cause than solution to her problems, but rather the problem that 'The truth is, neither Eve Black nor Mrs White is a satisfactory solution. Neither of them is really qualified to fill the role of wife, mother or even a responsible human being. A victory for either would be disastrous.' Furthermore, Luther explains that there has been no breakthrough in discovering repressed memories from 'childhood, or should I say childhoods', that would explain the MPD and offer potential for de-repression and cure. It is at this moment Eve Black arrives at the office to warn Luther that Eve White attempted suicide and, furthermore she, Eve Black, is now experiencing periods of blackout too. Composed in a two-shot, Luther uses hypnosis to try to go deeper with Eve White, but, while he is distracted taking notes, the spectator observes Eve/Woodward undergoing a new transformation, slowly emerging as the composed and commanding 'Jane'. As Walker explains it is 'clear to the audience that Dr Luther, who is visible on-screen, has not participated in the emergence of Jane'.[65] Walker sees this as a significant shift in the narrative with regard to the female protagonist(s) taking control of their recovery, and narrative, from Luther. The doctor's confusion and slow realisation is revealed in a long mid-shot as his expression slowly changes. In a restaging of the film's opening, Luther goes to get Day for his opinion, asking 'Can you take another one?'

In Cooke's subsequent voiceover he explains, 'And so now Dr Luther had three inadequate personalities to complicate and confuse his search for one stable and complete woman.' This triggers a representative montage of the three alters, as he continues: 'Which would it be? The rollicking and irresponsible playgirl, the defeated wife, or the pleasant young woman who had no memory?' Finishing the montage with Jane on a date with boyfriend Earl, she explains her MPD and tells him that the condition is the reason she cannot accept his proposal of marriage. The film cuts back to Luther's office, where he undertakes a final session with Eve White, in which she expresses her expectation and desire to be replaced by Jane, who she feels will be a good mother to Bonnie. Luther calls forth Jane, who then explains an experience from the previous weekend which she felt was significant. This triggers the film's first flashback scene, overlaid with Jane's voiceover recollections in the present, in which she observed Eve White going under the house to retrieve a ball while playing with daughter Bonnie. This triggers a zoom-in to a further flashback-within-a-flashback, where she is suddenly 'a little girl under the house'.

Luther than calls Eve White back, who under hypnosis, is then able to complete the flashback, as the music on the score soars, she shouts 'momma please don't make me!' Woodward then reproduces the identical response of a suddenly emergent Eve Black, as shown near the end of the 16mm *A Case of Multiple Personality* film, where she wipes away Eve White's tears and looks surprised at them. Following Eve Black's re-emergence, there is an uncharacteristically emotional scene between her and Luther where she says goodbye to him. He calls up Jane to ask her 'what it all means?', which retriggers the flashback to her childhood in which her mother calls her out from under the house to get ready for her grandmother's funeral, during which she is forced to kiss the face of her dead grandmother's corpse. Jane then realises she can recollect other memories from her childhood as well as the disappearance of the other alters, highlighting their successful integration into Jane through the 'de-repression' process, which was initiated by Luther but completed by Jane. Two years on, Drs Luther and Day receive a letter from Jane on the 'second anniversary of that day in the office', which we hear read in voiceover by Jane. A dissolve from the psychiatrists' office to a three shot of Jane, new husband Earl and Bonnie driving together eating ice-creams, reassures 'And still no more Eve White and no more Eve Black. That's why we decided it was safe at last to have Bonnie with us. And so here we all are . . . going home together.' The film ends therefore, with a resolute 'cure' and, as a result, the possibility of a reorganised modern family unit.

While the film can certainly be understood in the context, therefore, of the post-war readjustment narrative, as Lloyd and Johnson do,[66] in its use of modern psychiatric intervention to reclaim marriage and the housewife role, it also affords some agency to Jane in taking control of her psychological and social refashioning. Furthermore, it celebrates the liberatory potential (and mediating role) of Eve Black in this process, in her breaking out of gendered and generic boundaries within the film, and mourns her loss in a way that it does not for Eve White. Does this indicate that there are moments of more progressive ideas of modern womanhood in *The Three Faces Eve*?

The film, and book, through their unsympathetic portrayal of husband Ralph – as simultaneously frustratingly stupid and psychologically and physically abusive – make an argument for divorce (though not against marriage). This includes, though expressed more subtly in the film, the problem that Eve/Chris has an unfulfilled sex life with Ralph. As Thigpen explains in a 1955 letter to Costner Sizemore, deriding her first marriage to Ralph and celebrating her second marriage to Don, 'at that time you were in a miserable marriage situation . . . Sex life was an ordeal and you could not thoroughly enjoy one of the most rewarding of all experiences.'[67] The film raised only minor censorship issues, but those it did focused on these issues of sex, marriage and motherhood rather than on mental health representation. In dealings with the Production Code Administration, initial reports demanded one major change to the submitted synopsis. Where it discusses the divorce, the section stating 'Eve tells Dr Luther she is filing for divorce. Whatever the formal charge, Dr Luther knows she is filling for divorce from Ralph for infidelity with her other self', this whole passage is crossed out and replaced, in pen, with 'Ralph divorces her!'[68] Even after these changes, the Legion of Decency pinpointed the issue that the film 'reflects the acceptability of divorce' – in addition to the 'suggestive costuming, dialogue and situations' of Eve Black – as grounds for their 'B' rating.[69]

Critical and legal contention over *The Three Faces of Eve*

Rather than the usual Los Angeles premiere, the film was premiered in Augusta, Georgia, on 18 September 1957, where Thigpen and Cleckley had their practice. Nunnally Johnson and Alistair Cooke attended the screening and 'Patron's Dinner' held to honour Thigpen and Cleckley. Before the screening, Johnson presented the psychiatrists with gold plaques, from the president of 20th Century Fox, which recognised their 'contribution to the motion picture industry and the whole world.'[70] As highlighted above, Costner Sizemore was not invited to the screening for fear of its effect on her mental health (and, therefore, arguably the validity of the film's narrative closure).

Costner Sizemore explained cynically in *A Mind of My Own*, 'My alters had been barred from the premiere in Augusta, Georgia, because Drs Thigpen and Cleckley believed that seeing it would be detrimental to the stability of the patient who, they had wrongly claimed, was cured.'[71] Although she was 'barred' from the premiere, she saw the town gearing up for the 'festivities' on a trip for a medical procedure a few days prior, and saw numerous images of Woodward portraying her in shop windows and the cinema marquee ('That's not right', she despaired, 'she did not look like' me).[72] In *I'm Eve*, she expresses 'the more she searched for Chris in the premiere events, the less able she was to find Chris in herself. Her whole being became abstract, absent.'[73] Following the event, Thigpen reported back to her, 'The doctor work went on as usual – almost anyway – but the "girls" in the office were so excited they could hardly think about anything but the premiere. Everything went off remarkably well, I thought. The picture was well received here, and we all felt that Joanne Woodward did a splendid job. I wonder if your family sent you the newspapers about the Premiere and if not if you would like me to send them to you?'[74] The following March, Costner Sizemore would experience this feeling of absence again when Woodward received an Oscar for her 'role as the "real-life neurotic with three personalities"'.[75]

Critics almost universally praised Woodward's performance (except the extremely critical review in *Time*), but the reviews were more mixed with regard to how well the source material and subject matter had been – and could be – translated to Hollywood genre filmmaking. A British reviewer explained, 'As a unique case in the field of psychiatry, this is probably of profound interest to some, but it doesn't wholly convince as entertainment.'[76] This reviewer was particularly perturbed by how the amount of time spent in the therapy room 'affords few opportunities for Cinemascope' – psychiatric authenticity and the cinematic are seen at odds here. Others agreed, stating, 'The psychiatric sessions, while possibly authentic, could readily confuse the layman.'[77] *The Times*, on the other hand, felt that the 'most interesting moments are, indeed, when the audiences turn into invisible third presence in the consulting room of Dr Luther', praising it as a 'serious and well-made film'.[78] Similarly, *The Guardian* also praised the film as 'a true record which succeeds in being entertainment', in contrast to similar themed Hollywood films – 'The same true story had already been exploited in another film, *Lizzie* . . . the difference between the two films is precisely that between the usual essay in Hollywood melodramatics and a real attempt to do justice to an extraordinary subject.'[79] Similarly, genre was key to the US middle-brow press's reception of the film.

Many of the critics evoked a clear gendered politics of taste in assessing the success or failings of *The Three Faces of Eve*, particularly in situating the film within a largely unwelcomed recent trend of a resurgence of the 'unmistakably angled "women's films"' with its trope of bifurcating women into good and bad characters, but with the modern twist of housing them in the same body.[80] The *New York Times'* Bosley Crowther's patronising article identified *The Three Faces of Eve*'s 'piteous account' as 'precisely the sort of thing that would've had the women awash with self-involvement back in the days of Good Queen Bette Davis' reign. It would have been irresistible with Olivia de Havilland.' Crowther is, surprisingly, very positive about writer, director, producer Nunnally Johnson's 'commendably detailed job' in adapting this 'actual case report by two psychiatrists' and then tracing 'the psychological developments with almost documentary clarity' on-screen. Instead, he aimed his criticism at the female audience's identification with the film's bifurcated character(s) (referred to by Crowther, offensively, as a 'psychological freak') which is seen to be the basis of the 'women's film' genre. He continued, 'Could anything be more inviting to "audience identification"? Here is a woman who is both good and naughty without any responsibility . . . She doesn't even have to solve the mystery. That's a job for her psychiatrist.'[81] While Philip Scheuer of the *Los Angeles Times* also positioned the film in relation to the trend of rebooting the 'woman's picture', he is far more self-conscious about the problematic nature of this trade term – 'women, I find, resent it (and really, you can't blame them) as something fairly derogatory, suggesting they are as a race apart or as incapable of thinking as individuals. This, I hasten to stay, is not a connotation in which I use it.'[82]

Positive reviews of the film tended to foreground genre terms such as 'psychiatric case history' or 'psychological drama', while negative reviews tend to associate it with the older traditions of the 'woman's film' or 'melodrama' discussed above. In his later review of the film, Crowther complained that this 'melodrama', while 'based on a clinical study . . . when you come right down to it, this is simply a melodramatic exercise – an exhibition of psychiatric hocus-pocus, without any indication of how or why.'[83] There is a disconnect for Crowther between the scientific basis (male) and mode of audience address (female). Despite the dismissal of this genre film as a means of communicating its psychiatric basis, a surprising number of the reviews misdiagnosed Eve as having 'spilt personality',[84] rather than the diagnosis of 'multiple personality' which is clearly stated from the film's introduction onwards. Others blamed the film's generic hybridity (a form of 'split personality') for its failing, suggesting '[Nunnally] Johnson shifts back and forth – striving for comedy at one point and presenting a documentary case history at another'.[85]

Costner Sizemore did not see the film until 16 November 1974, when it was scheduled to rerun on television. In *A Mind of My Own*, she discusses the complex, conflicted feelings she experienced in anticipating and then watching the film with her family. First, 'emptiness and longing . . . in tune with the mood' of the credit sequence with its 'eerie' score; a 'twinge of our perpetual fear: *What in God's name has this movie shown the world about me?*' triggered by Cooke's referencing Jekyll and Hyde; sadness at the missed opportunity for Jane to go to Hollywood to make a cameo in the prologue; then, after an initial numbness, growing admiration of Joanne Woodward's performance of her and her alters: 'At one point I gasped, realising that while the actress was portraying the "switch" of personalities, the phenomenon seemed authentic, as if one of my psychic sisters were actually emerging from within her.'[86]

After the film, she suggested, the family's 'collective tension' was replaced by an 'overwhelming sense of relief' at her representation within the film, but also a personal feeling of her own fragile and fragmented recollections of past selves: 'I only knew *the others* as the result of my mind's recall – a motion picture not much different from what we had just watched. A second-hand familiarity.'[87] She further reconciled with the film in 1978 (after *I'm Eve*), when she was invited to London to be the 'guest of honour' at a special screening of *The Three Faces of Eve* programmed by the British Film Institute at the National Film Theatre. During the screening, she suggests, she felt 'decades of resentment and pain exorcising themselves' on receiving a standing ovation on her way to the stage to address the audience. She experienced this as the 'single most glorious moment of my life' as it was public recognition for her central role in the film at last.[88]

While Costner Sizemore reconciled with the film in the late 1970s, this was the beginning of her legal contention with 20th Century Fox over the rights to her story, and the start of her public denouncement of her former therapists over their version of her story. Her contention with 20th Century Fox began over the rights to *I'm Eve*, for which they purchased the option (with a 'built-in renewal') and then did not produce, which Costner Sizemore interpreted as a way to 'simply prevent me from challenging the 1956 agreement'.[89] A decade later, however, she successfully sued the studio for the rights to her life story following interest from Sissy Spacek in co-producing and staring in a film based on her new book *A Mind of My Own*. 20th Century Fox blocked the project, claiming that in the original contract, brokered by Thigpen and Cleckley, one of Sizemore's alters had signed over the film rights to 'all versions of my life story hereafter published' in perpetuity. Costner Sizemore's attorney, Carol Rinzler, contended that the studio was aware that she was 'still in the grip of the disorder',[90] as the contract was signed by all her alters, and that she was 'unduly influenced' by Thigpen to sign away the rights to her life story.[91] Costner Sizemore reached a settlement with 20th Century Fox, and in her statement on the case she stated that while she was 'enormously grateful' for Thigpen's initial diagnosis and treatment, she contested their book and the film's neat closure of their 'cure' of her MPD, as 'she endured it for 18 more years.'[92]

With the publication of *I'm Eve*, she began her challenge to Thigpen and Cleckley's version of the story, in which they 'cured' her by integrating the three alter personalities in 1953. She was treated by eight therapists and her condition was not resolved until 1974, after four years of treatment with Dr Tony Tsitos who identified twenty-two alters, of different ages and sexes, and a more involved history of childhood trauma and abuse – both of which are more representative of cases of MPD/DID. In addition to her reproaches in her books, from 1975 she also denounced her former therapists – for their inadequate diagnosis and treatment and for the exploitation of her story – in extensive and ongoing lecturing tours, during which she advocated for patients' rights as well as the formal recognition and nuanced understanding of her former condition (including within the DSM).

Costner Sizemore's lecture tours can be understood in the context of the rise of the psychiatric survivors movements and patient advocacy groups which emerged from the anti-psychiatry movement (discussed in Chapter 5), but were distinct in being patient-driven rather than professionally led. A formalised MPD survivors movement was established later, in 1984, with the formation of the International Society for the Study of Multiple Personality and Dissociation (ISSSMP&D). This was more top-down, in being formed by a group of psychiatrists and psychologists interested in MPD, but 'the movement has had an egalitarian look.'[93] In assessing Costner Sizemore's role in this, Hacking explains, 'She did not so much join the movement as serve as a perfect exemplar of the new vision of multiplicity that emerged in the 1970s – including misdiagnosis or mistreatment by an earlier generation of doctors.'[94]

Hacking sees the case behind a subsequent high-profile 'multobiography' *Sybil* (1973) and its film adaptation (1976) as heralding the 'multiple movement' rather than *The Three Faces of Eve*.[95] *Sybil* again starred Woodward, but this time as psychiatrist and psychoanalyst Cornelia Wilbur, whose pioneering treatment with the titular character (played by Sally Field) involved 2,534 office hours. Hacking suggests 'Sybil became the prototype for what was to count as multiple', particularly in the aetiology of the condition – the result of childhood sexual abuse – and the understandings of the alters– mechanisms to protect the main personality from these traumatic episodes, both at the time and in the present.[96] In passages of her 1989 book, in which she details her integration, Costner Sizemore draws a distinction between herself and Sybil Dorsett's experiences, with Costner Sizemore highlighting her more prominent and active role in the processes of integrating her alters. She contrasts the total control of Sybil's therapist, Wilbur, who uses hypnosis to regress her alters to the same age and then bring them forward to Sybil's own age, to her 'primarily self-willed' organisation of 'her own personalities and life', which did not involve any regression on the part of her therapist Tsitos. She attributed this integration in July 1974 not to Tsitos, but to her own work and learning, 'the culmination of nearly twenty years of therapy'.[97]

In the 1980s, Costner Sizemore's expertise was formally recognised in her appointment to the human rights committee of the Dorothea Dix hospital (North Carolina's first and largest psychiatric hospital named after an early mental health advocate) and being invited, by pioneering FBI agent and profiler Robert Ressler, to be an expert consultant for a 'serial killer' case. In this capacity, she watched videos of interviews with Kenneth Bianchi, the 'Hillside Strangler', switching between alters to advise if she felt that he was faking the condition for an 'insanity plea' (the controversy over which is discussed in Chapter 6). She studied his eye movement (as psychologist in the late 1960s had studied hers in the 16mm films) and from this decided that he was faking.[98]

Costner Sizemore continued to give lectures and appearance on television into the 2000s, drawing on her experiences and expertise. In 2007, she was invited back to Augusta, Georgia, to be guest of honour and to give a talk at a fiftieth anniversary screening of *The Three Faces of Eve* at the Imperial Theater (the Miller Theater was undergoing renovations at the time).[99] Before her death in 2016, Colin A. Ross, a psychiatrist specialising in disassociation, wrote a book titled *The Rape of Eve*, written in consultation with Costner Sizemore, that detailed the 'Svengali-like' Thigpen's exploitation and control of her up until his death in 1999.[100] In her *New York Times* obituary, when questioned on the validity of Ross' claims, her son Bobby Sizemore suggested that while Thigpen deserved some credit for his mother's diagnosis, 'there was some truth there' in *The Rape of Eve*.[101]

The Feminine Mystique and the *Mad Housewife*

As discussed above, the book and film of *The Three Faces of Eve* sought to understand Eve/Costner Sizemore's symptoms, at least initially, in the context of her unhappy marriage and home life, while situating a more modern and satisfying approach to being a wife, mother and homemaker as being the marker of her psychological integration. The film stops well short, therefore, of pathologising the role of housewife altogether, as would emergence in the following decade with second-wave feminism's 'widespread projection of the lack and power and failure of individual development on to the persona of woman at home'.[102] The best-selling book that is typically attributed with sparking second-wave feminism in the United States is Betty Friedan's 1963 book *The Feminine Mystique,* which addressed 'the pervasive problem that has no name'[103] – the unhappiness of post-war women. The book was based on research with suburban housewives conducted from 1957 (the year of *The Three Faces of Eve*'s production and release) and discourse analysis of media and advertising. This data was marshalled to challenge assumptions that women would be fulfilled by marriage, motherhood and housewifery alone, and, conversely, that education, work outside the home and engagement with politics would ultimately make them unhappier. She coined this assumption the 'feminine mystique'.

Post-war psy scientists helped to perpetuate this discourse – including the 1950's analysts featured in *Life* magazine who were discussed earlier in this chapter – with Friedan seeing 'Freud as the ultimate source of America's "Feminine Mystique"', originally through the misogynistic ideologies underlying his and subsequent Freudian analysts' ideas, including 'penis envy', and subsequently through the simplification and circulation of these in popular mass media.[104] Friedan saw a circularity to 'the problem that has no name', in that many of these unfulfilled middle-class wives and mothers – suffering from deep-seated malaise, in spite of taking up the prescribed roles that pseudo-Freudian media told them would make them happy – 'sought psychoanalysis to cope with their troubles, only to feel more enmeshed and desperate'.[105] Rejecting Freudianism as a workable model for women, while conceding the 'basic genius of Freud's discoveries',[106] Friedan looked instead to psychologist Abraham Maslow's self-actualisation theories, popular in the late 1950s and early 1960s, to argue that the 'feminine mystique' was blocking women's basic need for positive human growth and self-realisation. She demanded, therefore, not just equal rights to employment and pay, but also 'equal psychological opportunities'.[107]

While 'second-wave feminism initially defined itself against analysis',[108] Freidan and her contemporaries also saw the potential of psychological and psychotherapeutic ideas to provide support to feminist arguments – for Friedan this included Maslow, but also pioneering female psychoanalyst Karen Horney (1885–1952), who challenged the essentialism of Freudian theory, primarily his concept of 'penis envy', and is as a result credited as the founder of feminist psychology. The Women's Movement's central mechanism of 'consciousness-raising' (CR) must also be understood in the context of contemporary humanistic psychotherapeutic trends (such as Carl Rogers' client-centred psychotherapy and its use within 'encounter groups',[109] albeit marshalled for explicitly political aims. In the late 1960s, the CR practices of group discussion and support were the bedrock of the radical feminist groups emerging in metropolitan centres, where there was a 'respectful attention to emotion and a desire to communicate the subjective feeling of women's everyday lives, from anguish to anger'.[110] In an article advocating for consciousness-raising as a mechanism to mend rifts in psychiatric nursing, Randolph and Ross-Valliere express 'Anger is an important, necessary, and productive aspect of a CR group.'[111] CR groups helped women to tap into their emotions to drive social change – this included anger, which 'many women have been socialized to believe' is 'unacceptable'.[112] The distinction between CR sessions and 'therapy' was very important to the movement, with, for example, Carol Hanisch's influential essay 'The Personal is the Political', demanding that 'analytic sessions are a form of political action'.[113]

The film *Diary of a Mad Housewife* was adapted by screenwriter Eleanor Perry from Sue Kaufman's novel. During the adaption process the two women, both educated Jewish feminists, struck up a productive and supportive creative dialogue. Work in feminist psychology and English literature have drawn links between Kaufman's novel *Diary of a Mad Housewife* (1967) and Friedan's *The Feminine Mystique* in that both powerfully evoke the 'discontent, demoralisation and rebellion' of the 'affluent suburban housewife', and use its as a rallying call at this nascent moment for the Women's Movement.[114] In the post-war era, Eleanor Perry (née Rosenfeld) combined a career as a psychiatric social worker with (co)writing articles, novels and plays, some 'on mental hygiene and psychiatric subjects' for the Cleveland Mental Hygiene Association.[115] She achieved her first major successes in the late 1950s, with the staging on Broadway of her and her then husband's, Leo G. Bayer, play *Third Best Sport* (1957). In 1960, the recently divorced writer married aspiring director Frank Perry and, drawing on her psychiatric background, wrote a screenplay for the film *David and Lisa* (1962), which they raised the money together for, and which her husband directed. The film, based on a short story by American psychiatrist and author Theodore Isaac Rubin, is the story of the nurturing relationship that develops between two young patients, David and Lisa, at a residential psychiatric treatment centre. The Perrys received, mostly, an extremely positive critical reception and subsequently Oscar nominations for screenwriting and directing.[116] This professional partnership produced five subsequent films, including their final film together *Diary of a Mad Housewife*, which also marked the end of their marriage.

In a 1971 *Film Comment* interview, she cited her personal motivations for adapting *Diary of a Mad Housewife*, because, referring to her first marriage, 'at one time I was a mad housewife', and reading Kaufman's novel she recognised 'everything I had known and thought and felt about marriage in a certain affluent American middleclass'.[117] She continued, 'At last somebody was telling that truth about the soul-kicking activities of the housewife . . . I thought Miss Kaufman said it all splendidly with wit and insight'.[118] She went on to situate the film's message in relation to the 'spread of the Women's Lib movement', in that housewife Tina learns, across the film, that to be a 'fully realised human being' she must not rely on any man (neither husband nor lover) for 'her self-image or her self-esteem.'[119] Perry stresses that she largely retained the 'insights' of Kaufman's novel, but insisted on one major change, the ending. 'Sue Kaufman keeps Tina and Jonathon together and implies that the marriage will become workable once he achieves some insight through psychoanalysis.'[120] Perry's decision to change the book's ending when 'dramatizing [Kaufman's insights] for a visual medium'[121] is significant in relation to the feminist understanding of psychoanalysis – as innately patriarchal – and its distinction from consciousness-raising.

In the opening scene of *Dairy of a Mad Housewife*, the camera tilts up to Tina's (Carrie Snodgress) sleeping face as she is woken by her neurotic and abusive husband Jonathon, who we see through Tina's point of view shot as his loud, cheery whistling switches to judgement on her sleeping. He goads, 'I wish I could understand what's a matter with you these days', before offering a list of criticisms of her 'exhausted' disposition, her appearance (her 'too skinny' figure, her 'god-awful' hair), her habits (smoking), and later, her cooking, her house-cleaning, and so forth. He justifies his criticism by saying, 'My wife is reflection of me. I only say this because I am deeply concerned about you Tina.' Throughout the scene, Tina says nothing. The scene is indicative of the film's wider strategy, using Jonathan's incessant criticism, passive-aggressiveness, gaslighting and other forms of psychological abuse to provoke escalating anger in the spectator, while Tina, mostly, remains quiet and acquiesces to these expectations and demands from her husband. At other points in the narrative, Jonathan switches to taking up a childlike demeanour, especially when demanding to be looked after when he is ill, situating himself *also* as the vulnerable and disempowered one, therefore giving Tina no position to speak from. The film could be seen to acts as a form of consciousness-raising – provoking empathy and, more importantly, anger at Tina's treatment by men. When she is later coerced into an affair with a sadistic writer (who at one point Tina threatens 'to report you to Women's Lib'), she initially finds some sexual fulfilment but soon discovers this to be an equally abusive relationship. At the end of the film, Tina and the spectator learn that her husband has lost all their savings on a foolish vanity project, and he is begging her to stay with him nonetheless. This leads into the aforementioned revised final scene.

The decision Perry made was to end the story not with Jonathon in therapy, but with Tina 'searching for help' through group therapy. Rather than advocating for this psychotherapeutic intervention, however, Perry uses this as a narrative device to further strengthen the film's feminist argument against the ideology of the 'feminine mystique', with the metatextual dimension of using the group therapy session (attended by a range of men and women of different ages) to stage, she explained, the opposing gendered 'reactions we heard about the book ... indicating how aroused and passionate assorted people can become over the problem of the housewife'.[122] When it is revealed at the end of the film that the narrative we have just watched was, at least in part, her recollections to the group in this therapy session, she is immediately assaulted with a tirade of opinion and abuse from the other participants. Following an initial panning shot of faces delivering angry, at times surreal, responses to her story – 'You are just a spoilt middle-class bitch, just like my ex-wife, so I know of which I speak'; 'My husband is devouring my life juices, just as your husband is devouring your life juices' – the camera comes to rest on Tina's steadfast face as the credits roll and the group's increasingly curt opinions wash over her ('leave him', 'divorce him', 'split', 'get a lawyer'). The scene and the film most certainly do not advocate for traditional psychotherapy or group therapy but, it could be argued, contributes further to the sense of the film as an exercise in consciousness-raising. As Perry suggested, the film is 'not about madness. Tina is certainly in the grips of neurotic conflicts, on the edge of drinking too much and altogether fragile, but she is less crazy-mad than outraged-mad.'[123] And, as the film's critical reception attests, the spectator is, in the absence of Tina's response, encouraged to experience her anger and take up the position of the 'outraged-mad' housewife.

The film was released on 10 August 1970 to mostly positive critical reception, with Carrie Snodgress' Golden Globe-winning performance particularly praised. The reception of the film suggests that it worked in provoking, even projecting Tina's anger into several critics, enacting a form of consciousness-raising. Roger Ebert of the *Chicago Times* explains, 'What makes the movie work, however, is that it's played entirely from the housewife's point of view ... We're irritated by the things the character puts up with.' He continues, 'when you've finished watching this movie you start getting mad at' the 'egotistical, cruel, insecure, immature, and bitchy' husband. He concludes, 'But then, then ... you start thinking about the title and the point of view of the movie, and you realize this is indeed a diary; that we're getting the housewife's version of the story.'[124] Ebert highlights his empathic response to the film, not just feeling sympathy for the character, but taking up her subject position and feeling and expressing her anger. Countering a few negative reviews that dismissed husband Jonathon as a 'clumsy caricature',[125] *Variety* appreciated him as 'a character so delineated that one wants to throw something at the screen'.[126] Grace Gluek of the *New York Times* also felt affected by Tina's unexpressed anger towards her 'exasperating, male chauvinist mate' and experienced the housewife's domestic imprisonment in the 'claustrophobic trap full of high-class consumer goods'.[127] However,

Gluek does not necessarily experience the portrayal of the 'masochistic' Tina and her disempowerment at the hands of both husband and 'narcisso-sadist lover' as feminist, stating, 'This picture will not, repeat not, be found on any women's lib list for 10 best.'[128]

Some of the trade press reviews disagreed with Gluek's interpretation, with, for example, the *Independent Film Journal* telling exhibitors that there is 'strong box office potential' in this narrative of a 'trapped America house-wife', explaining 'her filmed "diary" arrives at a time to boost further the women's liberation movement. Certainly the young marrieds, especially the wives, will be standing in line to see *their* story on the screen.'[129] While some critics adopted a gendered politics of taste akin to the one marshalled against *The Three Faces of Eve* – Jay Cocks' acerbically negative review of the film dismissed it as 'a snide, skin-deep *Cosmopolitan*-style short story'[130] – *Variety* welcomed the film's updating of the genre of the woman's film for a modern female, perhaps feminist, audience. Murf commended, 'It seems overdue for the trade to update his definition of a woman's picture. Used nowadays mostly in derogation of the weepy sudsers of a bygone generation . . . *Diary of a Mad Housewife* is a modern woman's pic, the primary market for which are under-40 femmes.'[131] This review corresponds with Perry's intentions and, she suggested, the audience response to the film on release.

In a 1974 radio interview with film critic Arthur Knight for his 'In Con-versation' series, in which he introduces Perry as someone 'very much associated with the cause of women's liberation', she states that there is an 'enormous audience of women in the thirties, forties, fifties who never go to movies because they have no one to identify with'. She suggests that *Diary* proved that there is such an audience and feels that more successes like it could enable an 'era of women's movies'. She continued that the film had the 'kind of success where there are lines around the corner all night, but also all day. And who was in those lines, mad housewives' who identified with Tina and her struggles, and in her 'saw themselves . . . it meant something to them.' Positioning the film in relation to the Women's Movement, she acknowledges that she would 'go much farther now with' the film, feeling now that 'it stopped at the place we're only just beginning now'.[132]

After *Diary of a Mad Housewife*, Perry divorced from her director hus-band, instigated by him, and they subsequently pursued separate careers. In her next and final film, the failed 'women's lib western' *The Man Who Loved Cat Dancing* (1973), she was 'left out of creative decisions and mistreated because she is a woman' even though she was given a co-producer credit.[133] In the 1970s, she challenged the patriarchal structure of the film industry, through industrial action, protests, news articles, and, in 1979, a thinly dis-guised autobiography, *Blue Pages* (1979), 'in which a female screenwriter is exploited by her filmmaker husband in the male-dominated jungle of

Hollywood'.[134] In the early 1970s, she was also involved in feminist direct action. At the 1972 Cannes Film Festival, Perry was part of a group that protested Federico Fellini's film *Roma* (1972), the poster for which featured a nude, three-breasted 'she-wolf' which Perry decried as an 'ugly distortion of the female anatomy [and] a humiliating offense to women everywhere'. As the *Chicago Tribune* reported, Perry and five other women 'stirred up a hornet's nest when they set up ladders in front of the Carlton Hotel before the showing . . . and threw four cans of red paint on the Fellini poster'. When police turned up to arrest them, 'Mrs. Perry screamed *mechant* (a French word meaning wicked and evil) and ripped epaulets from their uniforms.'[135] Perry suggested that that her involvement in the Women's Movement had motivated her, for the first time, to enter the male-dominated sphere of directing. She said that while previously she unequivocally answered 'no' to the question of whether she would like to direct, 'Today the answer is yes. My conscious has not so much been raised as uncovered by all the pieces I have read about the Women's Liberation movement and the few meetings of assorted groups I have attended.'[136] Eleanor Perry was never to direct a film, however, her career blocked – it was asserted by Perry and subsequent critics – by her feminist politics. She died in 1981, aged sixty-six with her *New York Times* obituary celebrating her as 'one of the movie industry's strongest feminist voices'.[137]

Conclusion

This chapter has looked at two films that straddle the emergence of second-wave feminism, which employ the contested idea of 'madness' as a way to understand and express the shifting expectations and roles of American women across this period, and the impact of psychological ideas and expertise in progressing and impeding women's psychological and social developments. *The Three Faces of Eve* was analysed in the wider context of post-war women's experiences and struggles, but it is also important not to forget – as many critics did then and now – that this is the story of a real woman, Chris Costner Sizemore, and her very specific diagnosis with multiple personality or dissociative identity disorder. In gender terms, it offers an extreme but revealing case study of the elision of a female patient's experience and expertise from the documenting and circulation of her case history which, while preferred as for her own protection, demonstrates the twin disempowerment of being a woman and a psychiatric patient. Though Costner Sizemore was able to find her voice across a number of multobiographies, within popular culture she continued to be defined, right up until her death, by her (mis) representation as Eve, an identity imposed by her male psychiatrists.

Eleanor Perry was able to break out of her housewife role to become an acclaimed screenwriter, drawing upon both her background in psychiatric nursing and an expanded sense of identity and opportunity as a feminist. In the context of the emergent Women's Movement, *Diary of a Mad House-wife* combines Betty Friedan's challenge to psychoanalysis' normalising underpinnings – in highlighting that its titular housewife's madness is bred of socially motivated anger rather than psychological neurosis – but also points to alternative psychotherapeutic sensibilities within feminism. With the switch to group therapy in the film's final scene, it is revealed that the spectator has actually been subsumed in the silenced housewife's perspective – listening to her account of the marriage in which 'she's noble and long-suffering, and of course he's a witless bastard'[138] – and as a result is invited to feel angry for her and with her, more in the manner of a CR group member than the unemphatic group therapy attendees she encounters. While Perry's films, which drew on her psychiatric and feminist experience and expertise, offered alternatives to the limited roles for women in Hollywood films, her career was curtailed because she was considered, by many in the industry, to be too outspoken about the systematic disavowal of women in the industry and on-screen.

Radical collaborations: 'anti-psychiatry' on-screen

A 1972 *Guardian* article reporting on the contentious clinical ideas under-pinning the new British film *Family Life* (1971), characterised its political intention as the 'work of radical filmmakers spread[ing] the ideas of radical psychologists'.[1] Inspired by R. D. Laing's ideas on the aetiology of schizo-phrenia, *Family Life* was a 'big screen' reworking of the 1967 BBC television play *In Two Minds* (1967), made by the same production team of producer Tony Garnett, director Ken Loach and screenwriter David Mercer, in con-sultation with progressive psychiatrists Laing, Aaron Esterson and David Cooper. However, Merete Bates' portrayal of a unidirectional influence from the pages of psychiatric texts to the screen, misapprehends the complex critical and creative interactions of psychiatric and media professionals that shaped the co-production and circulation of these two films. *In Two Minds* and *Family Life* emerged from the filmmakers and psychiatrists' converg-ing professional and political convictions that the well-being of individuals and society was being hindered rather than helped by 'orthodox' psychiatric practices and the media forms that perpetuated their power. As this chapter will explain, *In Two Minds* and its source text, Laing and Esterson's *Sanity, Madness and the Family* (1964), subvert the expectations of the BBC's factual medical programming and the psychiatric case history genre to undermine the ideological surety of these dominant genres within their fields.[2] These 'radical' films must be understood in the context of the wider contestations and cross-pollinations within and between the fields of mental health and media in Britain and America during the long 1960s detailed in this book. Specifically, *In Two Minds* represents a confluence of what Crossley defines as the 'field of psychiatric contention'[3] – which included 'anti-psychiatry', but also the post-war mental hygiene movement and the emergent user/survivor and parent advocacy groups of the early 1970s – and an analogous field of media contention, driven not by commercial or even creative imperatives, but primarily by political ones.

This chapter draws upon practitioner interviews conducted with producer Tony Garnett and director Ken Loach, and archival research conducted at the BFI National Archives, BBC Written Archives, the R. D. Laing Archive at the University of Glasgow, the British Board of Film Classification (BBFC) Archive, and the Wellcome Collection.[4] It employs these sources in a diachronic analysis of the production, mediation and reception of *In Two Minds* and *Family Life*, which explores their circulation within shifting clinical, media and political contexts as the 'rebel'[5] ideas within the films became increasingly mainstream. Can we even consider the ideas of 'the Mick Jagger of psychiatrists'[6] Laing as 'radical' by 1972?

The first half of the chapter challenges previous research on the production of *In Two Minds* through its foregrounding of the vital, hands-on contributions of Cooper and Esterson, who are often elided in the emphasis on Laing's roles.[7] In doing so, it contributes to a recent revisionist drive to rewrite their contributions into histories of 'anti-psychiatry'.[8] The second half of the chapter contributes to recent scholarship that questions the idea of a polarisation between anti-psychiatry and psychiatric 'orthodoxy' by approaching this issue from a media perspective.[9] While the popular press' reception of *In Two Minds* and *Family Life* did intensify an adversarial relationship between 'rebel' anti-psychiatrists and hard-line behaviourists such as William Sargant, the wider mental health field largely welcomed the films' contributions to mental health awareness and sought to use their publicity to counter the idea of a 'battle' within British psychiatry. This includes leading UK mental health organisation, NAMH looking to Loach and Laing as models for engaging contemporary audiences as it rebranded to MIND in 1972. This chapter contributes to the book's wider aim of developing historical understandings of the complex interactions between the fields of media and mental health, but also seeks to intervene in recent scholarship that challenges the idea of a clear split between anti-psychiatry and mainstream psychiatry.

British psychiatric culture in the long 1960s

Sociologist Nick Crossley's *Contesting Psychiatry* offers a history of the changing landscape of the mental health field in post-war Britain, and the social movements whose resistance to psychiatric orthodoxy provoked these changes. This sociological study is useful in mapping the interactions of competing mental health organisations and advocacy groups 'who converge around common areas of concern (whether in agreement or disagreement)', and the diffuse currents of discourse and demands they circulated during the post-war period in Britain.[10] At the centre of this field of contention in the long 1960s period, for Crossley, is the struggle between psychiatric orthodoxy, which is seen to favour biomedical models of understanding and treating mental illness, and the emergent 'anti-psychiatry' movement, associated with progressive/radical psychiatrists such as Laing and Cooper, who advocated for psychotherapeutic approaches and the de-institutionalisation of treatment.[11] The anti-psychiatry movement originated in the late 1950s as a series of challenges to dangerous and coercive physical treatments like electroconvulsive therapy (ECT) and psychosurgery (such as lobotomies), but, according to Crossley, by the early 1960s sought to challenge the 'very basis of psychiatry itself; its purpose, its foundational concept of mental illness and the very distinction between madness and sanity'.[12]

Recent scholarship has sought to challenge the idea of a clear break between mainstream psychiatry and the anti-psychiatry movement, characterising it as a 'journey away from the psychiatric hospital, but not necessarily away from psychiatry itself'.[13] Oisín Wall highlights how the British anti-psychiatric group, which formed around Laing, Cooper and Esterson, amalgamated and extended existing post-war trends within the mainstream psychiatric milieu – therapeutic communities, psychodynamic therapy, social psychiatry, de-institutionalisation and institutional reform – rather than initiating them. For example, the experimental therapeutic communities developed in the 1960s by the anti-psychiatrists 'took their lead from well-respected and established "mainstream" psychiatric practitioners like [T. P.] Rees, [Maxwell] Jones, and [Joshua] Bierer', who developed working models for therapeutic communities, both in and outside the hospital, in the 1940s and 1950s.[14] The key innovations of David Cooper's 'anti-hospital' within a hospital, Villa 21 (1962–1966), and the Philadelphia Association's more famous alternative community Kingsley Hall (1965–1970) was in the politicisation of these post-war models through their inculcation of anti-institutional and countercultural discourses. From the mid-1960s, Laing, Cooper and Esterson were united in their belief that the pre-condition for mental well-being was a conjoined personal and social liberation 'from the alienating and oppressive power of social institutions', including those of 'the family'. They argued that the 'structures of the family were repressive and destructive and . . . that these structures were mapped onto the authoritarian society and state'.[15] In this way, their work intersected and resonated with both New Left and countercultural discourses and audiences.

It was this bridging of psychiatric, political and countercultural concerns that brought anti-psychiatry into public discourse. In the late 1960s, the 'star' of this movement in the United Kingdom was Laing, who as Crossley explains, 'It was Laing whose books were bestsellers . . ., it was Laing whose ideas were turned into television plays and stage plays . . . who appeared regularly on British television and radio, even on such mainstream interview formats as the *Parkinson Show*.[16] Laing became a go-to media spokesperson for anti-psychiatry – despite his ambivalence about the term – gaining him a significant counterculture following and a level of public awareness.[17] This concentration on the charismatic Laing as the 'poster boy' for anti-psychiatry and, by the early 1970s, as talismanic countercultural 'guru' has been cemented in subsequent academic and media discourse – including the recent British drama *Mad To Be Normal* (2017) starring David Tennant. This has contributed to a corresponding minimising of Cooper and Esterson's important and distinctive roles in the ideas and interventions that became known as anti-psychiatry. This chapter seeks to contribute to a recent drive to 're-Cooper',[18] as well as 're-Esterson', the history of anti-psychiatry by foregrounding their fundamental roles in the making of these two films. This includes the vital roles Cooper and Villa 21 played in the research, production and staging of the films, and Esterson's centrality to the filmmakers' understanding and staging of the family dynamic.

In Crossley's account, anti-psychiatry emerged in the early 1960s to contest the biomedical understandings and treatments of mental illness that were favoured by the British psychiatric establishment. The key organisation he identifies as seeking to maintain the status quo in advocating for psychiatric orthodoxy between the mid-1950s and mid-1960s was the NAMH, known as 'the Association' within the mental health field. While the NAMH was formed in the immediate post-war era with the reformist agenda of thinking about mental health more holistically (as an issue that affected all and that should be addressed through social policy and education, as well as medicine), when the psychiatric establishment came under attack in the 1960s, the NAMH was seen to adopt the role of defenders of both orthodox psychiatric methods and government policy.[19]

The NAMH was formed in 1946 out of a merger of three interwar voluntary groups that, whilst having different focuses, were all driven by the rationale of the 'mental hygiene movement' which advocated for a medical understanding of mental illness.[20] This formalisation must be understood in the context of the post-war development of the welfare state, with mental health and parliamentary fields converging through their complementary interests and concerns.[21] By the start of the 1960s, the NAMH had become closely aligned with the psychiatric establishment, working closely with and being funded by government to advise upon and advocate for established approaches to mental health. Key elements of the mental hygiene movement's reformist agenda were reconciled with NAMH's more conservative turn in the long 1960s period. This included its ongoing support for the British post-war therapeutic community experiments and their innovators, including Rees and D. H. Clark, who were 'closely involved with the NAMH',[22] as well as NAMH/MIND committee member Dr Richard Fox, consultant psychiatrist at Severalls Hospital, Colchester, whose 'Group Home' experiment from 1964 – where older women patients were moved into shared rented housing – predates Kingsley Hall.[23]

Within its 'conservative' capacity as staunch defenders against internal and external critiques of psychiatric expertise, the NAMH adopted a paternalistic and censorial approach to educating the public (and particularly the working classes) about mental health, and saw television and cinema as the key media for spreading information and, more importantly, misinformation about psychiatric practices. As discussed in Chapter 2, the NAMH had a vested interest in film. In 1947, they formed the 'Film Visiting Committee' (FVC) with the purpose of protecting the psychiatric professions and practices against misrepresentation. Within this capacity, the NAMH reviewed films that dealt with mental health or represented psychiatric practices for their in-house journal *Mental Health*, judging them for clinical accuracy and influence on audiences rather than on dramatic or aesthetic terms. In 1963, the NAMH formalised its ongoing collaboration with members of the British Film Academy to form the Mental Health Film Council (MHFC). In forming this new organisation, which sat within and shared membership with the Public Information Committee, the NAMH expanded its remit to include film production, and organised courses to train members to make films countering misinformation spread within mainstream cinema. Some of these hygiene films were even screened in cinemas as supporting features.[24] With this shift into production the NAMH became direct actors within the cinematic field rather than just converging with it through consultation and comment.

In the mid-1950s, the NAMH became attuned to the importance of television in spreading psychiatric information. In 1956, it launched and sought BBC representation on its Public Information Committee with the primary agenda, 'To spread a knowledge of the principles of mental hygiene among the general public.'[25] It made a high-profile appointment in Mary Adams, former Head of Talks and Current Affairs (1945–1954) and then Assistant to Controller of Television (1954–1958). In this capacity Adams initiated the innovative BBC medical series *Matters of Life and Death* (1948–) and *Your Life in Their Hands* (1958–), and was a staunch advocate of the value of medical and science programming.[26] Adams was on the Public Information Committee from its first meeting in 1957 until the end of the 1960s. On her retirement from the BBC in 1958, the NAMH approached Huw Wheldon – a producer in the Television Talks department and presenter of flagship arts and culture programme *Monitor* (1958–1965) – so it had up-to-date representation from someone influential within the BBC. Wheldon declined the invitation, recommending Grace Wyndham Goldie, Assistant Head of Television Talks and Features at the time. In 1963, Doreen Gorsky (nee Stephens), feminist activist, innovator of women's programming, and then Head of Family Programmes at the BBC, was appointed chairman of the Public Information Committee and remained in this role until the early 1970s. These appointments of pioneering female broadcasters and, in Gorsky's case, feminist campaigners, to its committees challenge (or perhaps indicates underlying gender politics) the NAMH's 'staid image as a "twin-set-and-pearls"' establishment organisation by the 1960s.[27]

The NAMH's most ambitious intervention into television was its collaboration with the BBC on the development and production of the five-part mental health series *The Hurt Mind* (1957). It intended to present a comprehensive account of contemporary thinking on the causes and treatment of mental health, featuring discrete episodes on physical and psychotherapeutic approaches. The series was presented by Christopher Mayhew MP and featured a number of publicly recognised psychiatrists and psychologists, including T. P. Rees, Lionel Penrose, John Bowlby and William Sargant. *The Hurt Mind* was developed from preliminary BBC research into public attitudes to mental health, but was also used to conduct post-broadcast research to measure its 'effects'. Despite the desire to represent a balanced view of mental health provision, biomedical treatments featured more prominently across the series due to the agendas of some key actors. As NAMH minutes suggest, producer Andrew Miller-Jones intended the series to advocate for 'physical treatments including the new method of ECT', presenting it with an 'un-alarming look' that would have 'a reassuring effect on the public'.[28] The fourth episode focused on physical treatment and featured a presentation of a staged ECT procedure. This was studio-based, but edited and the set designed to give the impression of an outside broadcast (OB) from a hospital. A doctor in mid-shot introduces the procedure – edited to show a few close-ups of the equipment being used – and begins by administering muscle relaxant, foregrounded as the 'most important advance that has been made in this treatment' which 'has in fact taken the convulsion out of convulsive treatment'. He then simulates sending a 'carefully measured dose' of current through the patient twice, doing it a second time so viewers can 'watch his toes', stressing this subtle reaction is 'as much as you'll see'. The scene's mundane staging of the treatment and matter-of-fact exposition (the doctor introduces the scene as 'going through the motions of having ECT'), have close equivalences to the corresponding scene in *In Two Minds*, as discussed below.

The post-broadcast audience research conducted by the BBC's senior psychologist highlighted 'the most striking' change as a 'large increase in viewers' confidence in electric shock treatment (45 per cent were confident before and 65 per cent after) and a corresponding increase in approval of it as method of treatment.[29] The series' chief adviser, controversial biological psychiatrist William Sargant, saw this almost 50 per cent increase in confidence in ECT and other psychical treatments as an important balancing of the media's historical bias towards 'talking cures', stressing that 'previous film and radio publicity had already raised public approval of the use of psychotherapy and psychoanalysis as acceptable treatments'.[30] This was corroborated by the audience research which reported that, 'The series produced a more equal balance, increasing the reference to psychical treatment and reducing reference to psychological treatment.'[31] A number of psychiatric organisations and clinicians contacted the BBC to express appreciation for the programme's advocacy of medical approaches, but it also received some high-profile criticism. The *British Medical Journal* criticised the programme's depiction of ECT for 'increas[ing] the hypochondria and neurosis' of the British public, stating that 'a very large number of persons, we were given to understand, as a result got into touch to with their own doctors asking whether they could have electric shock treatment'. The author provoked 'it may be doubted whether those organising the programme thought this a desirable result'.[32]

The NAMH used its role as publicity for the organisation, co-producing a pamphlet titled *Mind Out of Balance* with the BBC to promote the series, and circulating it in conjunction with the Ministry of Health.[33] It heavily advocated for a proposed follow-up series of *The Hurt Mind* but this did not materialise. The NAMH and its members (Stafford-Clark and Sargant, in particular) continued to advise upon and appear in a range of BBC talk and documentary programmes in the late 1950s to mid-1960s, including *Lifeline* (1957–1962) and *Brain and Behaviour* (1964). In the early 1960s, mental health conditions and practices became the subject of individual and serial dramas too, most notably the ABC series for ITV, *The Human Jungle* (1963–1964), which followed a detective show-style structure of discrete weekly cases solved by British psychiatrist Dr Corder (Herbert Lom). Corder employs mostly psychoanalytic and psychotherapeutic methods of diagnosis and treatment, and his 'maverick ad-hoc approach' has been understood in the context of Laing's growing influence.[34] The show's generic and clinical underpinnings raised issues for the NAMH, who discussed whether to take 'further action' on this programme at a Public Information Committee meeting in June 1963.[35] NAMH-affiliated psychiatrist Dr Hugh Freeman acted as medical adviser on the show and, correspondingly, as the series develops, Corder is much more varied in his methods, prescribing antipsychotics drugs and ECT alongside offering psychotherapeutic interventions. Freeman described his advisory role as 'frustrating experience', as the scriptwriters 'didn't appreciate my efforts to make their stories conform to reality'. Later, he continued, 'when anti-psychiatry was in vogue, it was eagerly seized by television, often with primarily political motives,'[36] which he saw as culminating in Loach's *Family Life*. While *The Human Jungle* and the BBC comedy play *A Suitable Case for Treatment* (1962) have subsequently been interpreted in the context of Laing and anti-psychiatry, *In Two Minds* was the first 'drama' to explicitly draw upon his writings and expertise.

Media and psychiatric contention on British television

In Two Minds must be understood in the context of a wider contention within the BBC in the 1960s. It was one of BBC's *Wednesday Plays* (1964–1970), a series of one-off television dramas introduced by BBC's Head of Drama Sydney Newman (1962–1967). *The Wednesday Plays* gained a reputation for being socially engaged and formally innovative, provoking public debate and, on occasion, media controversy, including within the BBC.[37] The most well-known and critically acclaimed of these was Garnett and Loach's *Cathy Come Home* (1966), the story of a homeless couple whose children are taken into local authority care which was shot in an observational documentary style. This drama mobilised public and media debate, discussion in Parliament and triggered the formation of the homeless charity Crisis in 1967. *Cathy Come Home*'s generic innovation of the 'drama-documentary' triggered concern within the BBC where it was felt, particularly by former Head of Talks and Current Affairs Grace Wyndham Goldie, that the 'play' should have been produced by the documentary not the drama department.[38] This was a battle not just about generic boundaries, but also politics in that 'incorporation of documentary elements into drama could offer the means for evading institutional controls regarding political partisanship' that were applied to all factual programming.[39] Garnett and Loach have proffered that they used the relative 'openness' of the *Wednesday Play* format to express contrary political views to the 'official' BBC line, but saw the BBC's documentary and current affairs programmes as far from apolitical, unbiased and objective. Garnett criticised the BBC for its 'hypocritical and tendentious pretence of objectivity'[40] and for making programmes that were 'public relations jobs for establishment institutions'.[41]

The *Wednesday Plays* can be seen, therefore, as part of a wider momentum, referred to herein as a *field of media contention*, which, like 'anti-psychiatry', was motivated by a convergence of socialist politics with field-specific movements to 'transform both conceptions and practices' within the media and mental health systems.[42] It was these political confluences that brought together – both ideologically and psychically – the clinical–creative alliances that produced *In Two Minds*. *In Two Minds* was Garnett and Loach's subsequent collaboration for the *Wednesday Play* series, a 'drama-documentary' shot entirely on-location that tells the story of a young woman who 'suffers from a diagnosis of schizophrenia'.[43] The play was simultaneously a personal and intellectual project for Garnett, who explained that the film 'emerged from a terrible rage' and confusion he felt after his wife Topsy Jane, an actor best known for her role in *The Loneliness of the Long Distance Runner* (1962), was rendered 'unrecognisable' through treatment with drugs and ECT. When she was taken 'ill' during the production of *Billy Liar* (1963):

> Her mother sent her to the GP, and the GP sent her to the local 'bin', and they immediately plugged her into the mains. And fed her up with all those psychotropic drugs, that were even cruder than they are now, and she just got worse and stayed in that state until she died a few years ago.[44]

At the same time Garnett, who had a degree in psychology and a lasting 'intellectual interest' in Freud, encountered and was, 'like many people of my generation', inspired by the writings of Laing.

Laing's *The Divided Self* (1960)[45] and Laing and Esterson's *Sanity, Madness and the Family* (1964) were key influences and sources for the script, and were recommended to scriptwriter Mercer by Garnett.[46] Mercer had received acclaim for a previous BBC television play exploring the idea of madness as a strategy of revolt in *A Suitable Case for Treatment*, but stated that he had not read any of the anti-psychiatry literature in researching the play or subsequent film adaptation, *Morgan* (1965). During our interview, Garnett explained that the 'spark' for the film's script was the case study of 'Julie' at the end of the *Divided Self*, particularly her 'delusion' that a child had been murdered. While the ideas within *The Divided Self* and the 'Julie' case study were contentious, its structure follows the conventional form of the 'psychiatric case history' in plotting a narrative of a patient's history and treatment alongside the clinician's interpretations.[47] As discussed earlier in the book, this genre that has adapted well to popular media forms, and particularly Hollywood films, including *The Three Face of Eve* (discussed in Chapter 4) and Huston's biopic *Freud* (discussed in Chapter 3).

Formally, Laing and Esterson's *Sanity, Madness and the Family* is more unconventional in presenting the near-full transcripts of its interviews with eleven families 'with very few interpretations, whether existential or psychoanalytic',[48] and offering few conclusions on causes or cures. The book's formal and ideological challenge to the conventions of the psychiatric case history genre – in refusing to offer an explanation as to 'why' – was the book's overriding 'problem' for the reviewer of the NAMH's *Mental Health* journal.[49] The formal inventiveness of *In Two Minds* takes inspiration from

Sanity, Madness and the Family, structuring its first half around the ethnographic semi-structured interviews conducted with a young woman diagnosed as schizophrenic, Kate Winter (Anna Cropper), and her family by an unseen psychiatrist (Brian Phelan). As with Laing and Esterson's book, the play's generic innovation in presenting psychiatric material was also questioned for its boundary-breaking. Laing, Esterson and Cooper's roles in the conceptualisation and production of the play were far more than merely providing source material, with Cooper in particular central to the inception of the project prior to Loach's involvement and even prior to Mercer's agreement to write it.

Tony Garnett approached Cooper and Laing in January 1966 to ask the psychiatrists to meet to up with himself, scriptwriter Mercer and Ken Battersby, the original choice for director, to discuss ideas for a 'a film about some people who suffer from the diagnosis Schizophrenia'.[50] Laing was initially reluctant, but Cooper attended this meeting at Mercer's home, during which the scriptwriter, following a 'useful discussion with Dr Cooper', agreed to write the screenplay. This meeting seems to have also consolidated the idea of drawing on material gathered for *Sanity, Madness and the Family*, specifically the interview tapes with Ruth Gold and her family.[51] In late February, Garnett wrote to Laing and Esterson seeking permission to use their research with the Golds for the film, and to seek their advice 'at all stages' of the production.[52] The three psychiatrists agreed to act as advisers, with Cooper and Laing taking up the roles of chief technical advisers (each were paid £100). Laing subsequently contacted the Golds to ask if he could bring Mercer to meet them 'in order to enable him to learn, first hand from you, what some of the problems are'.[53] Garnett did not remember this meeting with the Golds happening, but much of Ruth's experiences of a 'feeling of unreality' and the Golds' negating family dynamic and contradictory communication correspond with the characterisation of the Winters; this includes the dialogue oscillating between the poles that Ruth/Kate drink too much and do not drink at all.[54]

While Laing and Esterson's writings were vital, Cooper arguably provided the most significant and consistent contribution: advising during pre-production; consulting on 'procedures of referral and treatment' for Mercer's script; reading and commenting on draft scripts (with Laing); advising on and providing access to locations; appearing on set to provide technical advice; and advocating for the film in the press following broadcast. In our interview, Ken Loach identified Cooper as the most useful to him as director, working directly together on location as well as introducing him to ideas and people at Villa 21. Loach explained, 'We knew him better than Ronnie Laing, or at least I did. And he was very helpful. And very interesting to talk to about his ideas.'[55] Following their initial discussions, Cooper arranged for

Garnett and Mercer to spend a day at Villa 21 and at other clinical settings, including its sister hospital Harperbury, which were used as research for the script as well as locations for shooting. Cooper was on set at some of these locations, most notably advising on the clinical language and conduct of the training for the film's final contentious scene shot at the Middlesex Hospital medical school, and the ECT scene shot on location on the ECT ward of Cooper's own Shenley Hospital.[56] It was arranged for the crew to watch an actual ECT treatment prior to shooting the scene with actor Anna Cropper, and Garnett requested they shoot some close up footage of the real patient being injected with the relaxant. The hospital refused to allow the close ups with a real patient, because, as Garnett explained, the hospital administration and many of the doctors were suspicious of Cooper and his experimental ward and, therefore, of the intention of the film.[57]

Laing was also 'very generous with his time', providing advice to Garnett and Mercer during pre-production and scriptwriting at a couple of (drunken) lunch and dinner meetings and at Kingsley Hall, the residential treatment centre where Laing (sometimes) lived and worked.[58] Mercer and Garnett also visited Esterson at his private practice in Hampstead. Garnett highlighted Esterson's involvement as 'actually central to the film' in getting 'under the skin of the thing'. 'I made up my mind to follow Aaron's idea, which we we're not in the business of blaming anybody, we're in the business of understanding a family dynamic.'[59] Garnett highlighted Esterson as a 'very different personality', as 'very quiet, unpretentious, there was no performer in him', which perhaps in part accounts for the underestimating of his contributions in histories of anti-psychiatry as well as production histories of *In Two Minds*. Esterson also provided Mercer and Garnett with recordings of the interviews that were compiled in *Sanity, Madness and the Family*.

The first half of *In Two Minds* is structured around interviews with Kate and her family members, with dialogue that draws upon Laing and Esterson's interview recordings and transcripts for *Sanity, Madness and the Family*, and combines an intimate televisual interviewing style and fly-on-the wall aesthetic reminiscent of recent 'human interest' documentary programmes such as *Man Alive* (1965–1969). The play begins with a close-up of a young woman being interviewed about her conflict with her mother (see Figure 5.1). Her audio fades and an expository voiceover, paraphrasing the opening line of *Sanity, Madness and the Family*, explains over footage of the increasingly agitated interviewee:

> For some time I've been studying the families of schizophrenic patients. What you will see is extracts from interviews with the family of one of these patients, Kate Winter. When Kate re-entered hospital my research into her case had of necessity to cease.[60]

Figure 5.1 An agitated Kate Winter is interviewed by an off-screen psychiatrist in the opening of *In Two Minds* (1967)

At this moment Kate's audio returns and she screams. Through the first half of the play, the doctor interviewing the Winters remains off-screen, with the viewer experiencing him only as a disembodied voice. The camera position oscillates between the unseen doctor's point of view, and a more observationally 'neutral' position of the imaginary documentary film crew.

The second half of the play is more formally experimental drawing upon contemporary European 'art cinema' techniques, with Kate's re-admission to hospital triggering a shift 'from "objective" observation to "subjective" perception',[61] as the viewer experiences her inner mental world. The camera adopts Kate's point of view and the viewer hears her inner monologue expressing an internalisation of her parent's negative view of her 'bad self'. The film's final scene offers a further perceptual shift in adopting the tropes of the BBC's factual medical programmes. In doing so the play's conclusion offers a converging critique of 'orthodox' psychiatry and the media apparatuses that sustain it, as Kate is presented as an object of clinical observation paraded in front of medical students. Garnett pointed out in discussion that head of drama, Newman, objected to this pessimistic structure:

> He said he didn't like the film because it gave people no hope. And couldn't we have done the two sequences the other way round. So she started off being treated by orthodox psychiatry and then afterwards by what he called 'the good guys' and then she'd feel better.

Garnett insisted, drawing from his wife's experience, that if Act 1 had been with the orthodox psychiatrists, then 'there'd have been nothing left of her to get better, and in any case it wasn't the point we were trying to make'.[62] For Garnett the film was about protesting against the use of physical psychiatric interventions not about advocating for psychotherapeutic approaches.

The final scene of *In Two Minds* – upon which audiences and critical reception almost universally focused – offers a converging critique of biomedical approaches to mental health and the media forms that perpetuated their dominance. The BBC's documentary and talk formats dominated medical programming in the 1950s and 1960s,[63] and, despite their claims to be objective and apolitical, until the late 1960s promoted a very deterministic view of science and medicine as a positive trajectory towards 'progress and prosperity [for] the world at large'.[64] *In Two Minds* offers a challenge to this positivist view in revealing the damage caused by 'modern' biomedical treatments such as ECT and highlighting the ideological underpinnings of their matter-of-fact presentation in programmes such as *The Hurt Mind* and *Your Life in Their Hands*. It is interesting in this regard that the BBC pressured Garnett to contact the NAMH to take up their offer to be technical advisers on *In Two Minds*, but he ignored their request.[65]

The final scene fades from a disorienting montage of Kate's simultaneously mundane and distressing experiences on the ward, to a medium close-up of her hunched over as a consultant asks, 'Kate how are you this morning?' As Kate responds 'incomprehensively', the camera zooms out to a medium long-shot revealing that Kate and the consultant are in a lecture theatre, and she is being presented as a 'fairly typical case history' to an audience of medical students.[66] The scene is reminiscent of a television talk, a principal genre employed by the BBC for presenting scientific and medical information that was derived from radio, in which, quoting contemporary BBC documentary producer Robert Barr, 'expert opinion or information is conveyed directly from the authority to the viewer'.[67] The consultant recounts Kate's case history, the 'double narrative' of the patient's history and psychiatrists'[68] interpretation, explaining that there is no causal link between Kate's behaviours and her 'family history', in fact 'no detectable relationship between her various symptoms and her environment'. The contentious 'hopeless' structure of the play serves a clear ideological function in provoking the viewer to question the psychiatric authority that the 'clinical picture is a fairly clear one'. Having witnessed Kate's family dynamic, and the 'double binds'[69] to which she has been subjected, her 'delusions of persecution, for example, that her mother was killing her and killed her aborted child', as the consultant interprets it, seem more grounded in the material reality of a schizophrenogenic home environment than the consultant's claims of purely psychical causes within Kate. On completing his narrative of Kate's case history, the consultant opens the floor to the medical students to offer their opinions on diagnosis and treatment.

When a student asks the consultant a question about whether ECT 'does anything more than simply shake the patient up?' the editing cross-cuts to footage of an ECT treatment being administered to Kate, but with the dialogue from the consultant in the lecture theatre continuing to create a synchresis between the two medical contexts (see Figure 5.2). The consultant talks through the on-screen procedure as the relaxant is injected into Kate's arm, and, he explains indifferently, 'now something between the teeth, that's to stop dislocation of the jaw. Notice how the electrodes are placed.' Close ups show Kate's reactions – her hands clenching, her feet jolting – as the detached doctor administering the treatment jokes about a forthcoming job interview. The consultant's voiceover from the lecture theatre continues:

> Of course we don't know how it works all we know is that it does work quite remarkably. Do you know how this treatment originated? Yes, yes it was pigs. More or less an accident really. Naples I think. My God if we wait to find out why these things work we'd be waiting a long time.

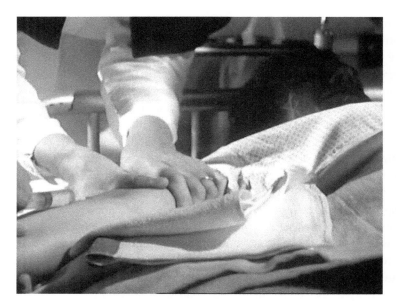

Figure 5.2 At the end of *In Two Minds*, the editing cross-cuts to Kate's ECT treatment, filmed on location at Shenley Hospital

Cutting back to the lecture theatre setting, the students start to pose some more challenging questions, concluding the film with one male student's provocation: 'With all due respect sir, you seem to be studiously avoiding any environmental factors ... Surely both before as a cause of her illness and after as a means of treatment, one's got to take into account her home background?'

The 'mundane' presentation of ECT in *In Two Minds* is in stark contrast to Hollywood's dominant aesthetic of 'violent convulsion' following delivery in unmodified form (without anaesthesia, muscle relaxant or oxygen) bemoaned by psychiatrists and pro-ECT medical historians in contemporary films such as *Shock Corridor* (1963), *Shock Treatment* (1964) and *One Flew Over the Cuckoo's Nest* (1975).[70] Rather, this scene's oscillation from 'live' talk to pre-recorded documentary footage is in keeping with innovations in British factual scientific and medical programming at the time. As Boon explains, by the late 1950s advances in outside-broadcast equipment meant scientific and medical TV talks no longer had to be studio-based, so a new genre of 'built OB' programmes such as *Your Life in their Hands* emerged that made use of real venues, such as hospitals, to lend authenticity to the productions, but that might combine live OB with telecine film inserts.[71] The ECT scene in particular is highly reminiscent of the corresponding one in the 'Physical Treatments' episode of *The Hurt Mind*, which cuts from a studio-based talk format in which expert guest William Sargant advocates for ECT as 'the most important of these new methods', into what appears to be live OB of a 'staged' treatment. The *In Two Minds* sequence presents and narrates the procedure almost shot-for-shot and word-for-word as in the earlier programme. This is not to suggest that the scene was a direct recreation or response to *The Hurt Mind*, but that in exploiting audience's familiarity with BBC's talks and documentary programmes like it, the film was able to expose and undermine the illusion that medics and the media formats that perpetuated their power operated outside ideology.

The BBC Audience Research Report (29 March 1967) for *In Two Minds* estimates that the 1 March broadcast was seen by 18.1 per cent of the population, representing an audience of almost 10 million. Questionnaires conducted with a representative sample of 335 audience members recorded 'appreciative response of well over half the reporting sample', who praised its authenticity, immediacy and grounding in research, suggesting that it offered 'new insights' into important issues 'we usually choose to ignore'. A number of responses identified this positive mental health awareness function with one medical social worker commending, 'A brilliant documentary. I am sure many more people now understand what schizophrenia is all about.' This respondent's interesting generic misrecognition is not discussed in the report, though genre is raised as a key problem for some other respondents.

Highlighting the hegemony of factual formats of medical programming, negative responses stated that it should have been 'a straight documentary' or a 'talk by an expert', while another respondent, designated as 'housewife' explained, 'I know not enough is known about mental illness, but to make a play about it is horrible.'[72] Here the perception of appropriate genres overrides the necessary mental health awareness function.

The production team would have likely welcomed the fact that the play 'aroused some misgivings (not shared by all the sample, however) as to whether treatment in mental hospital is as good as it should be', with some interpreting it as 'an awful indictment of the mental hospital'. Viewers were said to be 'particularly disturbed by the final scene in which a psychiatrist discussed Kate's case history with a group of students, in her presence', which was seen to be 'distressing to people of nervous disposition' and 'those connected with the mentally sick'. Like drama head Newman, some bemoaned that the play's conclusion offered 'little hope', while others were simply confused or put off by some of the play's more experimental narrative and formal techniques, stating that it was 'disjointed', 'bitty' and 'difficult to follow', and disorienting in its use of 'extreme, close-ups'. Though responses varied widely in terms of positive or negative views, they were unanimous with regard to viewers reporting feeling unease at the play's conclusion.

Following the broadcast, a special edition of BBC2's *Late Night Line Up* set up a discussion between screenwriter Mercer, Laing and psychiatrist Sargant. Sargant's attack on the play focused on diagnostic accuracy (was Kate a schizophrenic?) and the documentary style misleading the public, rather than the ideological implications of psychiatric labelling. Sargant followed up his appearance on *Late Night Line Up* with a letter to *The Times* bemoaning that the BBC had not offered orthodox psychiatry an equal platform to advocate for its methods. He complained that it was not until 11.45 on BBC2, 'when there was comparatively few viewers, that a psychiatrist was able to reassure what must have been millions of frightened and anxious people wondering . . . whether modern psychiatric treatment and conditions in mental hospitals were really as they were portrayed' in this primetime BBC1 play.[73] Sargant's letter promoted a flurry of responses from clinicians, a former patient, and Mercer restating the argument for his screenplay.[74] A consulting physician from St Thomas', where Sargant worked, attacked his 'ill-founded over-confidence' in psychiatry's modern diagnostic and treatment methods,[75] while an ex-patient attacked 'all the learned doctors and psychiatrists' who had been so 'righteous recently in the newspapers, and on television, about the cures for mental disorders'. She writes of her own experience, 'We have accepted, at the moments of least resistance, their appalling wires attached to our heads; we have accepted the continuing after effects of loss of memory . . . We survive, perhaps. But cured – No.'[76] Sargant's response to this patient's emotive letter is dismissive, restating his statistics on the success of ECT, and using it as an opportunity to state that it is not the 'function' of (anti)psychiatrists 'to "change" radically or "indoctrinate" patients'.[77]

NAMH's journal *Mental Health* had provided extremely limited space for the discussion of the ideas of or comment by anti-psychiatrists up to this point, excepting ambivalent reviews of some of their books.[78] Following the broadcast of *In Two Minds*, however, it offered screenwriter David Mercer a two-page article to 'answer the critics of his television play', particularly Sargant, and explain Laing's 'controversial contention' that behaviour labelled by orthodox psychiatry as schizophrenic is a 'special strategy that a person invents to live in an unliveable situation'. More than half of the article introduces Laing and his contemporaries' ideas, employing but not directly quoting Laingian language and metaphors, rather than discussing the play itself. This includes contextualising issues of psychiatric labelling in relation to military behaviour deemed appropriate even heroic within the context of the Vietnam War, situating, like Laing (and Cooper) in this period, psychiatric contentions in relation to wider New Left and countercultural arguments.[79]

It is interesting, therefore, that the journal's first real engagement with the anti-psychiatry group's ideas are mediated by a BBC screenwriter reflecting on his interpretations of them. When Mercer, two-thirds into the article, turns to justify his adaptation, he explains that, 'The play was in no sense an attack on the humanity of those who had to deal with her, but a questioning of their assumptions about madness and sanity'. Mercer moves on to discuss his argument on *Late Night Line Up*, challenging Sargant's distinction between the field of mental health and the 'province of politicians' by stating that the logic and practices of psychiatry 'is insidiously entangled with the rationale of our society'.[80] In addition, the journal's 'Mental Health Scene' section led with the contention triggered by the play, described as 'a semi-documentary based on case histories described by Dr. Laing', reporting Sargant's letter advocating for 'modern physical methods' in *The Times* and the reposts it provoked. It went on to praise the 'informative features' in the mainstream press, discussed below, that they felt countered Sargant's fears that 'the public might be alarmed and misled'.[81] The NAMH sought to offer some advocacy for the value of the play and reconciliation between the two camps.

The mainstream press reception of *In Two Minds* was on the whole very positive – irrespective of format or political leaning – praising the play for being both 'dramatically and clinically persuasive'.[82] Many of the reviews, like the audience responses, focused on the film's final scene and the unease and uncertainty the ending provoked. *The Sun* newspaper's review, for example, focused entirely on the play's final five minutes and concluded, 'A shocking play. Liable, like electric shock treatment, to dislocate the jaw'.[83]

Other reviewers commended the producer's generic innovation of the 'play-documentary'[84] with its 'device of presenting the play as a series of interviews'.[85] The reviewers felt that this allowed for a sense of enhanced realism and expository probing of 'little understood shock treatment'[86] beyond what was achievable in 'real documentaries'.[87] However, others saw its generic-hybridity ('the new television genre of talking point plays') as a cause of dramatic failure, with the *Daily Telegraph* stating, 'It was too much of a medical report to be a satisfying drama.'[88]

The tabloid newspapers in particular used the play as an opportunity to foreground (even escalate) polarisation within the mental health field, 'Psychiatry in Great Britain is in an uneasy state. The rift between *orthodox* psychiatry and its opponents is continually widening.' The *Express* article continues that *In Two Minds* put across the views of a 'rebel group of people interested in mental health' who 'totally oppose the old view, the orthodox view, of how to treat "mad" people'. The article introduces the ideas of 'Dr Ronald Laing, one of the rebels' and 'one of Dr. Laing's strongest supporters', David Cooper, who 'believes that if you use electro-shocks or operate on the brain, you lessen people as personalities, something you have no right to do.' The article also gives voice to the 'orthodox' opinion of psychology professor Hans Eysenck, working within the Institute of Psychiatry (IoP) at the Maudsley Hospital, who castigates 'people like Laing and Cooper' as 'anarchists' who 'do not back up their views with any scientific evidence'.[89] While Laing was becoming a familiar figure within educated and countercultural circles,[90] both the *Daily Express* and *Daily Mail* articles use the play as a way to introduce his 'rebel' ideas to their readership; the other reviews make no reference to Laing or his contemporaries by name. This reception challenges the oft-made but exaggerated claim that 'R. D. Laing's cultural authority and influence in the 1960s cannot be overstated.'[91] The reception of *In Two Minds* highlights a lack of mainstream awareness of his work, and therefore the importance of the play in bringing these ideas into the public sphere.

In addition to highlighting *In Two Minds* as introducing the television public to 'the heart of [the] current argument'[92] within the field of psychiatric contention, the play's reception also identified its 'propagandist-documentary style of treatment'[93] as a trigger for contention within the media field. Following the play's broadcast, the *Daily Express* reported that 'a new battle is blowing up' at the BBC between producers of documentary and drama regarding the effects of blurring of boundaries between the two generic forms. It reported the 'open anxiety' of the documentary department that these 'new forms of so-called dramas' were 'leaving the public in doubt about whether they are watching truth or fantasy and exposing them to a new and potentially alarming method of propaganda'. This provocation of audience uncertainty was identified as explicitly political. The journalist suggested that the drama department were not subject to the same demands on fact-checking and bias, and highlighted the inaccuracy of *In Two Minds* in displaying the symptoms and effective treatment of schizophrenia, 'in the opinion of most psychiatrists', as testament to this.[94] Writing for BBC's *The Listener*, Anthony Burgess also expressed serious concerns about *In Two Minds* being a 'dangerous hybrid' of forms. Whilst seeing it as 'superbly done', his vitriolic review railed that '*In Two Minds* was worse than pornography, for pornography offers, if not discharge in itself, at least a signpost pointing to discharge.'[95]

While *In Two Minds* prompted some psychiatrists to write to the BBC to bemoan its twin deception in presenting, as Dr M. E. Ward suggested, a 'fundamental psychiatric error ... as though it were a documentary', others saw the film as an important and engaging intervention into understanding schizophrenia.[96] Mercer's response to Ward's letter claimed he had received 'sixty or so letters' from 'general practitioners, psychiatrists, child psychologists and mental nurses' commending and corroborating the play's clinical underpinnings, while the medical school in Glamorgan and sociology department at the University of Edinburgh had contacted the BBC to ask if they could have a copy of the film to screen to their students.[97] Laing also contacted the BBC to arrange for the play to be screened at an international conference on 'The Origins of Schizophrenia' at the University of Rochester (United States) at which he was presenting in late March 1967. As the space given over to Mercer suggests, the NAMH were beginning to see the necessity of engaging with and understanding the increasingly publicly circulated anti-psychiatric ideas and its charismatic personalities. In 1968, NAMH's Mental Health Film Council invited Laing to participate in an October 1968 meeting titled 'Psychiatry and the Communicators'. The meeting brought together leading television executives, filmmakers, journalists, politicians and clinicians to discuss the ways in which psychiatry was and might be presented in the media. Laing accepted the invite to attend and participate in the discussion with invited delegates, including BBC's new Head of Drama Michael Bakewell, Penelope Mortimer, author of the recently adapted novel *The Pumpkin Eater* (1962), and a number of the people involved in *The Hurt Mind* including Sargant.[98] This attempt to reconcile, even incorporate elements of anti-psychiatry into their advocacy rather than defend against it indicates the emergence of a discursive shift that would culminate in the MIND rebrand.

The diffusion of 'anti-psychiatry' into the mainstream

From 1963, R. D. Laing made appearances on a number of TV talk programmes discussing mental health issues, but after *In Two Minds* he was, according to his son and biographer Adrian Laing, entering a 'new, unchartered league of fame. People wanted to know his opinion on everything – drugs, madness, religion, politics, childbirth, Vietnam, love and violence.'[99] These primetime appearances talking on a range of topics, as well as press reports on controversies such as the banning of a 1967 documentary on LSD he made for ITV arts programme *Tempo*, broadened public awareness of Laing and his work, but also sowed the seeds of media caricature of him and his association with the 'counterculture'. For example, in the bawdy British film comedy *The Bliss of Mrs Blossom* (1968), Bob Monkhouse plays the 'unorthodox' Harley Street psychiatrist Dr Taylor as a caricature of Laing. With a Scottish accent, long sideburns and countercultural dress, the media-obsessed Taylor charges erratically around his psychedelic office before launching himself at his client and promising, 'You're not lost now, I'm with you from now on, except when I'm on television.' Monkhouse's performance also bears potential influence from Peter Seller's Viennese psychoanalyst and 'lascivious adulterer' Dr Fritz Fassbender in the bawdy comedy *What's New Pussycat?* (1965), Woody Allen's first adapted screenplay.

The production and reception of the 1971 feature film remake of *In Two Minds*, retitled as *Family Life*, has to be understood in this context, as Laing's increasing celebrity fed into the shifting landscape for the fields of mental health and psychiatric contention. Garnett saw revisiting the themes of the earlier play within commercial cinema as a way to bring these personal and intellectual provocations to a wider and more international audience. He persuaded the reluctant Loach and Mercer to team up with him again, and, following the commercial and critical success of his and Loach's first feature film *Kes* (1969), was able to secure co-financing of the £175,000 film from Anglo-EMI and the National Film Finance Corporation. The film is more conventional in its style and narrative structure than *In Two Minds*, maintaining a more distanced observational mode that is more recognisable as Loach's social realist oeuvre. The key narrative shift for the purpose of this chapter is with regard to the enlarged role and on-screen presence of the progressive psychiatrist Dr Donaldson, within one-to-one psychotherapy sessions shown in flashback, and newly introduced scenes set in an experimental ward within an NHS hospital. The script explains that this ward is 'run on similar lines to Villa 21 at Shenley' with 'daubs and paintings on the walls, pieces of paper – no "order" in the conventional sense' (see Figure 5.3).[100] The protagonist Janice (Sandy Ratcliff) is voluntarily admitted to this therapeutic community overseen by Donaldson, and starts to respond well to the treatment. However, the ward becomes, like Villa 21, a 'political battleground' that reveals the limits of institutional reform,[101] and is closed down by hospital authorities. Janice has to return to the conventional psychiatric

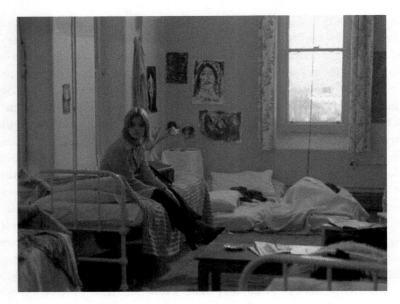

Figure 5.3 Janice settles into a Villa 21-inspired experimental ward in *Family Life* (1971)

wards and to biomedical treatments, including ECT. She is momentarily 'liberated' when boyfriend Tim rescues her from the hospital, but this is curtailed when her parents agree to have her involuntarily committed, and the film concludes, like *In Two Minds*, with the lecture theatre scene in which the consultant exhibits her to students as a 'typical case history'.

Dr Donaldson was played by a real doctor, Dr Mike Riddall, who worked as a psychotherapist in private practice 'but had spent some years in National Health hospitals'.[102] The extensive use of the scenes of the therapy sessions (rather than interviews) conducted by Donaldson/Riddall with 'schizophrenic' Janice and her parents, and the group therapy sessions he conducts within the experimental ward, allows for much more exploration of the approach and value of the psychotherapeutic method. Loach highlights Riddall's role as lending more than medical authenticity, in his use of psychotherapeutic skills in bringing forward an emotional truth in individual performances and in the dynamics between the actors/characters. Loach explains:

> Obviously, the family in the film is a fictional family, but Mike was very subtle and clever at exploring the real personalities of the people we brought in to play the other characters. In a way what emerged was almost a documentary about the people in the film.[103]

In addition to this influential on-screen role, Riddall provided 'day to day advice' on set regrading hospital routine, medical procedures and bureaucracy; persistent annotations on the shooting script to 'ask Mike' attest to this daily role. This everyday advice was in addition to Laing's reappointment as uncredited technical adviser. The decision to remove Laing's name from the film's titles and from any UK publicity – a blow for the producers given Laing's degree of celebrity by the early 1970s – was motivated by concerns raised by Laing and his union, the Medical Defence Union (MDU), regarding possible litigation. Following lengthy correspondence between Kestrel Films, Laing's secretary, the MDU and the British Medical Association Central Ethical Committee, executive producer Irving Teitelbaum sent 'confirmation that Laing's name should not be included nor should reference be made to his writings in the film production thereby reducing the risk of Laing being charged before the General Medical Council'.[104]

Mercer's script revisions highlight some significant inputs from Laing, however, including the complete rethinking of the meeting of the General Management Committee where it is decided not to renew Dr Donaldson's contract and, therefore, to close the experimental ward. The original scene featured heated allegations of 'very disturbing and irregular' goings on – including 'dark suggestions of sexual goings on between staff and patients' within the ward as justification for its closure, which chimes with Cooper's Villa 21 recollections of a 'fantasy existing in the minds of many staff outside the unit that rape, sexual orgies and murder [were] daily occurrences in the unit'.[105] However, Mercer explained, 'Laing has made it clear to me that none of the "undercover" or unconscious, or half-conscious alignments of staff which might exist against Donaldson would be revealed.'[106] Therefore, despite converging clinical, political and economic objections to the ward and Donaldson, the Superintendent insists 'as far as this committee meeting is concerned it is an administrative matter'.

The scene cuts to Janice and a number of other women being marched down a drab hospital corridor, then a curtain being pulled back as she is invited by a nurse into a white ECT treatment room. The placement of this scene following the sacking of Donaldson and the closing of the experimental ward, sets up a clear causal logic and converging economic and political motivations for (Janice's) ECT treatment. The scene is shot largely in mid-shot from the foot of the bed, observing delivery of the modified treatment in a similar fashion to *The Hurt Mind* and *In Two Minds*' sequences. In this scene we do not hear an authoritative commentary, however, rather we hear Janice's repeated weak and pitiful protests, 'I don't want it', 'I don't want an injection', 'I don't want to go to sleep', 'ouch, ouch'. After the treatment Janice is wheeled into the corridor and placed in line with nine other patients in recovery position following the same treatment, confirming the economic logic and conveyor belt approach to ECT. The film cuts to the consultant Carswell explaining to Janice's parents that 'our first objective is to get people in Janice's condition out of hospital and back to normal life', then a subsequent scene of Janice back in factory work, further reinforcing the role of converging social institutions – the hospital, the family – in serving the economic system at the cost of mental well-being.

The studio publicity for the film anticipated, even courted, contention within and between the medical and media fields, with the 'Exploitips' section of the pressbook explaining that '*Family Life* has created vast controversy with those members of the psychiatric world who have seen the film'. It continued that 'members of psychiatric departments of the local hospital were invited' to press screenings, and it was 'generally found that there is considerable difference of opinion both with the press and the medical profession'.[107] As with *In Two Minds*, *Family Life* mostly received positive reviews from across the spectrum of the popular press, specialist film publications and even some medical journals. The reception also demonstrated much more awareness and acceptance of the clinical and political convergences of anti-psychiatry underpinning the film. The mainstream press reception of *Family Life* almost universally used the term 'Laingian analyst',[108] 'Laingian therapist'[109] or 'Laingite psychiatrist'[110] as a shorthand for Riddall's character, highlighting the increased popular awareness of Laing by the early 1970s. The reviewers aligned more with the ideas of Laing and anti-psychiatry, even within right-wing publications such as the *Daily Mail* and *The Times* which commended the 'progressive psycho-therapy based on R. D. Laing's ideas' while condemning the 'production line methods of drugs and shock therapy'.[111]

Though *In Two Minds'* basis in 'rebel' Laing's ideas were considered radical and contentious, by *Family Life*'s release it was orthodox psychiatry's use of 'lock 'em and shock 'em' treatments that were the subject of media controversy and disgust. This represents a significant shift in media discourse on anti-psychiatry that was part of a wider transformation in the field of mental health. Correspondingly, some medical journals included reviews of *Family Life* (which was unusual), and were supportive of its psychiatric critique. This included a lengthy article in *General Practitioner*, which consulted psychotherapist and former Kingsley Hall resident Joseph Berke for his professional view on the film,[112] and a positive review in the NHS' in-house journal *British Hospital Journal of Social Service Review*. The NHS journal, like a number of newspapers, stressed that the producers were 'not attacking the health service but the acceptance by many of its workers of the categories within the system'.[113]

The reception of *Family Life* should be understood in the context of 'a variety of different reactions' within the field of psychiatric contention in the late 1960s and early 1970s, which 'carried some of the energy and controversy of anti-psychiatry, but had their own effects'.[114] These include a clinical, cultural and media terrain that was more aware and understanding of anti-psychiatry's (and particularly Laing's) demands for psychiatric revolution; the 'radical transformation' of the NAMH into MIND as it adopted a civil rights approach that, in certain respects, aligned with anti-psychiatry discourses;[115] and the emergence of new mental health networks and social movement organisations that sought to address anti-psychiatry's limitations. By the time of *Family Life*'s release in December 1971, the NAMH had launched its MIND campaign that led to the organisation's rebranding in 1972. The reorientation to MIND – with its focus on advocating for patients rather than the profession – was in part a response to the media's damage to the public image of orthodox psychiatry.[116] The rebranded *MIND* journal published a laudatory seven-page review of *Family Life* that hailed it as 'the most important film on a mental health subject to appear for many years, perhaps the most important, full stop'.[117] While the same publication's article on *In Two Minds* in 1967 had characterised Mercer's screenplay as giving voice to Laing's 'controversial contentions' regarding schizophrenia, conversely *MIND* characterised *Family Life* as being about 'the controversy surrounding methods of treatment in psychiatry' such as ECT.[118]

The *MIND* film reviewer, John Payne, positioned himself in opposition to 'the psychiatrists who are bent on administering drugs and ECTs', and sympathetic to 'both Laing and David Mercer . . . questioning . . . the basic idea that there are mad people and sane people and mad people must be cured, i.e. the philosophy of psychiatry'.[119] He foregrounds the ECT scene as 'a deeply disturbing sequence this, hinting at wide and indiscriminate use of "shock treatment"; Janice's experience is not an isolated case resultant of one over-zealous "shock 'em and drug 'em" psychiatrist, but an expose of a wider failing in institutional mental health care that prioritises economic imperatives at "the expense of the individual patient".'[120] While Payne suggests that the film 'will undoubtedly be disturbing, even to the best-adjusted cinema-goer', he hopes it reaches the 'wide audience it deserves'.[121] There is a clear discursive shift away from the NAMH's paternalistic approach to protecting the public and the profession from negative depictions of psychiatry, to advocating for the rights of individual patients. This was in line with MIND's emergent civil rights agenda, campaigning on behalf of patients in respect of issues such as involuntary 'sectioning' and the coercive use of ECT (both appearing in *Family Life*).

In the subsequent issue of *MIND*, *Family Life* prompted a further five-page article discussing the film in relation to the wider concern that 'mass media seems to be polarising psychiatry artificially'.[122] The article, based on an interview between MIND colleagues Payne and Dr Richard Fox (pioneer of

'Group Homes' at Severalls), sought to play down the idea of a fundamental
split within an increasingly integrated mental health field, instead highlighting popular media, and television in particular, as the source of contention.
Fox states that Television talks and documentaries seek a 'good old studio
punch up' between 'extremes who go down well in television, one extreme
being Dr William Sargant' and the other, Laing, as 'good "meat" for dramatic
material.'[123] While the NAMH had sought to use these television formats,
and divisive figures like Sargant, to bring psychiatry into public view, in the
MIND article Fox concluded, 'I'm developing the feeling that we are seeing too much psychiatry on television.'[124] For *MIND*, television's polarising
approach to mental health is in stark contrast to Loach's film with its 'halting
pace' and narrative 'packed with subtleties and nuances'. Extending his com-
mendation beyond Loach to the whole production team, in his review Payne
continues that 'the direction has the sensitivity which is becoming Kestrel's
hall-mark.'[125]

Following *Family Life*, MIND's Mental Health Film Council collaborated
with Kestrel Films (Loach and Garnett's production company) and the Spas-
tics Society (now Scope) on *Like Other People* (1972), a documentary film
about a Down syndrome couple, Margaret and Willie, who live in a mixed-sex
hostel, which revealed the moral policing of sexual relationships of disabled
people in the early 1970s. MIND's publicity for the film positioned it as a 'plea
for the rights of all handicapped people – the right to emotional and sexual
fulfilment, the right to relationships, the right to marry'.[126] The film, directed
by Paul Morrison and produced by Irving Teitelbaum (the associate producer
on *Family Life*) won the first Grierson Award for documentary and was later
screened as part of BBC's *Man Alive* (1965–1981) with a subsequent live discussion hosted by Desmond Morris.

If the reception of *Family Life* in one respect demonstrates the hegemonic incorporation of elements of anti-psychiatry discourse into the
transforming field of mental health – and the emergence of MIND in particular – in other respects it anticipates the evolution of nascent mental
health advocacy and social movements arising to address anti-psychiatry's
limitations. A lengthy article in the countercultural *International Times* demonstrated the timeliness and authenticity of the film by amalgamating their
review of the film with testimony from ex-patients received both directly
to the magazine and via the mental health network, People, not Psychiatry
(PNP), the formation of which David Cooper was involved in. These letters
exposed 'examples of the dehumanisation' experienced by people sectioned
and treated with physical methods, highlighting cases in which 'the treatment enjoyed by [the respondents] is, if possible, rather worse than that
shown even in *Family Life* (and that is pretty bad)'. As a result, the film was
applauded as 'an invaluable primer for anyone attempting to understand . . .

the way in which the psychiatric system acts as an agent of social control.'[127] At the other extreme, parent groups drew on accounts of family members to promote an anti-anti-psychiatry perspective that was becoming consolidated in groups like the Schizophrenia Association, who lobbied the British Board of Film Censors in 1973 – with the reluctant support of the Ministry of Health – to reverse their classification decision on the film. The Schizophrenia Association castigated *Family Life* as 'New Left' propaganda that represented a 'grossly exaggerated picture of the effects of electroconvulsive treatment' and 'presents psychiatrists as tricksters and half-wits'.[128]

Family Life was not commercially successful at the UK box office, despite near universal praise by critics, many of whom attributed its artistic merits and authenticity to the fact it 'totally ignores the demands of commercially successful film making'.[129] Other critics blamed distribution and promotional issues, including the film's release in the run-up to Christmas and the ban on making links to Laing's involvement in the UK press and publicity.[130] The film was far more successful in the United States and France, where much was made of 'the Mick Jagger of psychiatrists' Laing's connections to the film. In October 1972, *Variety* reported a 'windfall' for the US premiere (released in America as *Wednesday's Child*) on a two-week run in New York, citing Laing's nightly post-screening panel appearances as the reason for this box office success. This, it reported, had prompted the film's distributor to revise its release strategy to 'slot pics [sic] openings around the country with a national tour which Dr. Laing is about to undertake'.[131] In France the film was 'an instant hit' as 'Ronnie [Laing] had just been translated into French and the French intelligentsia were just getting onto him. So they loved the idea of the film.'[132] The film was heavily promoted and discussed in relation to Laing's ideas and celebrity rather than the relatively unknown filmmakers. Accordingly, this 'made Ken's [Loach] reputation in France, which has kept him going ever since'.[133]

Conclusion

During the process of writing this book, we were saddened to learn that Tony Garnett had died following a short illness. Garnett was a pioneering television and film producer who, as his friend and collaborator Ken Loach explained, 'understood the basic conflict at the heart of society, between those with power who exploit and those who are exploited', and harnessed the familiarity of popular media genres to provoke public awareness and agitation at these power imbalances.[134] *In Two Minds* has been characterised as 'very much Tony's project',[135] but as this chapter has demonstrated, the play's production was an inherently dialogic process motivated by converging political motivations to unmask the ideologies operating within and across the social institutions (healthcare, the media, the family) in which the producers were enmeshed. In Crossley's terms this represents a synergistic alliance between actors from the fields of psychiatric contention and a corresponding field of media contention, but also resonates with more recent revisionist histories of anti-psychiatry that seek to challenge the idea of a clear split between anti-psychiatry and British medical 'orthodoxy'. The reception of *In Two Minds* highlights the TV play's key role in introducing and circulating the actors and ideas comprising the 'anti-psychiatry group'[136] into popular discourse – challenging assumptions of Laing's ubiquity at this time – but also the simplification of a polarisation of British psychiatry into two opposing camps as predominantly a media contrivance.

Five years on, *Family Life* was produced and circulated in a context in which awareness and appreciation of 'anti-psychiatry' was more integrated into converging clinical, media and cultural terrains. This included the UK's leading mental health organisation the NAMH/MIND looking to both Laing's 'guru image'[137] and Garnett and Loach's Kestrel Films as models for successful public communication, as it shifted its attention from advocating for the profession to protecting patients' rights. From *The Hurt Mind* to *In Two Minds* to MIND, understanding these media interventions into mental health through their influence upon both institutional practice and popular discourse demonstrates the significant historical role of popular media in not only circulating but also contesting medical knowledge and its impacts on society, an issue that will be explored further in the final chapter.

Aetiology of a murder: forensic psychiatry and the evolution of true crime

In the epilogue to *Psycho*, discussed in the Introduction, in which forensic psychiatrist Dr Richman explains Norman Bates' motivations, he is interrupted by the chief of police, who accuses him of 'trying to lay some psychiatric groundwork for some sort of plea this fella would like to cop?' Richman interjects with a dismissive laugh that, 'A psychiatrist doesn't try to lay the groundwork, he merely tries to explain it.' This short but charged exchange speaks not only of a widespread awareness of the insanity plea, but also a tension around its (mis)use and the roles and relationships between law and psychiatry therein. In August 1959, ahead of *Psycho*'s production, renowned psychiatrist and penal reformer Karl Menninger published an article in *Harper's* magazine defending his profession from such claims, stating, 'We psychiatrists don't want *anyone* excused.' Menninger moves on to bemoan lawyers' lack of 'conception of the meaning or methods of psychiatric study and investigation', assuming psychiatrists can have a 'quick look at a suspect' and diagnose them with something called 'insanity'.[1] From the late 1950s and throughout the 1960s, Menninger and his colleagues at his family's Menninger Clinic campaigned against the 'frightening vengeance of old penology' – and particularly capital punishment – as ineffective and 'morally wrong', instead arguing for the psychiatric study and treatment of even the most serious criminals.[2]

This chapter will focus on two genres that evolved within the long 1960s to explore the relationships between criminality, psychiatry and the law: the courtroom drama and true crime, sometimes in hybrid form depending on the source material used for the former. In addition to psychological thrillers such as *Psycho*, *The Collector* and *Repulsion* (discussed in Chapter 2), these genres were adapted to explore the relationships between criminality and individual psychology, and the implications this had for society. Issues of causality and criminal responsibility underly both genres, often, given the seriousness and sensational nature of the crimes, involving contextually specific considerations of the insanity defence and/or capital punishment. In his 1967 book *The Insanity Defense*, Goldstein states that for 'over a century, the insanity defence has attracted more attention than any other criminal issue ... entirely unrelated to the numerical importance of the problem'.[3] Popular films have both drawn upon and contributed to the visibility of the insanity defence issue and the related capital punishment debate. The legal source material is easily translatable to film due to its dramatic nature and narrative quality with the trial of the defence 'treated as if it was a contemporary morality play'.[4]

The chapter will look at two Hollywood films based on narrativised accounts of true crimes and trials involving insanity pleas, Otto Preminger's *An Anatomy of Murder* (1959), based on a book of the same name by a Supreme Court justice, and Richard Brooks' *In Cold Blood* (1967), based on Truman Capote's non-fiction novel. The latter will be the main focus of the chapter. The film is interesting in the way that it goes beyond Capote's criticism of the limitations of the insanity plea to make a more reformist argument for a psychiatric rethinking of crime and punishment, which Capote did not agree with. In this way it aligns with and makes symbiotic arguments with concurrent research by the film's psychiatric advisers within the Menninger Clinic's Division of Law and Psychiatry. Drawing on extensive discussions with a number of psychiatrists at the Menninger Clinic, and the film's chief technical adviser Dr Joseph Satten in particular, *In Cold Blood* received a warm critical reception and was praised by mental health publications as a model for positive psychiatric consultation. However, some critics challenged Brooks' decision to align with the Menninger's anti-punishment agenda in using the film to campaign against capital punishment and advocate for psychiatric approaches to preventing crime.

Law, psychiatry and true crime

Psycho was produced in the context of a then recent landmark US Court of Appeals case – *Durham v. United States* (214 F. 2d 862 (D.C. Cir. 1954)) – that had controversially set a precedent for a more expansive definition of legal insanity in America. The United States had long adhered to the British legal system's M'Naghten rule (1843) that assumes defendants are 'legally sane' – and therefore criminally responsible – unless it can be proved that they were suffering from a mental disorder that meant they were not conscious of what they were doing or that it was wrong. In the 1960s, almost two-thirds of US states operated exclusively based on this rule.[5] With the

Durham rule (1954), however, if it could be proven, through psychiatric evidence, that a defendant had acted because of a mental disorder, then they could submit an insanity plea even if they were aware of their actions and knew that it was wrong at the time. The psychiatric profession welcomed the Durham rule, but US state courts almost universally refused to adopt it, 'using the occasion to reaffirm [their] faith in "free will" and deterrence', and their opposition to the broadening out of mental illness to encompass all crimes, including psychopathy. Goldstein sees this in the context of the courts' wider hostility and scepticism regarding psychiatry as a science.[6]

Though only a couple of US states officially adopted the Durham rule, this more expansive definition of legal insanity set a wider standard, with many states maintaining M'Naghten but supplementing it with the Irresistible Impulse test (first adopted by the Alabama Supreme Court in the 1887 case of *Parsons* v. *State* (81 Ala. 577, 2 So. 854)). This added a principle that a defendant should not be held responsible if they could not control their actions, even though they knew their actions were wrong. By the mid-1960s, around one-third of US states considered this rule alongside M'Naghten.[7] This more complex and contested definition of criminal insanity expanded the role of the psychiatrist as impartial expert within the courtroom, being called upon to assess the defendant's psychological condition at the time of examination, their intersecting life and case history prior to the act, to diagnose the exact 'mental disease' that the individual is suffering from, the nature of the crime within these contexts, and, ultimately, from all this, to estimate the mental state of the defendant at the time of the crime.[8]

A number of films of the 1950s and 1960s explored the intricacies and efficacies of the insanity defence, including *Compulsion* (1959) based (loosely) on the Leopold and Loeb trial (Chicago, 1924), and Anglo-American co-production *Man in the Middle* (1964) about a murder trial involving an American army officer in India. The most high-profile of these films was Otto Preminger's *Anatomy of a Murder*, adapted from the 1958 book by Michigan Supreme Court justice John D. Voelker (under the pen-name Robert Traver) which was a fictionalised account of a real 1952 legal case over which he presided. In the courtroom drama, small-town lawyer Paul Biegler (played by James Stewart) defends Frederick Manion, a US Army lieutenant who admits to murdering an innkeeper, while driven 'temporarily insane' because, he claims, the murdered man had raped his wife. Employing the old legal precedent and testimony from an army psychiatrist, Biegler is able to convince the jury that the defendant had acted under an 'irresistible impulse'. The army psychiatrist, Dr Smith, proffers that in his professional opinion Manion 'was temporarily insane at the time of the shooting'. When asked if he was able to distinguish right from wrong at the time, he notionally dismisses the M'Naghten rule by stating 'it doesn't make

too much difference'. He clarifies that Manion was suffering from 'dissociative reaction, a physic state that creates an almost overwhelming tension
that the person in shock must alleviate'. This temporary state, he explains, is
more widely 'known as irresistible impulse'. The prosecution tries to counter
the defence's expert witness by putting a different psychiatrist on the stand
with the opinion that Manion 'was not in the grip of irresistible impulse'. But
Biegler is able to undermine the prosecution psychiatrist's view by getting
him to admit that Dr Smith's opinion was 'made under better circumstances'
because he was able to examine the man.

   Although there was no psychiatric adviser on the film, author Voelker/
Traver acted as its legal adviser, in which capacity his expertise was used to
challenge (in many respects successfully) the Production Code Administration's prohibition of the use of 'clinical language'.[9] The film's clinical language
provoked controversy on its release, and even its temporary banning in Chicago. This was overturned when Preminger filed a motion in federal court,
where it was ruled that the film's dialogue was appropriate and realistic to
its legal context.[10] The attempt to ban the film prompted a backlash from
film critics, particularly the *New York Times'* Bosley Crowther whose article
titled 'Attempted Murder' attacked the Chicago censors attempt to 'kill a
fine film'.[11] The film received an extremely positive reception, with most
reviews deeming the boundary-pushing clinical language in the film appropriate to its subject matter, even though it had 'never before been heard in
an American film with the Code Seal'.[12] Critics praised Preminger's film as
'almost documentary in its stark black and white photography and meticulous reproduction of courtroom language, law and procedure', and ability
to match, even surpass, the realism of the novel.[13] Crowther explains, 'Following the line of "Mr Traver", even to the point of shooting all his film in
the actual up-country of Michigan where the fictional murder case is set,
Mr Preminger has fittingly developed the sharp illusion of a realistic look,
uninhibited and uncensored.'[14]

   These discourses of authenticity, fidelity to sources and appropriate style
would set the tone for the critical reception of an emergent cycle of true
crime films based on recent non-fiction novels. In the late 1950s and 1960s,
a cycle of best-selling true crime books depicting recent homicide cases, and
subsequent Hollywood adaptions of these books, emerged to feed public
interest in the phenomenal escalation and shift in the nature of murder in
the United States. Following a long downward trend in the national murder
rate, it doubled for the period 1964–1974 and the character of these murders
shifted significantly towards stranger killing (victims murdered by people
they do not know). This resulted in a sizeable increase in unsolved homicides. The period also saw significant and corollary changes in the judicial
and psychological characterisation and treatment of suspects, defendants

and criminals.[15] All of these factors coalesced to escalate and change the nature of true crime discourse in newspapers, magazines, books and films, as the unknowable, psychotically motivated murderer became a staple across these media forms. Jean Murley explains, 'the kind of killers treated in true crime books changed during the 1960s, largely due to the change in the most sensationally gruesome crimes being committed, and the growth of a large media-machinery that could hype and inflame fears about such crimes.'[16]

Murley also highlights this period as the moment when true crime began to establish the psychological and biographical conventions we identify with it and, largely as a result, its recognition as a serious literary and, to a lesser extent, filmic genre. She explains that 'until the 1950s, literary true crime consisted of warmed-over collections of old and tired cases, and murder narration outside of the magazines stagnated.'[17] In shifting towards the individual biographies and psychologies of recent murderers, late 1950s and 1960s true crime writing drew upon and aligned itself with recent psychological developments in trying to understand, even empathise with, the personal histories that led to the psychopathic and sociopathic personality disorders driving these individuals (or in many cases, pairs of individuals) to kill. To become a respectable literary genre, the repetition and seriality of earlier crime writing – which often revisited the same old cases, most infamously Jack the Ripper – was eschewed for explorations of highly topical 'crimes-in-context' and the individual psychologies and circumstances that produced them. Murley sees this literary mode as becoming 'fully embodied' in Capote's *In Cold Blood* and Gerold Frank's *The Boston Strangler*, and reaching its 'full frightening potential in film versions of these books.'[18]

Truman Capote's 1966 book *In Cold Blood* details the murders of four members of the Clutter family, who were from the small farming town of Holcomb, Kansas, in the early hours of 15 November 1959.[19] He began his extensive research in Kansas with residents and investigators on the case prior to the capture of suspects Perry Smith and Dick Hickock, who were arrested six weeks after the murders. The trial was held 22–29 March 1960 in Garden City, Kansas. The defence pleaded 'temporary insanity' for both defendants and raised a motion that they undergo comprehensive psychological testing. This was denied and instead, three local general practitioners were appointed to examine their mental states. They agreed that Smith and Hickock were sane at the time of the murders and, therefore, able to be tried under the M'Naghten rules. Hickock's lawyers sought the opinion of a junior psychiatrist from Kansas' Larned State mental hospital, Dr W. Mitchell Jones, who did diagnose signs of mental illness in Smith and potential neurological causes in Hickock's case, but within Kansas state law the psychiatrist could only state 'yes' or 'no' to the defendant's sanity at the time of the crime. Based on this limited testimony, the jury found them guilty of murder with their crimes carrying the mandatory death sentence. They spent five years on death row at the Kansas State Penitentiary, during which time they unsuccessfully appealed, on three occasions, to the US Supreme Court on the grounds of their determination as legally sane, their inadequate defence and jury bias. Both men were executed by hanging on 14 April 1965.

While on death row, Capote undertook a series of interviews with Smith and Hickock, becoming interested in and close to Smith in particular. This resulted in his more sympathetic portrayal (as more sensitive and more the victim of his upbringing) than Hickock, even though Smith was the one, according to the book, who physically committed the murders. The book was not completed until after Smith and Hickock's executions. It was first published as a four-part serial in *The New Yorker* magazine in September–October 1965, then published as a best-selling novel to considerable, but not universal, critical acclaim in January 1966; Kenneth Tynan of *The Observer* was extremely critical, seeing the book as cynical and dishonest in both Capote's 'cold' style and the exploitation of the tragedy for 'cold cash'.[20] Written in a style that combines a subjective authorial positioning with the long-form reporting of facts, referred to as 'new journalism', the book is structured in four parts. The first, 'The Last to See Them Alive', oscillates between the Clutter family's and Smith and Hickock's perspectives, recounting the build-up to the murders on 14 November and the discovery of the bodies on the morning of 15 November; 'Persons Unknown' covers the aftermath of the murders from 16 November, focusing on Smith and Hickock's activities in particular; 'Answers' details the investigation, arrest and questioning of Smith and Hickock, switching between theirs' and the investigators' perspectives, particularly that of lead detective Al Dewey; and, finally, 'The Corner' recounts the trial, Smith and Hickock's wait on death row and their execution.

This final part includes a nine-page section[21] – discussed in detail below – that stands out from the rest of the book, because it eschews Capote's literary style to instead quote directly, in many cases verbatim for long passages, from psychiatric reports and academic sources. In the book, Skålevåg suggests, 'the forensic psychiatric witness enjoys a privileged position among the host of witnesses to whom the account offers a voice.'[22] In these nine pages, Capote evidences the ideas and arguments that have until this point been evoked through more poetic imagery or integrated into character dialogue. In 'The Corner' (and specifically these nine-pages) Capote focuses on the insanity defence and evidence admissibility, staging a contestation between law and psychiatry. Capote blames the limitations of M'Naghten (Kansas was not one of the fourteen states that supplemented it with irresistible impulse) for making psychiatrist Dr Jones 'impotent' to employ his expertise in a way that might meaningfully influence the jury's decision.

Jones was only able to respond 'yes' or 'no' to the two questions to which he was called on to respond: was he able to reach a conclusion on each defendant's mental state; and in his opinion did they know right from wrong at the time of the murders? Jones was not able to give any details of his examination and resultant opinions on Hickock and Smith's mental health, and Capote implies that if he had been able do to, as in *Anatomy of a Murder*, the jury might have arrived at a different outcome. However, 'while the courtroom makes the forensic expert "impotent", the text in *In Cold Blood* restores his power by permitting him to testify as to the complexity of [Perry and] Dick's mental state[s]'.[23]

Putting the reader in the position of a juror in a retrial – with access not only to inadmissible evidence but also to psychiatric research that had yet to be published – Capote quotes directly from Jones' lengthy psychiatric evaluations of both men (it is never explained how he obtained the reports). Jones' evaluation of Hickock focuses particularly on the need for further examination to assess whether a 'serious head injury' had caused residual brain damage. Such a neurological issue may explain his antisocial tendencies and the 'emotional abnormality' which presented in the crimes. He concluded that Hickock 'shows fairly typical characteristic of what would be called a severe character disorder'.[24] His evaluation of Smith (or what is presented to readers) is more detailed and definitive, stating from the outset that 'Perry Smith shows definite signs of mental illness', which, it is suggested, is at least in part the result of the 'brutality and the lack of concern on the part of both parents'.[25] Jones identifies 'particularly pathological' traits in his personality, including 'his "paranoid" orientation towards the world', 'an ever present, poorly controlled rage', 'emotional detachment' and 'mild early signs of a disorder of his thought process . . . a magical quality, a disregard for reality'.[26] He concludes that while more detailed psychiatric examination would be needed for a definitive diagnosis, 'his present personality structure is very nearly that of a paranoid schizophrenic reaction'.[27]

Capote goes on to immediately validate these reports by stating that a 'widely respected veteran in the field of forensic psychiatry, Dr Joseph Satten of the Menninger Clinic in Topeka, Kansas, consulted with Dr Jones and endorsed his evaluations of Hickock and Smith'.[28] Suturing Satten into the book as character, Capote suggests that the forensic psychiatrist identified Smith, in particular, as fitting the profile for a particular type of murderer that he had recently identified in his research. Capote goes on to quote or paraphrase, almost in its entirety, from Satten's 1960 *American Journal of Psychiatry* article written and researched with Karl Menninger, Irwin Rosen and Martin Mayman, titled 'Murder Without an Apparent Motive – A Study in Personality Disorganisation'.[29] The article (and Capote's quotation of it) starts with the law's simplistic division of murders into 'two groups, the "sane" and the "insane"', then highlights the 'difficult problem' arising within the courtroom when presented with 'murderers who seems rational, coherent and controlled and yet whose homicidal acts have a bizarre, apparently senseless quality'. Capote quotes further, 'In general, these individuals are predisposed to severe lapses in ego-control which makes possible the open expression of primitive violence, born out of previous, and now unconscious, traumatic experiences.'[30] The authors had examined and diagnosed a number of such cases – apparently 'sane' men who had committed seemingly unmotivated murders – as part of the appeals process, and as a result identified Smith as a case of this 'specific syndrome'.

Across the above case, Satten and his contributors identified childhood histories of 'extreme parental violence' and 'severe emotional deprivation', which he asserts 'is closely linked to early defects in ego formation and later severe disturbances of impulse control'.[31] The 'murderous potential' of these wounded individuals, he suggested, could be activated 'when the victim-to-be is unconsciously perceived as a key figure in some past traumatic configuration'.[32] Many such crimes were committed, therefore, whilst in a 'dreamlike dissociative trance'.[33] Capote moves on from directly quoting Satten's article to suggest that subsequently – seemingly in direct conversation with him – Satten 'feels secure in assigning [Smith] to a position among their ranks.'[34] Capote then goes on to combine (even confuse) Satten's direct question and his own speculation:

> ... when Smith attacked Mr Clutter he was under a mental eclipse, he was deep inside a schizophrenic darkness, for it was not entirely a flesh-and-blood man he "suddenly discovered" himself destroying, but a "key figure in some past traumatic configuration": his father? the orphanage nuns who had derided and beaten him? the hated army sergeant? the parole officer who had ordered him to "stay out of Kansas"? One of them, or all of them.[35]

Capote completes his/Satten's psychiatric profiling of Smith by directly quoting from Smith's confession, 'I didn't want to harm the man. I thought he was a very nice gentleman. Soft spoken. I thought so right up to the moment I cut his throat.' Smith continues, 'Maybe it's just that the Clutters were the ones who had to pay' for the hurt that others had caused him. Capote concludes this unusually expert-driven section of the book by paralleling Satten and Smith's (and seemingly his own) assessment of motivation, stating 'by independent paths, both the professional and the amateur analyst reached conclusions not dissimilar.'[36] Whilst Skålevåg suggests this is the 'closest Capote comes to a conclusion', he states that this 'closure' is problematic. While, 'The Corner' marshals the discourse of forensic psychiatry to highlight shortcomings in the judicial process (the limitations of M'Naghten), ultimately on the questions of justice and capital punishment, and psychiatry's role and responsibility therein, Capote has 'discouragingly little to say'.[37] This is not the case with the film adaption, which engaged with and employs the expertise and ideas of Satten and other members of the Menninger Foundation for less ambiguous and more ambitious aims.

The case for psychiatric criminology in Brook's *In Cold Blood*

Hollywood's interest in Capote's non-fiction novel proceeded its commercial and critical success. A number of high-profile directors – including *Anatomy of a Murder* director Otto Preminger, who wished to cast Frank Sinatra as Smith – fought over the rights for the film; this was literally the case with Preminger, who had a physical altercation with Hollywood agent Irving Lazar over the rights. However, Capote wanted Richard Brooks to write and direct the film version, as he felt that Brooks, best known then for *Blackboard Jungle* (1955), *Cat on a Hot Tin Roof* (1958) and *Elmer Gantry* (1960), was the only director 'who agreed with – and was willing to risk – my own concept of how the book should be transferred to film'.[38] Brooks was also committed to the project, in part because of the true crime subject matter, and in part because of its potential to work as an anti-capital punishment vehicle – a 'concept' for the adaptation that Capote did not share.

For the screenplay, Brooks largely maintained the structure of Capote's novel, but reduced and expanded the detail from the four sections, including heavily reducing the courtroom scenes and expanding the build-up to the executions. This corresponds with his political intentions with the film, discussed in detail below. He also made a major change in bringing in a reporter character called Bill Jensen – in some ways a substitute for Capote, but also to voice Brooks' own feelings on the aetiology of the crimes and on capital punishment. In the film's diegesis, reporter Jensen, like Capote during the research process, befriends lead investigator Dewey and has discussions with him about the crimes, the legal case and the executions. The character of the reporter was used by Brooks to introduce some of the research by Satten on the psychology of the criminals into the dialogue. During a discussion with Dewey prior to the arrests, Jensen hands over an article to him and explains:

> This report was written six months before the Clutters were killed. It's called 'Murder Without Apparent Motive'. At the Menninger Clinic right here in Kansas, a study was made of four killers. They all had

certain things in common. They all committed senseless murders. They all felt physically inferior and sexually inadequate. Their childhood was violent. Or one parent was missing or someone else had raised them. They couldn't distinguish between fantasy and reality. They didn't hate their victims, they didn't even know them. They felt no guilt about their crime and got nothing out of it. And most important, they told the police or a psychiatrist that they felt the urge to kill before they committed murder, but their warnings were disregarded.

Like Capote, Brooks felt Satten's research was important enough to the understanding of the aetiology of the murders (and how better to prevent them) that he was prepared to directly insert it into the dialogue, even if it disrupted the narrative flow.[39]

The reporter character was also used to communicate the director's intended anti-capital punishment message, particularly in a final speech just prior to the executions where he equates the senselessness of Smith and Hickock's crimes with those of the justice system: 'What's it all add up to? Four innocent and two guilty people murdered.' After the film's release, Capote stated that he objected to both the introduction of the reporter character and the film's anti-capital punishment polemic.[40] Brooks was not satisfied to rely entirely on Capote's account in the book, undertaking additional research with federal investigators, local law enforcement and prison guards at the Kansas State Penitentiary. For the research trip to the prison, Brooks was accompanied by the film's composer Quincey Jones, who he insisted score the film despite resistance from both Capote and Colombia Pictures.[41] Brooks most in-depth research was with Joseph Satten and his fellow psychiatrists, psychologists and psychoanalysts in the Division of Law and Psychiatry at the renowned Menninger Clinic in Kansas, who were acknowledged for their 'Technical Assistance' in the film's opening credits.

The Menninger Clinic was established in Topeka, Kansas, in the 1920s, with its sanatorium, treating patients based on Freudian principles, opening in 1925. This basis in Freudian psychoanalysis was maintained into the 1960s and is acknowledged by Capote in his characterisation of Satten and his co-authors' 'psychoanalytic hypothesis' on these apparently motiveless murders, citing 'early defects in ego formation' and resultant inabilities to control unconscious drives.[42] The clinic's founder, Dr Karl Menninger – 'by all accounts, the leading psychiatrist in America circa 1960'[43] – was committed to Freudian principles, including Freud's controversial and contested dual-drive theory of the 'death instinct'. Following a 1934 trip to Vienna where he met and discussed ideas with Freud, Menninger committed to bringing experienced émigré psychoanalysts – some of whom had worked with or been analysed by Freud (including Grotjahn, discussed in Chapter 3) – to America to further develop and enhance his Kansas clinic based on a European view of psychoanalysis.[44] The 'Murder Without Apparent Motive' paper must also be understood in the context of the Menninger Clinic and its co-founder Karl Menninger's aligned interest in reforming the state's mental health and penal systems, believing both mental disorders and crime were preventable and treatable. In the early 1960s, Satten was tasked by Menninger with setting up and heading up the Division of Law and Psychiatry at the clinic. Within this capacity, Satten established consulting links between Menninger psychiatrists and agencies, including the Federal Bureau of Prisons, the Topeka Police Department and county courts throughout Kansas. The Division of Law and Psychiatry developed in parallel with the Menninger research on psychiatric causes and treatments of crime, which included the journal article Capote uses in the book and culminated in Karl Menninger's widely debated book *The Crime of Punishment* (1968).

In *The Crime of Punishment*, Menninger argues that 'punishment as practiced in penal settings is an injustice amounting to a crime'.[45] The book is a call for the complete eradiation of the 'crime of punishment' perpetrated by society and its institutions. Incarceration and the 'ultimate barbarity' of capital punishment, he argues, are based on principles and rituals of vengeance – which are not only cruel but also duplicitous in matching and reproducing the original crimes – and saw the public as complicit in demanding or, at least, tolerating this medieval system. He also critiques the roles and collusion of legal and psychiatric professionals in perpetuating a ritual – 'done only for show rather than with any intention of helping solve the problem'[46] – of pronouncing criminals 'sane' or 'insane' and then confining them in technically different but fundamentally similar prisons or secure mental units. He demanded a complete rethinking of criminality as mental illness, and therefore psychotherapeutic understandings and treatment of criminals motivated by principles of prevention and rehabilitation rather than punishment and vengeance. A draft of the book's seventh chapter on 'innate violence' – which draws on Freud's theory of the death drive to align society and its institutions (including the media) to the criminals – was shared with filmmaker Richard Brooks when he visited the Menninger Clinic to undertake extensive research during the scriptwriting process.

Over two days between 16 and 17 January 1967, Brooks visited the Menninger's Department of Preventive Psychiatry (in which the Division of Law and Psychiatry was situated) where he met with more than twenty forensic psychiatrists, psychoanalysts, psychologists and mental health nurses. In addition to Satten, who was present throughout the two days, this included two of the Menninger family of psychiatrists (Karl's' nephews Roy and William) as well as leading forensic psychiatrists Dr Ralph

Slovenko (author of *Psychiatry and Law* (1973)), Dr Syndey Smith, Dr Herbert Modlin and psychologist/psychoanalyst Dr Irwin C. Rosen (who co-authored the aforementioned article with Satten, Menninger and May-man).[47] The interviews resulted in six tapes of material, which were transcribed as a 160-page document –marked up and used by Brooks within the production process.[48] Although the transcripts identify Satten and Brooks always by name, others are mostly designated 'speaker', so it is only possible to directly identify them when referred to by name. Within the discussions, Brooks asks for psychiatric literature written by the people he is speaking to because he has not been able, as a non-medic, to access them. An additional file contains these materials that included the draft chapter from *The Crime of Punishment* (which makes direct reference to Capote's novel), and further articles on relevant topics by Menninger (the aforementioned 1959 *Harper's* article), Smith (delinquency and punishment) and Satten (crime, punishment and mental disorders, and the development of psychiatric criminology co-authored with Menninger).[49] These are also marked up with notes by Brooks.

The interviews conducted with Satten and his colleagues address a number of key issues and questions, often revisiting key aspects with a different grouping of professionals. The key issues that Brooks sought to come away understanding were: the psychology of Smith and Hickock and their complex and converging motivations for the crimes; how to authentically translate these into cinematic language, and, more ambitiously, to reproduce aspects of psychiatric examination through the medium of film; and what 'message' Satten and his colleagues would like to see communicated to audiences or leave them contemplating so he could align with their wishes. While checking the accuracy and authenticity of his draft script and direction are aspects of what Brooks was hoping to take away from the consultation, he wanted to go further in understanding the dynamics and motivation of the killers and how to gradually and meaningfully communicate this in cinematic terms such that it engaged audiences empathically. Using Hitchcock's *Psycho* as a comparison, he explained:

> It has to be done with the development of the story, rather than some experts telling you, 'Now, therefore, I would like you to know what this is all about.' The only successful picture of this nature was *Psycho* which was a poorly done film, in my opinion, and the only part of the film that was interesting was the summation by the psychiatrist at the end of the film in which he told what actually happened, and they didn't know what the hell he was talking about anyway. They just knew they shouldn't go to a motel where just one fellow runs it and lives in a house in the back.

Through this process of consultation, Brooks was seeking to move beyond what had been achieved within earlier psychological thrillers, and (co-) produce something more creatively ambitious and psychologically sophisticated. Furthermore, he saw potential symbiosis in both parties wishing to tell a more complex story about psychologically damaged criminals like Smith and Hickock. As Satten explained to his colleagues at the start of the process, Brooks is 'concerned with doing more with this film than simply having it a thriller', he 'is interested in our reaction as to what we as professionals concerned with the problem of crime and delinquency and some of the problems of homicide, what would we like to see said in this film, either generally or more specifically'.[50]

Brooks' first step was to go beyond what Capote had achieved (and indeed intended) in understanding the aetiology of these murders: where had they come from psychologically? He wished to understand the roles of environment and individual psychology on Smith and Hickock, as well as the psychodynamics of the crimes themselves. One of the other doctors at the clinic explained to Brooks, 'This is not Smith and Hickock. This is a Smith–Hickock combination, in which certain forces in Smith may bring out certain forces in Hickock.'[51] Satten clarifies, 'It is more than a combination of two people. It is a combination of two people who needed something from the other, each of whom needed something from the other and each of whom, not getting something from the other, so destroys something in the other.'[52] According to Satten, Smith needed Hickock's approval, and Hickock – who he believed had been indulged by permissive parents – needed Smith to be 'firm with him – say no to him'. Smith was scared of being deserted, as he had been by his absent and abusive caregivers, so he did not take up Hickock's invitation to stop him. For Satten, it was key to stress how these unconscious patterns within Smith and Hickock's individual psychologies, as a result of their childhood traumas, fed into the 'deep unconscious psychodynamics'[53] that drove them to act collectively in a way that they would not have done individually. He explains, 'There is some kind of sharing that takes place and with some people they both reinforce the anti-social, rather than the pro-social attitude.' He continues, the partner in crime 'becomes a representation of the parents or the forces who should have said no but didn't' and this reinforces an idea that 'maybe it's not so bad, maybe I can go ahead.'[54] Brooks highlights that this dynamic is not a feature of Capote's book – and in fact Hickock's psychology is largely neglected all together – so he had been struggling with how to dramatise it. Seemingly referring back to *Psycho*, Satten stressed, 'if you can show some of the forces that are operating in these guys accurately, sensitively, you don't need a psychiatrist in there'.[55] While Brooks' aim was to communicate this visually, he did add a line of dialogue, spoken by reporter Jensen in a voiceover over Smith and

Hickock on death row, that paraphrases from the interviews. 'According to an expert in forensic medicine neither one of them would've done it alone. But together they made a third personality. That's the one that did it.'

During their discussions, Brooks explained to Satten and Rosen that 'the epitome of drama is human choice', so he saw a potential clash here with the idea of the inevitability of the murders once 'Smith–Hickock' had committed themselves to the idea. In the interviews, Brooks, Satten and Rosen have lengthy and complex discussions about Smith and Hickock's crimes in relation to notions of choice, inevitability and 'fate' – a key concept for Smith, which Satten saw as a 'kind of disclaimer of responsibility'. Satten explained that because of the 'patterns that have been laid down' in Smith and Hickock's pasts, and the psychodynamic and unconscious 'displacements' they create in the present, once they committed to the murders '[t]heir freedom to make choices, kept getting progressively less and less'.[56] This idea resonated with Brooks ('That is good ... the moment they make the next step they are reduced and they keep getting reduced until finally they reach their moment ...') and shapes the film from its outset.

The film's credit sequence features intercut scenes of Smith and Hickock traveling to meet each other in Kansas, by bus and car, respectively. Over these images we hear the subjective sound of Hickock's voice reading out the letter, heard in Smith's head as he rereads it, inviting his 'friend' to meet him there so they can undertake 'the perfect score', thus creating a synchesis across the two planes of action. Having already intercut a few establishing shots of Holcombe and the Clutters' home, Brooks cross-cuts to idyllic domestic scenes within the Clutters' house (including foreshadowing of the basement and Herb Clutter shaving his neck with a straight razor). When daughter Nancy answers the phone, a match-on-action cuts to a distressed Smith on the phone in the bus station calling Revered Post at the Kansas State Penitentiary, from whom he is trying to get the phone number of another ex-convict friend, Willie-Jay. Willie-Jay is characterised as a contrasting good influence from prison, who he is hoping to meet instead, thinking he might save him from going along with Hickock's plans (he explains, 'It's very important. It's maybe the most important thing in my life'). Because of penal rules, the reverend is not allowed to pass on the information. As Brooks explains to Rosen and Satten, 'That is one possible road off, right at the very beginning, before he got on the freeway.'[57] This scene sets up a sense of fatalism reminiscent of classical Hollywood 'film noir', a style in which Brooks was well versed, but also, following Satten, sets up an early and key instance of the possibility of choices, but incremental reduction of these possibilities as individual and institutional failings gradually bring the two opposing worlds of Smith–Hickock and the Clutters together.

Another psychiatrist (who from the schedule appears to be Sydney Smith) explains that one of the most important but 'hardest concepts to grasp', is how, within these adult offenders, co-exists the chaotic 'emotional life of an infant which, at times, is capable of taking over', with its 'undifferentiated mixture of love, of hate, of violence, of need, of dependence, of rage'.[58] This, he suggests, is the context in which to understand the 'idea splitting, or the idea that within the personality, contradictory elements may be entertained yet, not influence each other', which underlies the seeming incongruous behaviour of Smith, such as caringly making Mr Clutter comfortable on a box before cutting his throat. Brooks responds that if he is 'going to dramatize the intermixture or the overlapping of reality and fantasy, of infantilism and adult human, at a given point in the story, that night for example, regardless of when it may take place, I also have to do it earlier'.[59] For Smith only, Brooks develops the plan to use flashbacks and fantasy sequences, triggered by stimuli within the film world, to capture 'this mixture you are talking about of this human being'. This includes an early sequence in the film in which three baby shoes hanging from the rear-view mirror in Hickock's car, trigger Smith's flashback/fantasy to a happy childhood memory of his rodeo star mother, father and siblings. Smith emerges from this daydream initially blissful but becomes agitated, asking Hickock how he could leave his three children if he loved them. Here, this 'intermixture' of Smith's infant past and adult present, and the displacement of his trauma and anger onto Hitchcock, as father, is enacted in this brief sequence. Brooks explains, 'that didn't happen so-so in the book'.[60]

Examples such as this highlight that Brooks was already developing some narrative and formal techniques for depicting Smith's psychology, and trialling them with the Menninger advisers. However, experienced director and screenwriter Brooks is, at times, quite passive in deferring to the psychiatric professionals on how best to visualise the psychologies of Smith and Hickock (and particularly Hickock) without defaulting to exposition (à la *Psycho*). When Brooks asks again how he should dramatise this, Satten restates that the psychiatrists' roles are in 'understanding, than too much about how to do it' which, he says, is Brooks' expertise – 'We really feel that we are not at our strongest in telling you how to translate the understanding into drama.' He continues, 'Our expertise is the understanding of the characters, the psychological forces and their reaction to the external sociological and cultural forces. If we understand ourselves, and convey this to you, we have done a tremendous amount.'[61] This prompts Brooks to share his key visual mechanism for demonstrating the complex 'displacement' (the 'unconscious substitution made of an innocent object for an originally feared and hated one' perceived to have been enacted within the murders.[62] Brooks divulges, 'I'm going to tell you something. I appeal to your confidence as professionals.' He goes on to explain his plans for use of substitution of Smith's father's face for Hickock's in the immediate build-up to the murders. When Smith and Hickock are arguing in the darkened basement and Smith says to Hickock, 'this is between me and you', Brooks, placing himself in the position of Smith in the film, explains 'and I turn the flashlight and it is not Hickock, but his father for a moment, it would knock you off your seat' (see Figure 6.1). Then during the ensuing chaos when Perry murders Herb Clutter, the editing cuts erratically between 'a face and another face and another face and even his own face . . . as they are all mixed up in his mind'.[63]

This complex and shifting displacement – moving beyond the idea of a unidirectional projection of anger and disappointment towards his own father onto Herb Clutter – resonates with Satten, who responds:

> . . . the more I think about it, the more I think that at that very last part of that experience, Hickock represented for Smith, the wish for a father. Partnership, deals, treasure hunt together, the venture that never succeeded, and the rage at Hickock was that he turned out to be just like his father, failing him.[64]

These ideas for translating the murder scene were enacted almost exactly as viscerally described by Brooks. Satten and Herbert Modlin corroborated the psychological underpinnings for how he was 'proposing to put it on the screen' as 'absolutely sound', but both expressed concern about 'how much can the audience take' as they, even as professionals with 'experience of this kind of thing', were suffering from 'emotional drain' after Brooks' description of the scene. Brooks counters these concerns by highlighting that the murder

Figure 6.1 The superimposition of Smith's abusive father over bullying accomplice Hickock visualises the killer's psychological motivations in *In Cold Blood* (1967)

scene will not be gratuitous and, more importantly, those 'few minutes must be in the proper place. By that time the audience will be prepared, at least, to have enough of the picture in mind and who these people are and what the elements are here in this drama.' He continues, 'it has got to be more than merely revulsion to what occurred. It has to be an irresistible force that cannot be stopped any longer.'[65] Brooks reproduces Capote's narrative structure here, in holding back the account of the murders and then revealing them in a lengthy flashback triggered by Smith's confession, but due to Brooks decision to vastly shorten the court case because the murders (the Clutters and Smith and Hickock), as Satten attests, are 'really the climax of the film' not the (mis)trial. As discussed below, this structural decision was the key point of contention in the critical reception of the film in regard to Brooks' intentions and ethics.

The third outcome that Brooks wished to take away from the visit to the Menninger Clinic was knowing what message the psychiatric professionals would like audiences to take away. Brooks had an explicit anti-capital punishment agenda that aligned with the clinic's view on the issue, but he was also sympathetic to their wider beliefs in the psychiatric motivations for violent crime and treatment of it in this context. When asked Brooks' question 'what do you want to see?', one of the doctors responded:

> You know, I keep thinking if I were doing this, the last line to the film would be, 'if I could just talk to the doctor'. And then I would have the rest of it, 'well, why didn't you tell him?' I would quote that because I think this is really important.[66]

The doctor is referring here to a statement by Smith, which was not included in Capote's book, which Brooks took from a police report and used in his script. Satten interjects, 'That to him was an unimportant fact, not worth even mentioning' – as Capote was not trying to advocate for psychiatric approaches to understanding and addressing crime – but notes that Brooks' 'point might be a little different' in revisiting the same case material.[67] Highlighting his different political intentions to Capote, Brooks explains 'I just don't think reporting it is enough.'[68]

Brooks took on the psychiatrist's request, including a line very similar in the film's much extended scenes prior to the executions. When Smith is alone with the Reverend Post prior to his execution, he tells him, 'If they'd had a head doctor here during my first stretch, then they'd have known I had a bomb ticking inside me. He'd have known I wasn't ready for parole.' This emotive scene employs other visual effects to build empathy for Smith. As he discusses his troubled relationship with his violent

Figure 6.2 The reflection of rain on the window suggests tears on Perry Smith's cheeks, as he awaits execution

father, raindrops pour down the prison cell window and are reflected on Smith's eyes and cheeks, suggesting tears on his cheeks (see Figure 6.2). When the reverend says soon after, 'I'm glad you don't hate your father any more', Smith responds helplessly, 'But I do. I hate him. And I love him.' This line is drawn directly from Satten's insights. When Brooks explains this scene, that Smith 'cannot disconnect himself from his father, even to the last moment and he doesn't hate his father, he loves him', Satten nuances, 'He doesn't hate him only.'[69] Minutes later when Smith is on the gallows, he again imagines his father's face, this time superimposed over that of the hangman.

The film's final image, and explicit anti-capital punishment statement, is Smith dropping through the trapdoor and bouncing, in slow motion, on the noose while the solitary sound of a heartbeat on the soundtrack slows and then stops (see Figure 6.3). The screen then darkens as the words 'In Cold Blood' appear. Rejecting Capote's hopeful epilogue, in which investigator Dewey meets and chats with Nancy Clutter's best friend Susan at the girl's graveside, Brooks explained to Satten, that the film must end 'in their [Smith and Hickock's] death. Not in the cemetery where you get some other story, because the story is these men and not some external figureheads.'[70] While Capote was happy to use Satten's research to highlight the legal failings – suggesting that inadmissible psychiatric evidence might have changed the insanity plea – he was ambivalent about capital punishment and penal reform. Brooks, who ardently opposed capital punishment, went considerably further in allying with Satten and the Menninger Clinic to argue that crime was a form of madness and should therefore be treated and not punished. As Satten explains to Brooks regarding his

Figure 6.3 *In Cold Blood*'s final scene sends out a clear anti-capital punishment message that is absent from Capote's novel

chosen take-away from the film, 'Suppose instead of an institution, those men have been in a psychiatric hospital?'[71] Satten continues that society needs to finally reject the 'fearful tit for tat response', as through psychiatric understanding and treatment, violent crime 'can begin to be prevented and in prevention is the only protection that we have in this society, and that is the message I would like'.[72]

Satten sees potential for the film to have a more concrete political impact, marshalling it in a 'next step' of not just raising awareness but persuading the American government and people that this is where funding should go. Satten asserts that the clinic has at least 'partial answers' to preventing crimes such as the Clutter murders, but this would require the 'building of and staffing of several institutions', and, as a result, 'new roads won't be built, or a bomb won't be built, or we have to get out of Vietnam'. Making a distinction to the wealth of funding for diseases such as leukaemia that effect 'normal' people, he states, 'suppose instead of talking about mental abnormalities that lead to homicides we were talking about psychical abnormalities that lead to death'. Brooks confirms to Satten, he 'wants to get into that', to provoke audiences not to worry 'about how they shall pay for it', but to leave the cinema knowing that there is an 'an answer to what you are all thinking tonight. Now are you willing to examine this?'[73] Buoyed by Brooks' alliance in political aims, Satten directs him to 'some of the things Karl Menninger has written, that I have written',[74] which he can use to nuance this argument for ongoing failings of the US penal system (as demonstrated by the escalating reoffending of Smith and Hickock) and to point to psychiatric alternatives in studying and treating violent offenders rather than locking them up or killing them.

Critics contest the ethics and aesthetics of
In Cold Blood

Media reporting on the production of Brooks' *In Cold Blood* set the agenda
and tone for much of the reception of the film; would the film recreate
and match Capote's style, authenticity and sensitivity for the material, or
was the medium of cinema itself simply not up to the job? In *Life* magazine's seven-page pictorial on the production of *In Cold Blood,* Jane Howard
detailed the 'eerie' parallels between the looks and lives of real killers Smith
and Hickock and the unknown actors who were restaging their murders on
location at the original crime scene. The magazine's cover featured pictures
of the actors, Robert Blake (Smith) and Scott Wilson (Hickock) filming
on location, but with them stood next to Capote rather than Brooks. She
praised Brooks' 'chilling insistence on re-creating reality', through his casting decisions and location filming, explaining, 'Like ghosts returned to the
Kansas wheat fields, two young men go through the events that give the
town of Garden City a macabre fame.'[75] Confusing past and present tenses,
Howard's description – like the accompanying images – characterised
Brooks' commitment to re-enact the Clutter family murders with uncanny
detail, as a conjoined ethical and aesthetic project. According to the article,
Brooks felt he needed to eschew the Hollywood gloss of Technicolor and
famous faces in order to be truthful and respectful not only to the events
and victims – including the killers, victims of social and psychological
deprivation – but also to his audience.

A number of articles and reviews positioned Brooks' commitment to
'real' actors and locations as a virtuous struggle between creativity and com-
mercialism, with the director as lone artist fighting the studio moneymen –
Columbia wanted popular stars Paul Newman and Steve McQueen to play
the roles of Smith and Hickock.[76] A *New York Times* article conducted prior
to commencement of filming was more challenging in questioning Brooks
on where the line between an ethical 'devotion to realism' and 'catering to
the morbid interests of the public' lay. The reporter asked the director how
he was going to 'avoid making a movie that was merely sensational on the
one hand, or just documenting on the other?' Invoking a cultural distinction between serious art and Hollywood horror, Brooks suggested that he
saw his role in capturing the ethos of the events as a 'kind of Greek tragedy
American style'. He continued, 'I'm not interested in Hitchcock stuff . . . Not
this piddly neurotic stuff. If I thought the movie did not have a relevance
to a general social problem, I wouldn't be making it.'[77] Brooks reproduces
the distinction from Hitchcock and his psychological thrillers – likely, as at
the Menninger Clinic, with *Psycho* in mind – to underscore the psychiatric
foundations and social relevance of his project.

The film was premiered in New York on 14 December 1967 and released nationally the next day, carrying the MPAA's 'Suggested for Mature Audiences' advisory. On the whole, the film received positive critical reception that felt it matched, in some cases exceeded, the quality and importance of Capote's non-fiction novel. Most praised the film's fidelity to the style, spirit and structure of the book, adopting a similarly 'meticulous' approach to documenting the events, recreating a 'look and sound of reality',[78] through its location filming in the real locales including the Clutters' home, through its 'crisp' black and white photography, and, in particular, the casting and performances of the two lead actors. On Blake and Wilson, even the indifferent Richard Schickel praised, '*In Cold Blood* is their film.'[79] Those who commended the 'probing' film for surpassing Capote's book, highlighted aspects that Brooks had honed with Satten during the Menninger visit. *Variety* explicitly identified the role of psychiatric expertise in shaping Brooks' 'careful exposition to his characters and their motivations' stating, 'No small factor in character delineation is the technical assistance from Dr Joseph Satten of the Menninger Foundation's law and psychiatry division.'[80] The *Hollywood Reporter*'s John Mahoney praised the screenplay for exceeding the novel in 'illuminating the human chemistry by which the two principles provided the mutual catalyst which resulted in their crime',[81] while *Motion Picture Daily*'s Richard Gertner identified Brooks' translation of this psychological understanding into visual terms, extolling, 'His handling of the fantasies and reveries of the past of Perry Smith is especially masterful; past and present have seldom so felicitously and unobtrusively been mingled in a film.'[82]

In an especially glowing review, which identifies the film as one of the finest of the decade, the *Saturday Review*'s Arthur Knight highlights the third key aspect Brooks and Satten worked on in the Menninger visit, communicating a clear 'point of view'. Knight commends that 'Brooks has not only managed to eliminate all sensationalism, but has imbued his film with the quality of social responsibility that I found somewhat lacking in the book.'[83] Knight felt that these aspects elevated the film not only above the source text, but also most commercial films, applauding Brooks' 'unremitting effort to make his film both clinically and historically as accurate as possible. Such a sense of responsibility is still, alas, relatively rare in the motion picture industry.'[84] Most reviewers that resisted or rejected Brooks' adaption of Capote's book, did so because they, like Capote, did not like his introduction of a message. Writing for *Life* magazine, Richard Schickel complained, 'At the film's end, Brooks allows himself to get preachy about capital punishment, almost as if he were under the impression that the book was a tract against it, which it most assuredly was not.'[85] While he sees the perceived apolitical stance of Capote's novel as superior, the *Newsweek* reviewer felt the issue was more that Brooks 'misses the point' of the novel. He states, 'Instead of dealing with anything so specific as the M'Naghten Rule, the film takes weary refuge in a familiar assault on capital punishment.'[86] This reviewer clearly understood, and approved of, Capote's more focused critique of this specific aspect of law and psychiatry's intersection.

In Cold Blood, and its murder scene in particular, became the focus of the acrimonious replacement of America's leading film critic Bosley Crowther, then in his sixties, who, it was announced in December 1967, was to be replaced as the *New York Times'* chief critic following twenty-seven years in the role. His replacement was to be Renata Adler, still in her twenties, who represented a new generation of critics. It was implied at the time and has since passed into academic dictum that Crowther's extensive and unremitting polemics against *Bonnie and Clyde* had revealed him to be out-of-touch with contemporary tastes, and the *New York Times*, eager to chase the new youth market, exploited this to replace him.[87] Before stepping down, Crowther wrote a laudatory review of *In Cold Blood*, which he welcomed as 'totally, gratifyingly different from its counterpart *Bonnie and Clyde.*' Using the review to have a final rant against his bête noire, Crowther contrasted the 'subjective and sympathetic portrayal' of *Bonnie and Clyde* to *In Cold Blood*'s 'sharply objective, unromantic and analytical' treatise on violence. Haberski argues that Crowther has been mischaracterised as conservative and pro-censorship in film scholarship, almost entirely based upon his criticisms of *Bonnie and Clyde*. Conversely, he suggests, Crowther was a crusader for the freedom of filmmakers and audiences throughout his career. His violent reaction to *Bonnie and Clyde* was the result of his dismay that the freedoms he had helped to fight for had been used to sensational rather than serious ends by a cynical new generation.[88]

Crowther saw *In Cold Blood*'s objectivity as emanating from the experience and approach of Hollywood veteran Brooks, a writer and director strongly associated with the type of filmmaking Crowther had long championed – 'downbeat' films combining documentary realism with social relevance.[89] This included the 'bold' and 'realistic' *Crossfire* (1947), based on Brooks' novel *The Brick Foxhole* (1945), which, according to Crowther, was the first film to deal with an anti-Semitic murder.[90] Making a patronising generational distinction, he praised 'how much more aware and adult [Brooks' film was] in its evaluation of the explosiveness of violence and crime' in comparison with *Bonnie and Clyde*. Crowther located the film's maturity in its conjoined ethical and aesthetic approaches, suggesting Brooks' use of a flashback structure for the murders 'builds up a horrifying sense of the slow terror and maniacal momentum of that murderous escapade' which enhances the spectators' experience of the 'cold brutality of the crimes . . . but completely without generating sadistic feelings in the audience'. By implication Crowther suggests that the (younger) audience for *Bonnie and Clyde* do enjoy such 'sadistic feelings'.[91]

A month later, Crowther's replacement Adler wrote a second *New York Times* review for *In Cold Blood*. Stretching over two pages, her lengthy polemic challenged Crowther's evaluation of the film on every aspect, announcing her arrival as the *New York Times*' new critical voice. Adler highlighted the film's fidelity to Capote's book, but for her this is where the problem lay, with its structure and characterisation serving to tease the audience while denying 'any truth beyond the scope of conventional journalism'. In attacking the film's simultaneous ethical and aesthetic failure – or more accurately deception – Adler linked the film not just to the 'elaborate tease' of tabloid journalism but also to the horror genre's appeals to the corporeal rather than the cerebral. She taunted, 'This is not the Grand Guignol, but . . . a serious study of violence etc., and a treatise on capital punishment. A liberal intellectual double feature. It is, of course, nothing of the kind.' She challenged Brooks' and Crowther's claims to objective realism and social responsibility, explaining that the 'pacing of the book (and now the movie) has been set up in such a way that only the killers have any reality at all'.[92]

Whilst Crowther praised the film's flashback structure for withholding explicit violence, Adler protested that it created a troubling identification and artificial tension in the audience. Drawing upon her observation of the sell-out crowds at New York's Cinema 1, she explained that 'the audience is relaxed, talking, laughing with the killers, waiting' for the first 90 minutes of the film before 'it perceptibly draws its breath' for the murder re-enactment for which it has been primed and promised by the film's dialogue and editing. Whilst Adler condemned the director's exploitation of 'every technique of cheap fiction', she saw the film's audiences as equally complicit, highlighting, 'The book, the movie, the killers, the audience are stalking the family together.'[93] Adler's critique of the film (and its audience) provoked a number of letters to a 'Movie Mailbag: *In Cold Blood*' section, all from men, justifying the film's (and resultantly their own) ethical stance. Only one backed Adler's response as the 'only true review' of *In Cold Blood*.[94] Brooks' film received other criticism from the younger generation of critics like Pauline Kael, Andrew Sarris and Roger Ebert. While Ebert praised the film for its realism, he condemned 'the self-conscious "art" that Brooks allows into his film. It does not mix with the actual events.' These included the manipulative overdubbing of 'conventional Hollywood spook music' and the subjective use of graphic matches to foreground a Freudian reading of events.[95] Sarris criticised Brooks and his film even more explicitly, for their indebtedness to the psychoanalytic storytelling techniques of classical Hollywood, complaining that 'the movie is motivated by the kind of facile Freudianism that is supposed to have gone out in the forties'.[96]

While some newer film critics criticised the film's 'facile Freudianism' and dogmatism in comparison with Capote's book, psychiatric publications in both the United States and the United Kingdom praised the film's approach and the role of psychiatric consultation therein. Perhaps unsurprisingly, Karl Menninger himself highlighted the film as surpassing Capote's novel in the published version of *The Crime of Punishment*. Contrasting Capote's book, Menninger praises Brooks' film version as 'infinitely more moving. The pointless murder is not shown, but the pointless execution of two offenders is shown in vivid detail. There is no fun in it, no relieved feelings of one killing to match another.'[97] Menninger goes on to quote extensively from Bosley Crowther's review of *In Cold Blood*, in which the now 'retired' critic commends the chilling effect of the 'final scene of the hanging, which realistically done, is like some mediaeval right of retribution'. For Crowther, but also Menninger and Brooks, the scene demonstrates the 'ironic playing out of society's ritual compensation for damage already done'.[98]

On its UK release, the NAMH's *Mental Health* journal commissioned Dr Patrick Gallwey, a pioneering psychoanalyst, prison doctor and forensic psychiatrist then working at Wormwood Scrubs Prison in London, to review the film. Gallwey praises the film as 'mostly rational, scientific and psychodynamic' in its approach to the material, and, like Crowther, contrasted its 'honest intent' to *Bonnie and Clyde*'s 'exotic, fanciful identification with brutality and psychopathy'. Narratively, he welcomes the decision not to depict the murders until the 'origin and nature of the psychopathology of the murderers' has been explored, 'so that understanding has a chance to mitigate outrage'. This is not so much a question of 'sensationalism', therefore, as instilling audience understanding (even empathy) for all the victims (including the murderers). Whilst acknowledging the limitations of film as a medium to deal with the complexities and convergences of motivating factors, he praises Brooks' marshalling of key formal aspects of characterisation, dialogue and 'special effects to visualise the disordered perception of Perry as he projects his traumatic past and confused identifications into the figures of his precarious past'. This focus on Smith – whose motivating 'riot of trauma' is easily translatable to cinematic storytelling – however, results in a lack of comparable analysis of Hickock, 'whose contained and efficient criminality is the real central issue in forensic psychopathology'. On this aspect, which Brooks had hoped to enhance from the book, Gallwey thought psychiatry and the film's priorities were not aligned. Ultimately, though, he appreciates the Menninger's psychodynamic insights (Smith–Hickock) and ideologies ('The Crime of Punishment') underpinning the film, both in the assertions that Smith and Hickock were 'individually incapable of this terrible crime, but together composing a fleeting and terrible unit', and its demonstration of 'the traps, for victims and society alike, of a rational, amoral, self-advancement view of crime' and its punishment.[99]

The British Board of Film Censor's passing of *In Cold Blood*'s hanging scenes specifically – 'the most realistic ever filmed' – was seen as news. A Motion Picture Export Association press release promoted that this was the 'first time a complete hanging has been allowed to be shown in such detail on the British screen' and quoted Trevelyan's justification that while 'the scenes are pretty gruesome . . . so were the murders which are also shown in some detail'.[100] The film was passed with an 'X' certificate in March 1968. The BBFC's passing of *In Cold Blood* and other high-profile Hollywood true crime films, including *The Boston Strangler* (discussed in Chapter 2), prompted them to revisit their longstanding policy on refusing to certify films that portrayed real crimes and court cases that had happened within the last fifty years. Since the start of the 1960s, the BBFC had been in discussion with a number of British film producers, the Home Office, the BBC (who had recently changed their own policy for the documentary series *Panorama*), the Independent Television Authority and a range of legal advisers. These discussions were prompted by a series of attempts to make a film about the crimes in the 1940s and early 1950s by serial killer John Christie, and the miscarriage of justice that resulted in the execution of the wrong man, Timothy Evans, before Christie's subsequent crimes and arrest. During this period of contestation over a Christie film within the BBFC, capital punishment in Britain was suspended by the Murder (Abolition of Death Penalty) Act 1965, and Evans was pardoned in 1966. In 1968, the plan to make a film based on Ludovic Kennedy's acclaimed anti-capital punishment book *10 Rillington Place* (1961), directed by Hollywood veteran Richard Fleischer and starring BAFTA-winner Richard Attenborough as Christie, forced the BBFC to revisit the rule.[101] The legal concerns about true crime in the United Kingdom were motivated less by concerns about the politics of challenging the legal system, and more about protecting filmmakers from libel charges. A 1970 BBFC document stressed that in considering *10 Rillington Place*, 'regard should be paid to the possibility that film of this kind might be regarded as a contempt of court, and involve film distributors and exhibitors (and possibly the producers) in court proceedings'.[102] In 1970, the BBFC shifted to a case-by-case policy on British true crime films, and *10 Rillington Place* was released with an 'X' certificate on 29 January 1971.

Conclusion

While scholarship on contemporary true crime media has identified its role as 'part of a dynamic legal process' in fostering a 'jurification' of audiences,[103] the film of *In Cold Blood* asked audiences not to assess whether

Smith and Hickock were innocent or guilty – or indeed whether they were acting under an irresistible impulse – but rather to pass judgement on the ethics and efficacy of the whole of the criminal justice system. For Brooks and his collaborators at the Menninger Clinic, the very fact of these crimes, committed by psychologically damaged individuals who had been failed multiple times by the institutions that housed them and sent them back into the world more damaged, made the penal system equally guilty of perpetuating and then reproducing Smith and Hickock's crimes. Satten and the Menninger Clinic had been campaigning for a different way of preventing and treating crime as mental illness, but 'for over twenty years nobody listens',[104] so in Brooks they found an ally with whom they could share a platform. The political and creative alliance fostered with Brooks demonstrates a form of consultation and celebration which, like the comparable allying of radical filmmakers and psychiatrists in Britain at the same time (discussed in Chapter 5), sought to extend beyond their chosen fields to make visible the fundamental failings at the heart of society. Similarly, Brooks, as he explained to Satten, saw the potential of their alliance in tapping into the current climate of the counterculture and anti-war movements, the 'spread of feeling among the people, and prey on that and say, "Here is something else that you must be concerned about"'.[105] The polarised critical reception of the film – and particular its rejection by the new generation of critics to whom *Bonnie and Clyde* spoke – suggests that the message coming from this older generation – Brooks, Crowther and the Menninger's devout Freudians – did not necessarily land with its intended, enlightened audience.

Conclusion: aftershocks

In 1972, two British films titled *Asylum* were released into cinemas. The first was a schlocky anthology horror film written by *Psycho* author Robert Bloch, the second a verité-style anti-psychiatry documentary 'starring' radical psychiatrist R. D. Laing. While generically and tonally these films could not be further apart, their central premise of blurring the distinction between patients and psychiatrists receiving and giving care within a mental health facility has clear if not concerning parallels. In the Amicus horror film *Asylum*, it is ultimately revealed that the patients have murdered the psychiatrist and 'taken over the asylum'. In the documentary *Asylum*, director Peter Robinson becomes both active participant and documenter of the communal living in an experimental therapeutic community for 'schizophrenics' run by and shared with Laing and his colleagues in the Philadelphia Association. When considered together, the two films reveal the widespread diffusion of psychiatric ideas in film discussed in *Demons of the Mind*. By the end of long 1960s period we are detailing, the contentions provoked by these films was negligible. In autumn 1972, as the 'Mick Jagger of psychiatrists',[1] R. D. Laing toured America promoting Robinson's *Asylum* and *Family Life*, while Amicus' *Asylum*, a film considered uncertifiable by the British censors ten years earlier, passed through the BBFC with no cuts and was released to casual derision and condescension rather than controversy. Derek Malcolm of *The Guardian*, for example, invoked a grudging nostalgia for this 'extraordinarily archaic new horror film', which he found 'totally, hilariously absurd'.[2] The cinema culture into which the two *Asylum* films were released was fundamentally different from the one in which the 'crude, sensational exploitation' of *Peeping Tom* (1960), and even *Psycho*, were released twelve years earlier.[3]

Demons of the Mind has demonstrated how, across the long 1960s, mental health professionals intervened in cinema culture in unprecedented ways, changing how films were conceived, produced, censored, exhibited and received. The influences and interactions of psychiatric and cinematic expertise and ideas influenced film content and form; reoriented the nature of psychiatric consultation on film; accelerated fundamental shifts in film censorship; and provoked creative convergences of the material cultures of media and medicine. Across several chapters we have identified some significant transformations in film content and form. While, across its classical era, Hollywood had assimilated and popularised psychoanalytic theories (especially classical Freudian theory), its depictions of psy professionals and therapeutic practices were, on the whole, formulaic and tended to oversimplify and conflate different fields and approaches. They also elided any contestation between and within the psy professions. Similarly, there was a tendency, by filmmakers, to confuse and conflate different conditions or disregard patient experiences. From the mid-1950s, however, Hollywood and British cinema sought to understand and communicate, not only a more nuanced description of psychiatric professionals and their practices, but also to understand and communicate these differences and the resulting contestations within and between these fields. This encouraged filmmakers to look to authenticated case histories and to other varied forms of psychiatric literature for story material, feeding not just their own intellectual and creative interests, but also a perceived public demand for 'authentic' psychological subjects.

It was in the melding of case history material with established film genres, which we might characterise as a broader long 1960s trend, that a series of production cycles emerged to feed a range of audience interests and desires. The success of *Psycho* triggered a production cycle of psychological thrillers that shifted the emphasis of that genre onto the stereotypically dangerous and pitiable antagonists, but also paved the way, both thematically and in pushing censorship boundaries, for a subsequent cycle of true crime films focusing on the psychology of the killers. This established the syntax and semantics for that genre that persist to this day. We might also identify the American 'de-institutionalisation' films released from 1963–1964 that troubled the BBFC – *Shock Corridor, The Caretakers/Borderlines, Shock Treatment, Lilith, David and Lisa* – as a cycle that was in many respects triggered by timely and topical concerns in the United States.

The injection of psychological realism was also seen to reboot and reorient the classical Hollywood genres of the 'woman's picture' and the biopic, while the popularisation of psychotropic drugs (LSD in particular) was the catalyst for a completely new film genre, the 'psychedelic film',[4] as well as short-lived offshoot cycles such as the 'Acid Western'.[5] The psychedelic film, or 'Hollywood LSD-film',[6] is a genre defined by (and in the BBFC's case emphatically condemned by) its ability to simulate (or supposedly 'stimulate') a psychotropic experience through its style and form – this was achieved by incorporating tropes and techniques from avant-garde and experimental film. However, a number of the other films dealing with psychological subjects from more 'mainstream' genres, like *Freud* and *Repulsion*, also incorporated perceptual experiments and innovated new film and sound technologies and techniques to represent psychological states and authentic phenomenological experiences. While many innovated these to avoid the cliches of earlier films, many of these psychedelic tropes have themselves become cliches used nowadays to evoke the 1960s in parodies and pastiches.

The key figure we have sought in the *Demons of the Mind* research and book has been the psychiatric expert, usually referred to as 'technical adviser' or 'medical adviser' in the films' credits. Coming from a range of different professional backgrounds and approaches – though universally white, middle to upper class and male – these advisers had profound influences on the films on which they worked. In analysing the production files for the films in our study, we revealed that the adviser role was far more akin to one of creative collaborator than consultant, often shaping the films' narratives, characterisations, style and form in profound ways, but also, in some cases, in getting these films made and seen (or, alternately, stopping them in their tracks). In the long 1960s period, filmmakers marshalled the power associated with psychiatric expertise and social status to lend legitimacy to their projects – whether on-screen, as in *Psycho*, or behind the scenes, as initially with *Freud* – but this is only one part of our story. Christine Costner Sizemore's archive and autobiographical accounts indicate that the coercive relationships she experienced with her psychiatrists were reproduced within the processes of production and propagation of *The Three Faces of Eve*.

However, other film projects we have considered, through analysis of archive materials and interviews, appeared genuinely co-productive in their alignments of creative intentions and collective desires to make political interventions. For *In Two Minds/Family Life* and *In Cold Blood*, progressive alliances between the filmmakers and psychiatrists/psychoanalysts allowed these films to bring controversial theories, which challenged the underpinnings of the psychiatric and penal systems, into the mainstream. In contesting scientific theories and prevailing notion of madness within and between psychiatric and legal discourse, these films tapped into the climates of unrest of the social protest and counterculture movements.

One of the most significant findings of *Demons of the Mind*, was the vital role of psychiatric consultation in film censorship and classification, in America and Britain, in the long 1960s. Chapter 1 highlighted the Catholic Legion on Decency's complex relationship with psychiatric expertise. Despite a long-held concern over the psy sciences challenge to religious authority, in the early 1960s the Legion conceded that they needed help from psy experts to determine whether or not audiences could handle more realistic psychiatric depictions. Around the same time in Britain, the introduction of 'in-house' psychiatric experts was responsible for shifting the BBFC's policy on films representing mental health conditions and institutions. As demonstrated in Chapter 2, across the 1960s the influence of 'psychiatrist friends' encouraged a shift of BBFC policy from one of prohibition to one of productive collaboration and promoting mental health awareness. While the appointment of John Trevelyan as secretary of the BBFC had already instigated a process of liberalisation (particularly in relation to the social realist films of the British new wave), the British censors were still inflexible on their prohibition on films dealing with mental health institutions and issues. It was the psychological realism of the aforementioned cycles of Hollywood production, the 1963–1964 'de-institutionalisation films' in particular, that prompted the BBFC to realise that it no longer had the requisite expertise in-house to make informed decisions. While the BBFC adopted a repressive policy on the 'stimulative' psychedelic films, on the whole, this transitional period – in which the BBFC brokered productive collaborations between filmmakers and the specialist psy professionals – fostered a more liberal approach to films dealing with mental health, which, by the 1970s, allowed the BBFC to hand authority back to filmmakers to negotiate these psychiatric elements without their involvement.

Whereas the use of psy professional accelerated the liberalisation of British censorship, in America the shift to a psychiatric basis for decision-making was not received as wholly emancipating. As discussed above, the Catholic Church's growing acceptance of psychiatry fostered a willingness within the Legion to rely on professional psychiatrists for their opinions, but they still had issues with many aspects of the psy sciences (particularly psychoanalysis) and maintained a suspicion that, in many cases, filmmakers were exploiting psychological ideas to legitimate sensational content. This new psychological realism, as in Britain, prompted the realisation that the Production Code Administration's policies needed a refresh. As discussed in Chapter 3, *Freud* showed the current guidelines to be outdated and unworkable – how could the classic theories of the father of psychoanalysis be 'unacceptable to the board'? – so, after considerable psychiatric consultation, the PCA moved to a policy of considering a 'specialised film' like *Freud* to be outside the usual guidelines. Though these psychological films had shown the Code to be redundant, it limped on for a few more years, from 1966 using the workaround of placing a 'Suggested for Mature Audiences' (SMA) label on films that did not fit the Code.[7] With this shift, the MPAA had unofficially started rating films, which was formalised by the Production Code's replacement with an age-based classification system, overseen by the new Classification and Rating Administration (CARA), in October 1968.[8] In this process, recently appointed head of the MPAA Jack Valenti brought in psy experts as board members or freelance consultants to CARA to advise on classification, with the first appointment to the board, in 1968, being child psychologist Dr Jacqueline C. Bouhoutsos. In 1971, Valenti appointed Dr Aaron Stern, a New York psychiatrist who been acting as a CARA consultant since 1969, as the new director of CARA. While this shift was intended to proclaim a change from a religious basis for decision-making to a modern scientific one, many within the industry – including members of the CARA board – did not experience Stern as a liberalising force.

In 1972, film critic and former CARA member, Stephen Farber published *The Movie Rating Game*, an insider's account of the of recent takeover of the American movie rating board by 'headshrinkers'. Farber explained that with the dictatorial Stern's appointment, the 'terminology may have been different when Legion of Decency watched over the motion picture, industry but the stern, autocratic tone has not changed'.[9] Farber's criticisms of Stern were extensive: he was making decisions alone without consulting other CARA members; he was overstepping his role (and expertise) in acting as a 'creative consultant' who 'take[s] part in the filmmaking process itself'[10]; and, most problematically, employing 'psychiatric jargon' to propagate his own repressive and conservative agendas – particularly in automatically classifying any film portraying homosexuality (which, Farber suggested, Stern maintained was a mental illness) or containing social criticism as 'X' certificate. Stern was certainly a divisive figure, with some in Hollywood, such as American Internal Pictures (AIP) chairman Samuel Z. Arkoff, attacking his policy of restricting young people from seeing any politically subversive content as 'thought-control'. Arkoff stated, 'He is using the whole country as a guinea pig for his own psychiatric beliefs.'[11] Others celebrated Stern's appointment, including veteran director Sam Peckinpah, who commended Stern's productive 'cooperation' in 'keep[ing] the integrity of *Straw Dogs* intact.'[12] Following considerable criticism for CARA's erratic and contradictory decisions under the psychiatrist's tenure, Stern 'resigned' from CARA in April 1974, though Bernstein suggests that he continued to have an influence on CARA decisions into the 1980s.[13] Farber's account of Stern's hubris, overstepping his role of psychiatric consultant, is an interesting contrast to Trevelyan's at-arm's-length brokering of 'creative-consultant' roles for Black and other psy friends.

Finally, a key, but unexpected, finding of *Demons of the Mind* was the vital aesthetic, rhetorical and authenticating roles that material culture played within the production of the films we analysed. Objects such as psychiatric instruments, laboratory equipment, diagnostic tools, psychological tests, perceptual apparatus, were marshalled as the embodied materiality of the

psychological ideas that these films circulated and contested. Different readings of these objects were provoked by their interaction with the cinematic
and sound technologies and special effects, which encouraged spectators to
experience the therapeutic interventions related to these objects as either
coercion or cure. A key example of this would be the ECT equipment and
mouth gags used in *In Two Minds* – as discussed in Chapter 5 – in which
the visceral, but authentic depiction of the equipment being used on Kate,
is juxtaposed with the mundane voiceover which, as audience and critical
reception suggests, provoked unease at how ECT is administered in such a
humdrum and routine fashion. The use of a modified ECT treatment in *In
Two Minds* and *Family Life*, is usefully contrasted to the equivalent scenes
in 'de-institutionalisation' films such as *Shock Corridor* and *Shock Treatment*
(both banned in the United Kingdom), but also the most famous and, in
the opinion of pro-ECT psychiatrists, damaging anti-psychiatry film, *One
Flew Over the Cuckoo's Nest* (1975).[14] In *One Flew Over the Cuckoo's Nest*,
and in the mid-1960s films, ECT is administered coercively, without muscle
relaxant, and, in some cases, misused as a form of aversion therapy or even
punishment.

   One Flew Over the Cuckoo's Nest (1975) – certainly the most famous anti-
psychiatry film, perhaps the most famous psychiatric film – might seem a
notable omission from a book about the relationship between psychiatry
and cinema. For us, it is interesting more for how it looks back retrospec-
tively, even nostalgically, to the long 1960s period we have focused upon.
Whereas Ken Kesey's 1962 novel and Broadway stage version (1963–1964)
are squarely in our period, the film adaptation of *One Flew Over the Cuckoo's
Nest*, based on elements of both, did not come to fruition for a further twelve
years. While Kirk Douglas, who started in the Broadway play, bought the
rights in 1963 and sought to get the film made, he was unsuccessful in getting studio backing. It was not until his son Michael Douglas took over as
producer a decade later that the film was greenlit. The film maintained its
setting in 1963, the year of *Shock Corridor* and *The Caretakers*, and Thomas
Szasz's (1963) coining of the term 'the therapeutic state'[15] to characterise the
repressive collaboration between psychiatry and government. The reception
of *One Flew Over the Cuckoo's Nest* interpreted the film in this context, not as
an intervention into current psychiatric orthodoxy, but as a nostalgic evoca-
tion of an earlier, more idealistic time. *Variety*'s critic Murf, who reviewed a
number of the films discussed in this book, suggested that 'this long-delayed
film . . . seemed more like a fabulous remake of a dated story rather than the
first film version of a noted book and play'. He suggested that to the under
twenty-fives, the film would be experienced as 'a not especially challenging
ensemble showpiece, which poses the now-familiar question, who is insane
– the keepers or the kept?' To those 'over that age barrier', he suggested, 'it is

intellectual nostalgia . . . Sadly, the ideas herein are today as earth-shattering as The Pill, as revolutionary as pot, as relevant as the Cold War.'[16]

One Flew Over the Cuckoo's Nest's 'mossbound Sixties' thrust'[17] was also critiqued by the *New York Times*' Vincent Canby, who felt the use of psychiatric contention within the film, as a metaphor for 'the political turmoil in this country in the 1960s', was not only ineffective, but also 'conveniently distract[s] us from questioning the accuracy of the film's picture of life in a mental institution where shock treatments are dispensed like aspirins and lobotomies are prescribed as if the mind's frontal lobes were troublesome wisdom teeth'.[18] The reception and, it could be argued, mainstream success of *One Flew Over the Cuckoo's Nest* (it swept the boards at the 1976 Academy Awards), suggest the film's status as an evocative epilogue to rather than vital part of *Demons of the Mind*. As *The Three Faces of Eve*, produced on the cusp of the long 1960s, marked both the zenith of the classical Hollywood psychiatrist and a warning sign of his undoing, so *One Flew Over the Cuckoo's Nest* stands as both nostalgic celebration and reminder of the limitations of this long 1960s period of converging cinematic and psychiatric contention.

Notes

Introduction

1. See, Stephen Rebello, *Alfred Hitchcock and the Making of Psycho* (New York: Marion Boyars, ([1993] 2013), p. 128

2. The project website for Demons of the Mind can be found at: http://www. psychologyandcinema.com. The project and book are named after the 1972 British Hammer Horror film *Demons of the Mind* (Peter Sykes 1972) which combined classic Gothic horror elements and X-rated gore with the 'central very serious idea of looking at the life of [nineteenth-century German physician Franz] Mesmer and the origins of looking at psychopathic behaviour and hysteria and treating them through hypnotism' (Sykes 2002) director's commentary on *Demons of the Mind* DVD (Anchor Bay 2002).

3. Tom Baoso, 'Mother Knows Best: The Voices of Mrs. Bates in Psycho', *Hitchcock Annual* (1994), p. 13.

4. Arthur Marwick, 'The Cultural Revolution of the Long Sixties: Voices of Reaction, Protest, and Permeation', *International History Review* 27(4) (2005): 780.

5. Arthur Marwick, *The Sixties* (Oxford: Oxford University Press, 1998), p. 7.

6. Joanna Moncrieff, 'Magic Bullets for Mental Disorders: The Emergence of the Concept of an "Antipsychotic" Drug', *Journal of the History of the Neurosciences* 22(1) (2013): 30–46.

7. Margaret O. Steinfels and Carol Levine, 'The XYY Controversy: Researching Violence and Genetics', *Hastings Center Report* 10(4) (1980): 1–31; Michael Hakeem, 'A Critique of the Psychiatric Approach to Crime and Correction', *Law and Contemporary Social Problems* 23(4) (1958): 650–82.

8. Marga Vicedo, *The Nature and Nurture of Love: From Imprinting to Attachment in Cold War America* (Chicago: University of Chicago Press, 2013).

9. John Darley and Bibb Latané, 'Bystander Intervention in Emergencies: Diffusion of Responsibility', *Journal of Personality and Social Psychology* 8(4) (1968): 377–83.

10. Ellen Herman, *The Romance of American Psychology: Political Culture in the Age of Experts* (Berkeley: University of California Press, 1995).

11. Eli Zaretsky, *Secrets of the Soul: A Social and Cultural History of Psychoanalysis* (New York: Vintage, 2004).

12. Michael Staub, *Madness is Civilization: When the Diagnosis Was Social, 1948–1980* (Chicago: University of Chicago Press, 2011); Oisin Wall, *The British Anti-Psychiatrists: From Institutional Psychiatry to the Counter-Culture, 1960–1971* (London: Routledge, 2017).

13. See, for example, Morten Hesse, 'Portrayal of Psychopathy in the Movies', *International Review of Psychiatry* 21(3) (2009): 207–12; Samuel Leistedt and Paul Linkowski, 'Psychopathy and the Cinema: Fact or Fiction?' *Journal of Forensic Sciences* 59 (2013): 167–74; Joan Swart, 'Psychopaths in Film: Are Portrayals Realistic and Does it Matter?' in Mike Arntfield and Marcel Danesi (eds), *The Criminal Humanities* (New York: Peter Lang, 2016), pp. 73–98.

14. *Paranoiac* pressbook, 1963. PBS-40683, BFI pressbook collection, London.

15. Tino Balio, *Grand Design: Hollywood as a Modern Business Enterprise, 1930–1939* (Berkeley: University of California Press, 1995), p. 179.

16. Peter Stanfield, 'Intent to Speed: Cyclical Production, Topicality, and the 1950s Hot Rod Movie', *New Review of Film and Television Studies* 11(1) (2013): 34–55.

17. Stephen Farber, 'New American Gothic', *Film Quarterly* 20(1) (1966): 23.

18. Gabbard and Gabbard, *Psychiatry and the Cinema*.

19. See, for example, Martin Halliwell, *Therapeutic Revolutions: Medicine, Psychiatry and American Culture, 1945–1970* (New Brunswick, NJ: Rutgers University Press, 2013); Michael DeAngelis, *Rx Hollywood: Cinema and Therapy in the 1960s* (New York: State University of New York Press, 2018).

20. David Miller, Jenny Kitzinger, Kevin Williams and Peter Beharrell, *The Circuit of Mass Communication: Media Strategies, Representation and Audience Reception in the AIDS Crisis* (London: Sage, 1998); Janet Staiger, *Interpreting Films: Studies in the Historical Reception of American Cinema* (Princeton, NJ: Princeton University Press, 1992).

21. *Paranoiac* pressbook, p. 3.

22. Sykes 2002.

Chapter 1: Morally acceptable madness

1. On the formation of the Hays Office, see Leonard Leff and Jerold Simmons, *The Dame in the Kimono: Hollywood Censorship and the Production Code* (Lexington: University Press of Kentucky, 2013); Lee Grieveson, *Policing Cinema: Movies and Censorship in Early-Twentieth-Century America* (Berkeley: University of California Press, 2004); R. Vasey, *The World According to Hollywood, 1918–1939* (Madison: University of Wisconsin Press, 1997).

2. For the role of Catholics in the creation of the Production Code, see Leff and Simmons, *The Dame in the Kimono*; Frank Walsh, *Sin and Censorship:*

The Catholic Church and the Motion Picture Industry (New Haven, CT: Yale University Press, 1996); Gregory Black, *Hollywood Censored: Morality Codes, Catholics, and the Movies* (Cambridge: Cambridge University Press, 1994); Gregory Black, *The Catholic Crusade against the Movies, 1940–1975* (Cambridge: Cambridge University Press, 1997).

3. The Catholic Legion of Decency changed its name to the National Legion of Decency in 1935, but we will refer to it as the Legion of Decency or the Legion throughout the book. For its history, see Walsh, *Sin and Censorship*; Black, *Hollywood Censored*; A. McGregor, *The Catholic Church and Hollywood: Censorship and Morality in 1930s Cinema* (London: I. B. Tauris, 2013).

4. McGregor, *Catholic Church and Hollywood*, p. 17. In 1957, the Legion changed A-2 to indicate 'morally unobjectionable for adults and adolescents' and added the A-3 classification (adults only). *Motion Pictures Classified by National Legion of Decency, February 1936–October 1959*, Preface, J. A. McNulty, p. vii. In 1965, they added the A-4 classification (for adults with reservations). 'Roman Catholics: The Changing Legion of Decency', *Time* 86(23) (1965): 93.

5. Movie studios took the threat of a Catholic boycott seriously. In the 1930s one in five Americans was Catholic. Concentrated in eastern urban areas like Boston and New York, Catholics were essential for a successful box office. See Black, *Hollywood Censored*, pp. 162–70.

6. For a history of Catholic responses to the psy sciences, see Renato Foschoi, Marco Innamorati and Ruggero Taradel, '"A Disease of Our Time": The Catholic Church's Condemnation and Absolution of Psychoanalysis (1924–1975)', *Journal of the History of the Behavioral Sciences* 54(2) (2018): 85–100.

7. Bruce Ross, 'Development of Psychology at the Catholic University of America', *Journal of the Washington Academy of Sciences* 82(3) (1992): 135.

8. *Motion Pictures Classified*, p. 222.

9. Ibid., p. 209. See also, the review in *America*, which was written by a member of the Legion's reviewer group. M. Sheridan, 'Review of The Seventh Veil', *America* 12 January 1946, p. 417.

10. *Motion Pictures Classified*, p. 182.

11. 'His Holiness Pope Pius XII's Discourse to Delegates Attending the Fifth Congress of Psychotherapy and Clinical Psychology, April 13, 1953', *Linacre Quarterly* 20(4) (1953): 97–105.

12. A discussion of Catholics' growing acceptance of the psy sciences found in Foschoi, Innamorati and Taradel, '"A Disease of Our Time"'.

13. Referenced in ibid., pp. 93–4.

14. Our analysis is confined to the period before the release of the Second Vatican Council's documents in late 1965.

15. *Motion Pictures Classified*, p. 108.

16. *Motion Pictures Classified*, p. 26.

17. 'His Holiness Pope Pius XII's Discourse', p. 100.

18. Ibid., p. 101.

19. Lucille Ritvo, *Darwin's Influence on Freud: A Tale of Two Sciences* (New Haven, CT: Yale University Press, 1990), p. 2.

20. Frank J. Sulloway, *Freud, Biologist of the Mind: Beyond the Psychoanalytic Legend*, 2nd edn (Cambridge, MA: Harvard University Press, 1992), p. xii.
21. Pius XII, Encyclical Letter, *Humani Generis*, Rome, St. Peter's, 12 August, 1950.
22. See Robert Kugelmann, *Psychology and Catholicism: Contested Boundaries* (Cambridge: Cambridge University Press, 2011).
23. The Catechism of the Catholic Church covers the relationship between Catholicism and free will; *Catechism of the Catholic Church*, 2nd edn (Vatican, 2000). The specific section on free will can be found at: 'Article 3, Man's Freedom', *Catechism of the Catholic Church*, Catholic Church, available at: https://www.vatican.va/archive/ENG0015/__P5M.HTM, last accessed 19 December 2022.
24. For the Catholic Church's approach to this issue, see Malcolm Jeeves and Warren Brown, *Neuroscience, Psychology, and Religion: Illusions, Delusions, and Realities about Human Nature* (West Conshohocken, PA: Templeton Foundation Press, 2009).
25. D. Hare, 'Reviewer's Comments', 27 November 1961, *The Mark* files, National Legion of Decency files, Records of the Office of Film and Broadcasting of the United States Conference of Catholic Bishops Communications Department, the American Catholic History Research Center and University Archives, Catholic University, Washington, DC. (hereafter LDA).
26. Fr. Sullivan, 'Memorandum on *Freud*', 13 November 1962, *Freud* files, LDA.
27. 'Prologue', 1 November 1962, *Freud* files, LDA.
28. Sullivan, 'Memorandum on *Freud*'.
29. Perin Gurel, 'A Natural Little Girl: Reproduction and Naturalism in The Bad Seed as Novel, Play, and Film. Adaptation', *Adaptation* 3(2) (2010): 132–54.
30. Jerold Simmons, 'The Production Code Under New Management: Geoffrey Shurlock, The Bad Seed, and Tea and Sympathy', *Journal of Popular Film and Television* 22(1) (1994): 2–10.
31. Letter from G. Shurlock to J. L. Warner, 14 December 1954, *Bad Seed* file, LDA. The Hays Office sent this same letter to Twentieth-Century Fox and MGM studios.
32. 'Review of The Bad Seed', *America*, 22 September 1956, p. 529; T. J. Riley, 'Can "Bad Seed" Bring Forth Good Fruit', *The Pilot*, 22 September 1956, pp. 1–7; T. J. Riley, 'Can We Inherit Criminal Compulsions?' *Catholic Messenger*, 4 October 1956, p 9.
33. All quotes in this and subsequent paragraph from Riley, 'Inherit Criminal Compulsions'.
34. On the history of hypnotism, see Alan Gauld, *A History of Hypnotism* (Cambridge: Cambridge University Press, 1994).
35. H. Greene, 'Memo: Changes Demanded by Legion of Decency', 31 December 1947, Mary Pickford papers, 283.f-2682, Margaret Herrick Library, Beverly Hills, CA.
36. Fr. Sickler, 'Reviewer's Comments', undated, *The Hypnotic Eye* file, LDA. Sullivan, 'Memorandum on *Freud*'.
37. See Robert Genter, '"Hypnotizzy" in the Cold War: The American Fascination with Hypnotism in the 1950s', *Journal of American Culture* 29(2) (2006): 154–69.

38. All quotes in this and subsequent paragraph from J. A. V., 'Memo for the Files', 4 November 1955, *The Search for Bridey Murphy* file, Production Code Administration collection, Margaret Herrick Library, Beverly Hills, CA (hereafter cited as PCA collection).
39. This and subsequent quote from Letter from T. F. Little to P. Duggan, 9 April 1956, *The Search for Bridey Murphy* file, LDA.
40. Letter from P. Duggan to T. F. Little, 20 April 1956, *The Search for Bridey Murphy* file, LDA.
41. All quotes and information in this paragraph from ibid.
42. Ibid.
43. Letter from P. Duggan to T. F. Little, May 1956, *The Search for Bridey Murphy* file, LDA.
44. T. M. Pryor, 'Search Continues for "Bridey" Star', *New York Times* 18 May 1956, p. 21.
45. 'Legion of Decency Classifications', 27 September 1956, *The Search for Bridey Murphy* file, LDA.
46. For a history of 'brainwashing', see Susan Carruthers, *Cold War Captives: Imprisonment, Escape, and Brainwashing* (Berkely: University of California Press, 2009); Charlie Williams, 'Public Psychology and the Cold War Brainwashing Scare', *History and Philosophy of Psychology* 21(1) (2020): 21–30.
47. See R. L. Frank, 'Prelude to Cold War: American Catholics and Communism', *Journal of Church and State* 34 (1992): 39–56.
48. See Marcia Holmes, 'Brainwashing the Cybernetic Spectator: *The Ipcress File*, 1960s Cinematic Spectacle and the Sciences of Mind', *History of the Human Sciences* 30(3) (2017): 3–24; David Seed, *Brainwashing: The Fictions of Mind Control. A Study of Novels and Films since World War II* (Kent, OH: Kent State University Press, 2004).
49. J. Scovotii, 'Reviewer's Comments', undated, *The Manchurian Candidate* file, LDA.
50. J. Ellis, 'Reviewer's Comments', undated, *The Manchurian Candidate* file, LDA.
51. E. J. Quigley, 'Reviewer's Comments', 4 April 1963, *The Mind Benders* file, LDA.
52. S. Miragliotta, 'Reviewer's Comments', undated, *The Mind Benders* file, LDA.
53. On the 'golden age' of psychiatry films, see Glen Gabbard and Krin Gabbard, *Psychiatry and the Cinema*, 2nd edn (Washington, DC: American Psychiatric Press, 1999), pp. 75–106.
54. David A. Kirby, *Lab Coats in Hollywood: Science, Scientists and Cinema* (Cambridge, MA: MIT Press, 2011).
55. For example, see Letter from J. Breen to H. Cohn, 19 March 1948, *The Dark Past* file, PCA collection.
56. S. Miragliotta, 'Reviewer's Comments', undated, *Repulsion* file, LDA.
57. S. M. Grabowski, 'Reviewer's Comments', 23 September 1965, *Repulsion* file, LDA.
58. 'Legion of Decency Classification', undated, *Repulsion* file, LDA.
59. Letter E. A. Loomis to W. Gordon, 8 June 1961, John Huston papers, f.175, Margaret Herrick Library, Beverly Hills, CA.

60. Letter from W. Gordon to T. F. Little, 28 April 1961, *Freud* files, LDA.
61. Copies of several priests' opinions on the script are available at the LDA.
62. Letter from J. C. Ray to T. F. Little, undated, *Freud* files, LDA.
63. A few of the responses from the clergy explicitly use the word 'dangerously'. For example, see Letter from P. Ciklic to W. Gordon, 5 May 1961, *Freud* files, LDA.
64. This and subsequent quote from W. F. Lynch, 'Re: Screenplay Freud', undated, *Freud* files, LDA.
65. See Katarzyna Szmigiero, '"We All Go a Little Mad Sometimes": Representations of Insanity in the Films of Alfred Hitchcock', *Culture Medicine and Psychiatry* 2022: doi.org/10.1007/s11013-022-09789-y.
66. See Jonathan Freedman, 'From Spellbound to Vertigo: Alfred Hitchcock and Therapeutic Culture in America', in Jonathan Freedman and Richard Millington (eds), *Hitchcock's America* (New York: Oxford University Press, 1999), pp. 77–98.
67. D. J. O'Connell, 'Reviewer's Comments', 7 May 1960, *Psycho* files, LDA.
68. J. Scovotti, 'Reviewer's Comments', undated, *Psycho* files, LDA.
69. O'Donnell, 'Reviewer's Comments'; O'Connell, 'Reviewer's Comments'.
70. Letter from J. Breen to L. B. Mayer, 2 November 1944, *Bewitched* files, PCA collection.
71. T. F. Little, 'Inter-Office Memorandum', 6 May 1960, *Psycho* files, LDA.
72. Letter from R. Holman to T. F. Little, 3 June 1960, *Psycho* files, LDA.
73. R. Morgan, 'Reviewer's Comments', 12 May 1964, *Marnie* files, LDA.
74. R. Morgan, 'Reviewer's Comments', undated, *Marnie* files, LDA.
75. Gerald Peary (ed.), *Samuel Fuller Interviews* (Jackson: University Press of Mississippi, 2012) pp. 33, 115.
76. For example, see M. Cerow, 'Reviewer's Comments', 2 July 1963, *Shock Corridor* files, LDA; C. Smith, 'Reviewer's Comments', 2 July 1963, *Shock Corridor* files, LDA.
77. For example, see E. Connor, 'Reviewer's Comments', 5 July 1963, *Shock Corridor* files, LDA; S. Miraliotta, 'Reviewer's Comments', 9 July 1963, *Shock Corridor* files, LDA.
78. Memo from P. Sullivan to T. F. Little, 16 July 16 1963, *Shock Corridor* files, LDA.
79. Nymphomania is currently known as hypersexual or compulsive sexual behaviour.
80. 'Memo', cited below, n. 81.
81. Letter from E. Morey to T. F. Little, 5 August 1963, *Shock Corridor* files, LDA.
82. 'Legion of Decency Classification', undated, *Shock Corridor* files, LDA.
83. On the change to NCOMP, see Walsh, *Sin and Censorship*, p. 318.
84. Harrington, 'Reviewer's Comments', 13 May 1966, *A Fine Madness* files, LDA.
85. W. A. Reilly, 'Reviewer's Comments', undated, *A Fine Madness* files, LDA.
86. See Jenell Johnson, *American Lobotomy: A Rhetorical History* (Ann Arbor: University of Michigan Press, 2014).
87. For example, see C. Garibaldi, 'Reviewer's Comments', undated, *A Fine Madness* files, LDA; P.T. Hartung, 'Reviewer's Comments', 9 May 1966, *A Fine Madness* files, LDA.

88. P. T. Hartung, 'The Screen: Review of *A Fine Madness*', *Commonweal*, 27 May 1966, pp. 284–5.
89. 'NCOMP Classification *A Fine Madness*', undated, Box 159, LDA.
90. J. Ellis, 'Reviewer's Comments', undated, *Through a Glass Darkly* files, LDA.
91. S. M. Grabowski, 'Reviewer's Comments', 14 March 1962, *Through a Glass Darkly* files, LDA.
92. K. Mitchell, 'Bergman at Berlin', *Tablet*, 14 July 1962, p. 12.
93. S. M. Grabowski, 'Reviewer's Comments', 9 January 1963, *David and Lisa* files, LDA.
94. This and subsequent quote from P. T. Hartung, 'Draft Review of *David and Lisa* for Commonweal', 4 January 1963, *David and Lisa* files, LDA.
95. Letter from T. F. Little to W. Reade, 17 August 1965, *David and Lisa* files, LDA.
96. The majority of the Legion's reviewers indicated the need to give the film a special recommendation in their reviews. Letter from T. F. Little to B. Lancaster, *A Child is Waiting* files, LDA.
97. Letter from P. J. Cunningham to T. F. Little, *A Child is Waiting* files, LDA.
98. Grabowski, 'Reviewer's Comments', 20 December 1962; *A Child is Waiting* files, LDA.
99. John F. Kennedy, 'Special Message to the Congress on Mental Illness and Mental Retardation', 5 February 1963, available at: www.presidency.ucsb.edu/documents/special-message-the-congress-mental-illness-and-mental-retardation, last accessed 19 December 2022.
100. For a history of these debates, see Edward Berkowitz, 'The Politics of Mental Retardation during the Kennedy Administration', *Social Science Quarterly* 61(1) (1980): 128–43.
101. Philip Scheuer, 'Judy Cried, but It Wasn't in the Script', *Los Angeles Times*, 5 February 1962, A5.
102. Letter from E. Flipo to P. Sullivan, 16 February 1963, *A Child is Waiting* files, LDA.
103. Letter from P. Sullivan to E. Flipo, 19 February 1963, *A Child is Waiting* files, LDA.
104. F. H. G., 'A Child is Waiting', *Christian Science Monitor*, 23 January 1963.
105. The film never makes clear the exact number of Jo's children.
106. V. A. Taylor, 'Reviewer's Comments', 1 November 1964, *The Pumpkin Eater* files, LDA.
107. F. Burns, 'Reviewer's Comments', undated, *The Pumpkin Eater* files, LDA.
108. C. Siebert, 'Reviewer's Comments', undated, *The Pumpkin Eater* files, LDA.
109. Edward Collins Vacek SJ, 'Evolution of Catholic Marriage Morality in the Twentieth Century from a Baby-Making Contract to a Love-Making Covenant – Part II: Code of Cannon Law to Vatican II', in Thomas Heston and Sujoy Ray (eds), *Bioethics in Medicine and Society* (London: IntechOpen, 2021), pp. 339–53.
110. J. Elin, 'Reviewer's Comments', 1 November 1964, *The Pumpkin Eater* files, LDA.
111. P. Coll, 'Reviewer's Comments', 23 October 1964, *The Pumpkin Eater* files, LDA.
112. Elin, 'Reviewer's Comments', cited in n. 113.

113. G. Wead, 'Reviewer's Comments', undated, *The Pumpkin Eater* files, LDA.

114. T. B. Coyne, 'Reviewer's Comments', 7 November 1964, *The Pumpkin Eater* files, LDA.

115. David Kirby and Amy Chambers, 'Playing God: Religious Influences on the Depictions of Science in Mainstream Movies', in Brigitte Nerlich, Sarah Hartley, Sujatha Raman and Alexander Smith (eds), *Science and the Politics of Openness* (Manchester: Manchester University Press, 2018), 278–302 at 289.

116. Foschoi, Innamorati and Taradel, '"A Disease of Our Time"', pp. 94–5.

117. K. Jensen, 'Movie: Joker', *Catholic News Service*, 3 October 2019, available at: https://thecentralminnesotacatholic.org/movie-joker, last accessed 4 January 2023.

Chapter 2: The BBFC's 'psychiatrist friends'

1. Tracy Hargreaves, 'The Trevelyan Years: British Censorship and 1960s Cinema', in Edward Lamberti (ed.), *Behind the Scenes at the BBFC: Film Classification from the Silver Screen to the Digital Age* (London: BFI/Palgrave Macmillan, 2012), p. 54. For Trevelyan's liberalising influence, see also, Anthony Aldgate, *Censorship and the Permissive Society: British Cinema and Theatre, 1955–1965* (Oxford: Clarendon Press, 1995).

2. David Caputo, *Polanski and Perception: The Psychology of Seeing and the Cinema of Roman Polanski*. (Bristol: Intellect, 2012), pp. 80–4; Tom Matthews, *Censored: The Story of Film Censorship in Britain* (London: Chatto & Windus, 1994), p. 164.

3. Sian Barber, *Censoring the 1970s: The BBFC and the Decade that Taste Forgot* (Newcastle upon Tyne: Cambridge Scholars, 2011), p. 122; Matthews, *Censored*, p. 172.

4. Julian Petley, 'The Censor and the State', in Daniel Biltereyst and Roel Vande Winkel (eds), *Silencing Cinema: Film Censorship around the World* (New York: Palgrave Macmillan, 2013), p. 163.

5. Annette Kuhn, *Cinema, Censorship and Sexuality, 1909–1925* (London: Routledge & Kegan Paul, 1990); Nick Crossley, *Contesting Psychiatry: Social Movements in Mental Health* (London: Routledge, 2006).

6. Kuhn, *Cinema, Censorship and Sexuality*, p. 8.

7. Ibid., p. 6.

8. See Crossley, *Contesting Psychiatry*.

9. According to some sources, David Cooper coined the term 'anti-psychiatry', in 1967, but it was and still is a loaded term. At various times Laing and others have explicitly rejected and distanced themselves from the term. See Thomas Szasz, *Anti-psychiatry: Quackery Squared* (Syracuse, NY: Syracuse University Press, 2009), pp. 25–68.

10. Crossley, *Contesting Psychiatry*, p. 29.

11. Nick Crossley, 'Transforming the Mental Health Field: The Early History of the National Association for Mental Health', *Sociology of Health and Illness* 20(4) (1998): 878.

12. Gavin Miller, 'David Stafford-Clark (1916–1999): Seeing through a Celebrity Psychiatrist', *Wellcome Open Research* (2017): 2–30. As Miller highlights, during this period increasing public interest in Laing's ideas prompted popular presses like Penguin to publish and reissue his and his contemporaries work, therefore extending public awareness of the ideas that were later designated as 'anti-psychiatry'.

13. Crossley, *Contesting Psychiatry*, pp. 97–8.

14. Ibid., p. 43.

15. See DeAngelis, *Rx Hollywood*.

16. Robert James, 'The People's Amusement: Cinemagoing and the BBFC, 1928–1948', in Edward Lamberti (ed.), *Behind the Scenes at the BBFC: Film Classification from the Silver Screen to the Digital Age* (London: BFI/Palgrave Macmillan), p. 20.

17. Petley, 'The Censor and the State', pp. 155–6.

18. Jeffrey Richards, 'The British Board of Film Censors and Content Control in the 1930s: Images of Britain', *Historical Journal of Film, Radio and Television* 1(2) (1981): 108.

19. James, 'The People's Amusement', p. 25.

20. Watkins quoted in David Hyman, 'Case Study: *The Snake Pit*', in Edward Lamberti (ed.), *Behind the Scenes at the BBFC: Film Classification from the Silver Screen to the Digital Age* (London: BFI/Palgrave Macmillan), p. 50.

21. Ibid.

22. The online AFI Catalog entry includes a good synopsis and overview of the social and political impact of the film in the United States: available at: https://catalog.afi.com/Catalog/MovieDetails/25735.

23. Paul Frith, '"It was Good to Get Out into the Fresh Air after Seeing this Film": Horror, Realism and Censorship in post-Second World War Britain', *Journal of British Cinema and Television* 14(1) (2017): 98–115.

24. Hyman, 'Case Study: *The Snake Pit*', pp. 50–1.

25. Ibid., p. 51.

26. See Aldgate, *Censorship and the Permissive Society*; Hargreaves, 'The Trevelyan Years'; James Robertson, *The Hidden Cinema: British Film Censorship in Action 1913–1972* (London: Routledge, 1993).

27. John Trevelyan, *What the Censor Saw* (London: Michael Joseph, 1973), p. 170.

28. Ibid.

29. Ibid., pp. 169–70.

30. Erving Goffman, *Asylums* (New York, Anchor, 1961); Thomas Szasz, *The Myth of Mental Illness* (New York: Harper, 1961).

31. Gary Morris, *Mental Health Issues and the Media: An Introduction for Health Professionals* (London: Routledge, 2006), p. 147; Peter Stanfield, *Maximum Movies: Pulp Fiction's Film Culture and the Worlds of Samuel Fuller, Mickey Spillane and Jim Thompson* (New Brunswick, NJ: Rutgers University Press, 2011), p. 118.

32. The name change to *Borderlines* (referring to the borderline patients featured in the film) was not due to the BBFC's recommendations, but rather to prevent

British audiences confusing the film with the screen adaptation of Harold Pinter's play *The Caretakers* also released in 1963.

33. Arthur Knight, 'The Caretakers', *Saturday Review*, 10 August 1963.
34. More commonly known as the Community Mental Health Act 1963, this legislation was part of John F. Kennedy's New Frontier legislative programme of social and welfare reforms, including federal funding for community mental health centres and research facilities.
35. Examiners Report', 29 June 1963, *Borderlines* file, British Board of Film Classification Archive, London (hereafter, BBFC Archive).
36. Letter from John Trevelyan to NKB [Newton Branch] 20 September 1963, *Borderlines* file, BBFC Archive
37. Letter from John Trevelyan to Montague C. Norton, 20 September 1963, *Borderlines* file, BBFC Archive.
38. Crossley, *Contesting Psychiatry*, p. 82.
39. Ibid., pp. 85–7.
40. Ibid., p. 80.
41. Letter from Mary Appleby to John Trevelyan, 14 October 1963, *Borderlines* file, BBFC Archive.
42. Letter from John Trevelyan to Mary Appleby, 17 October 1963, *Borderlines* file, BBFC Archive.
43. See Crossley, 'Transforming the Mental Health Field'.
44. Letter from Mary Appleby to John Trevelyan, 18 October 1963, *Borderlines* file, BBFC Archive.
45. Miller, 'David Stafford-Clark', p. 9. Sargant is a controversial figure who is alleged to have used experimental drugs on his patients without their knowledge or consent, and was involved in alleged covert military experiments using hallucinogenic drugs.
46. Letter from John Trevelyan to Montague C. Norton, 6 November 1963, *Borderlines* file, BBFC Archive.
47. Letter from Hal Bartlett to John Trevelyan (via Montague C. Norton), 27 November 1963, *Borderlines* file, BBFC Archive.
48. David Cooper set up an experimental therapeutic community, Villa 21, at Shenley Hospital, Hertfordshire in 1962.
49. Letter from Montague C. Norton to John Trevelyan, 3 March 1964, *Borderlines* file, BBFC Archive.
50. Letter from Mary Appleby to John Trevelyan, 20 December 1963, *Borderlines* file, BBFC Archive.
51. Letter from Hal Bartlett to John Trevelyan (via Montague C. Norton), 16 January 1964, *Borderlines* file, BBFC Archive.
52. Letter from Mary Appleby to John Trevelyan, 1 February 1964, *Borderlines* file, BBFC Archive.
53. Letter from Montague C. Norton to John Trevelyan, 3 March 1964, *Borderlines* file, BBFC Archive.
54. Letter from John Trevelyan to Montague C. Norton to 4 March 1964, *Borderlines* file, BBFC Archive.

55. 'Borderlines', *The Times*, 4 November 1965.
56. Patrick Gibbs, 'Borderlines', *Daily Telegraph*, 4 November 1965.
57. 'NAMH Public Information Committee Minutes', 15 June 1966, Wellcome Library, London.
58. 'Examiners Report', 1 August 1963, *The Collector* file, BBFC Archive.
59. It was Frankovich who reportedly approached William Wyler, at the request of screenwriter Kohn, to persuade him to leave the production of *The Sound of Music* (1965), on which he was unhappy, and direct *The Collector* instead. Max Wilk, *The Making of the Sound of Music* (New York: Routledge, 2007), p. 63.
60. Letter from John Trevelyan to Mike Frankovich, 7 August 1963, *The Collector* file, BBFC Archive.
61. Jay and Stephen Black, 'No Snake Pits in Britain', *Daily Mail*, 9 June 1949, p. 4.
62. Letter from John Trevelyan to Mike Frankovich, 13 August 1963, *The Collector* file, BBFC Archive.
63. Letter from John Trevelyan to John Kohn, 14 August 1963, *The Collector* file, BBFC Archive.
64. Letter from John Trevelyan to Stephen Black, 14 August 1963, *The Collector* file, BBFC Archive.
65. Dilys Powell, 'The Collector', *The Times*, 17 October 1965.
66. 'Lovelihead Examiners Report', 23 June 1964, *Repulsion* file, BBFC Archive.
67. Letter from John Trevelyan to Stephen Black, 29 June 1964, *Repulsion* file, BBFC Archive.
68. Letter from John Trevelyan to Stephen Black, 23 July 1964, *Repulsion* file, BBFC Archive.
69. Letter from John Trevelyan to Michael Klinger, 23 July 1964, *Repulsion* file, BBFC Archive.
70. Roman Polanski, *Roman by Polanski* (London: Heinemann, 1984), pp. 209–10.
71. Letter from Trevelyan to Eugene Gutowski, 27 July 1964, *Repulsion* file, BBFC Archive. Three years later, a *Daily Mail* story did reveal that Trevelyan was 'calling in a psychiatrist these days before deciding whether to pass some of the mind testing epics producers are turning out', including *Repulsion*, quoting but not naming Black who explained that his work for the BBFC was 'confidential'. 'Decider', *Daily Mail*, 9 February 1967, p. 4.
72. Letter from John Trevelyan to Gene Gutowski, 4 December 1964, *Repulsion* file, BBFC Archive.
73. Polanski, *Roman on Polanski*, pp. 209–10.
74. Letter from Michael Klinger to John Trevelyan, 1 June 1964, *Repulsion* file, BBFC Archive. Further evidence of the perception of Black's positive influence on censorship decisions, is a telegram to Trevelyan from Polanski asking for Black's involvement in the Board's consideration of *Rosemary's Baby* (1969). Letter from Roman Polanski to John Trevelyan, 3 January 1969, *Repulsion* file, BBFC Archive.
75. John Ezard, 'BBC and Film Board Give Order to Play Down on Drug Scenes', *The Guardian*, 29 December 1967, p. 3. The article explained that the BBC and BBFC had consulted and agreed on this policy.

76. Trevelyan, *What the Censor Saw*, p. 169.
77 As with Black, Trevelyan and Miller's correspondence indicate a friendship as well as a professional relationship, with, for example, the letters discussing the two men and their wives meeting up for dinner. Letter from Dr Derek Miller to John Trevelyan, 30 January 1968, *The Boston Strangler* file, BBFC Archives.
78. Letter from John Trevelyan to Stephen Lions, 9 October 1968, *The Boston Strangler* file, BBFC Archive. Miller was the first of the three to consult on the production; he was paid to read and comment on a draft script for *The Boston Strangler* in February 1968.
79. Letter from John Trevelyan to Stephen Lions, October 1968, *The Boston Strangler* file, BBFC Archive.
80. Nina Hibbin, 'Well-made Strangler Film Raises Censorship Concerns', *Morning Star*, 17 May 1969; Victor Davis, 'Should the Film be Shown Here?' *Daily Express*, 7 May 1969.
81. Derek Todd, 'Should We be Exploiting the Harmonics of Horror', *Kinematograph Weekly*, 1 June 1968, p. 12.

Chapter 3: Freud goes to Hollywood

1. Zaretsky, *Secrets of the Soul*, p. 308.
2. Ibid.
3. See David Fisher, 'Sartre's Freud: Dimensions of Subjectivity in the *Freud Scenario*', in Janet Bergstrom (ed.), *Endless Night: Cinema and Psychoanalysis, Parallel Histories* (Berkely: University of California Press, 1999), pp. 126–52; Peter Wollen, 'Freud as Adventurer', in Janet Bergstrom (ed.), *Endless Night: Cinema and Psychoanalysis, Parallel Histories* (Berkely: University of California Press, 1999), pp. 153–70; Marie-Andrée Charbonneau, 'The Freud Scenario: A Sartrian Freud – A Freudian Sartre?' *Sartre Studies International* 13(2) (2007): 86–112; Jeffery Meyers, 'The Making of John Huston's Freud: The Secret Passion', *Kenyon Review* 33(1) (2011): 178–99.
4. Gabbard and Gabbard *Psychiatry and the Cinema*, p. 97.
5. Ibid., p. 15.
6. 'Freud Rebuffs Goldwyn: Viennese Psychoanalyst is Not Interested in Motion Picture Offer', *Variety*, 24 January 1925, p. 13 .
7. Letter from Ernie Anderson to J. Huston and Wolfgang Reinhardt, 24 November 1961, John Huston papers, Margaret Herrick Library, Beverly Hills, CA (hereafter John Huston papers).
8. Gabbard and Gabbard, *Psychiatry and the Cinema*, p. 53.
9. Tim Snelson, '"Bad Medicine": The Psychiatric Profession's Interventions into the Business of Post-War Horror', in Richard Nowell (ed.), *Merchants of Menace: The Business of Horror Cinema* (New York: Bloomsbury Academic, 2014), p. 93.
10. John Huston, *An Open Book* (New York: Alfred A. Knopf, 1980). He was further inspired by witnessing and recording the result of psychotherapeutic treatment of soldiers in his wartime documentary *Let There Be Light* (1946).

11. Thomas Pryor, 'Hollywood Canvas', *New York Times*, 8 April 1958, p. 5.
12. John Huston, 'Focus on Freud: Huston Analyzes His Own Motivations in making a Psychiatric Biography', *New York Times*, 9 December 1962, p. 59.
13. Huston, *An Open Book*, p. 297.
14   Letter from Burly and Geach Solicitors to John Huston, 25 March 1958, John Huston papers.
15. Letter from Bartlett & Co. to John Huston, 25 March 1958, John Huston papers.
16. Letter from Edward Bernays to John Huston, 18 November 1961, John Huston papers.
17. Letter from John Huston to Edward Bernays, 16 January 1962, John Huston papers.
18. Letter from Marilyn Monroe to John Huston, 5 November 1959, John Huston papers.
19. Huston, *An Open Book*, p. 294.
20. Meyers, 'The Making of John Huston's Freud', p. 184.
21. Memo from Geoffrey Shurlock, 21 September 1960, PCA collection, Margaret Herrick Library, Beverly Hills, CA (hereafter PCA collection).
22. Memo from Geoffrey Shurlock, 21 April 1961, PCA collection.
23. Letter from Geoffrey Shurlock to Kenneth Clark (United Artists), 8 May 1961, PCA collection.
24. Letter from William Gordon to Edward Muhl, 21 June 1961, John Huston papers.
25. Letters from Geoffrey Shurlock to Kathlyn McTaggart, 22 September 1961; 5 October 1961. A concurrent Hollywood film, *The Chapman Report* (1962), raised comparable issues for the PCA. The film was based, via a popular novel by Irving Wallace, on the Kinsey Reports on sexual behaviour undertaken and published by Alfred Kinsey and a group of other sexologists. Perhaps unsurprisingly, therefore, the script contained multiple uses of the words 'sex' and 'sexual' which were required to be reduced considerably (or replaced with euphemisms) by the PCA. Letter from Geoffrey Shurlock to Frank McCarthy, 22 June 1961, PCA collection.
26. Letter from William Gordon to John Huston, 25 May 1961, John Huston files.
27. Ibid.
28. Zaretsky, *Secrets of the Soul*, p. 313.
29. Ibid., p. 314.
30. Letter from Martin Grotjahn to William Gordon, 20 June 1961, John Huston files. An analyst at the Berlin Institute of Psychoanalysis, Grotjahn, like Freud, fled Europe on the eve of the Second World War, moving to America and taking up a role at the famous Menninger Clinic, then setting up Southern California's first psychoanalytic training centre, the Los Angeles Psychoanalytic Institute.
31. Letter from Harry Milt (Director of Public Relations) to William Gordon, 12 June 1961, John Huston files.
32. Letter from Charles Curran to William Gordon, 23 May 1961, John Huston files.
33. Zaretsky, *Secrets of the Soul*, 308.

34. Letter from William Gordon to John Huston, 18 January 1962, John Huston files.
35. Ibid.
36. Letter from Loomis to Gordon, 8 June 1961, John Huston files.
37. Ibid.
38. Ibid.
39. In his stage instructions Sartre specifies a lecture hall 'which is exactly like the one in the famous painting "Une leçon clinique à la Salpêtrière"'. See John Paul Sartre, *The Freud Scenario* (London: Verso, 1984), p. 53.
40. Mark Micale, *Hysterical Men: The Hidden History of Male Nervous Illness* (Cambridge, MA: Harvard University Press, 2008), p. 4.
41. John Kafka, 'A Hypnosis Documentary Part of Huston's Freud', *Variety*, 15 November 1961, p. 2.
42. 'Freud in Action', *Los Angeles Times*, 28 January 1962, p. 28.
43. 'Freud's Epic Quest Begins', *Life*, 4 January 1963, p. 51.
44. Letter from Ciklic to Gordon, 5 May 1961, *Freud* files, LDA.
45. Letter from Loomis to Gordon, 8 June 1961, John Huston files.
46. Letter from William Gordon to John Huston, 12 June 1961, John Huston files.
47. Letter from Earl Loomis to William Gordon, 16 August 1961, John Huston files.
48. Ibid.
49. Letter from Earl Loomis to William Gordon, 4 September 1961, John Huston files.
50. Letter from Earl Loomis to William Gordon, 25 September 1961, John Huston files.
51. 'Huston Freud Ends Photography Phase', *Variety*, 24 February 1962, p. 4.
52. Memo, Earl Loomis to William Gordon, 20 December 1961, John Huston files.
53. See Miller, 'David Stafford-Clark (1916–1999)'.
54. In his autobiography, Huston claims that he asked 'one of the leading psychiatrists in England', Dr Stafford-Clarke, to visit him in Ireland to work on the script just prior to shooting to help him to resolve the issue of how to 'demonstrate the psychic mechanism of repression'. Huston, *An Open Book*, p. 299.
55. Letter from William Gordon to Edward Muhl, 4 May 1962, John Huston files.
56. Letter from Earl Loomis to William Gordon, 7 May 1961, John Huston files.
57. Letter from Gordon to Muhl, 4 May 1962, John Huston files.
58. John Huston, 'Focus on Freud: Huston Analyzes His Own Motivations in Making a Psychiatric Biography', *New York Times*, 9 December 1962, p. 59.
59. Ibid.
60. Carol Berkenkotter, *Patient Tales: Case Histories and the Uses of Narrative in Psychiatry* (Columbia: University of South Carolina Press, 2008), p. 14. This alignment of Freudian and Holmesian narratives received a carnivalesque treatment in Nicholas Meyer's 1974 novel *The Seven-Percent Solution*, which was adapted into a film, in which Alan Arkin plays Freud, by Universal Pictures in 1976. In book and film, the cocaine addicted Holmes goes into analysis with Freud. During the course of his treatment, Holmes and Freud investigate a kidnapping case with international implications and Freud uncovers a dark family secret suppressed in Holmes' subconscious.

61. Ibid., p. 2.
62. Arnold Davidson, *The Emergence of Sexuality: Historical Epistemology and the Formation of Concepts* (Cambridge, MA: Harvard University Press, 2001), p. 4.
63. Anne Sealey, 'The Strange Case of the Freudian Case History: The Role of Long Case Histories in the Development of Psychoanalysis', *History of the Human Sciences* 24(1) (2011): 45.
64. Ibid., p. 43.
65. See, John Forrester, *Thinking in Cases* (Cambridge: Polity, 2017).
66. Micale, *Hysterical Men*, p. 243.
67. David Sigler, 'Huston's Freud: Adapting the Life of Psychoanalysis', in Douglas McFarland and Wesley King (eds), *John Huston as Adaptor* (New York: State University of New York Press, 2018), p. 238.
68. Loomis was consulted on the wording for the foreword, asking if there was anything 'which an astronomer, biologist or psychologist would find objection?' Letter from John Huston to Earl Loomis, 12 May 1962, John Huston files.
69. Letter from George Golitzin to Charles Simonelli, 23 November 1962, LDA.
70. Letter from John Huston to Stephen Grimes, undated, John Huston files.
71. Letter from Stephen Grimes to John Huston, 8 June 1962, John Huston files.
72. 'Pictures: Quick Scenes, Cuts to Startle in 'Point Blank', *Variety*, 22 November 1961, p. 13.
73. Howard Thomson, 'The Screen: 'Pressure Point', *New York Times*, 11 October 1962, p. 4.
74. Memo, Grimes to Huston, undated, John Huston files.
75. Douglas Slocombe quoted in Roger Hudson, 'The Secret Profession', *Sight and Sound* 34 (1965): 114.
76. Ibid., p. 117.
77. William Gordon to William Bier, 3 July 1961, PCA collection.
78. 'Special Music used for Film's Dream Sequences', *Los Angeles Times*, 15 March 1963, p. 12. A year earlier, British film *The Innocents* (1961) had pioneered the use of synthesised electronic sound, using it for a comparable psychological effect. The sound design was created by an uncredited Daphne Oram, a pioneering electronic composer central to the BBC's Radiophonic workshop, who innovated a spectral synthesised soundscape to indicate protagonist Miss Gidden's (Deborah Kerr) psychotic experiences. As in *Freud*, this modern, disorienting technique stands in contrast to George Auric's main orchestral score and the haunting A Capella theme 'O Willow Waly'.
79. Memo, Earl Loomis to John Huston, 20 December 1962, John Huston files.
80. Sigler, 'Huston's Freud', p. 242.
81. Bosley Crowther, 'Freud Prevue in Hanover', *New York Times*, 12 November 1962, p. 37.
82. Philip Scheuer, 'Freud Traumatic Cinema Experience', *Los Angeles Times*, 13 December 1962, p. 97.
83. 'Huston in States as Freud Dates Multiply', *Variety*, 20 February 1963, p. 16.

84. 'Never Heard of Freud: Re-titled, US Pic Does OK', *Variety*, 9 October 1963, p. 5. This removal of Freud from the title for middle American audiences goes some way to corroborating Sartre's cynical comment, 'As you know, one can make a film four hours long if it has to do with Ben Hur, but a Texas audience won't sit through four hours of complexes.' Sartre quoted in Kenneth Tynan, *Right and Left: Plays, Films, People, Places and Events* (London: Longmans, 1967), p. 308.
85. Letter from John Trevelyan to F. L. Thomas (the Rank Organisation), 4 July 1963, John Huston files.
86. 'Freud', *Listener*, 19 September 1963, PCA collection.
87. 'Papa of Psychiatry' *Time*, 28 December 1962, PCA collection.
88. Powers 'Freud', *Hollywood Reporter*, 29 October 1962, PCA collection.
89. Tube, 'Freud', *Variety*, 13 October 1962, p. 6.
90. Scheuer, 'Freud Traumatic Cinema Experience', p. 97.
91. Elspeth Grant, 'On Films: Psycho-Allergy', *The Tatler and Bystander*, 11 September 1963, p. 545.
92. 'Freud', *America*, 26 January 1963, PCA collection.
93. Saul Rosenzweig, 'Caveat Emptor!', *American Psychologist* (1963): 534–5.
94. 'SR Goes to the Movies: *Freud*', *Saturday Review*, 5 January 1963, PCA collection.
95. Tube, 'Freud', p. 6.
96. 'Papa of Psychiatry', *Time*.
97. Cecil Wilson, 'For this Dark Tribute to Freud, They Should Take out the Seats and Give us Couches Instead', *Daily Mail*, 29 August 1963, p. 3.
98. Ernest Callenbach, 'Freud', *Film Quarterly* 16(4) (1963): p. 50.
99. *Rowan and Martin's Laugh-In*, Episode 13, Season 4, 1970.

Chapter 4: Mad housewives and women's liberation

1. See Betty Friedan, *The Feminine Mystique* (New York: W.W. Norton, 1963).
2. Ian Hacking, *Rewriting the Soul: Multiple Personality and the Sciences of Memory* (Princeton, NJ: Princeton University Press, 1995), p. 41.
3. Carol Lawson, 'Eleanor Perry Dies; Wrote Screenplays', *New York Times*, 17 March 1981, p. 14.
4. Tillie Olsen, *Silences* (New York: CUNY Press, [1978] 2003).
5. Ferdinand Lundberg and Marynia Farnham, *Modern Women: The Lost Sex* (New York: Universal Library, 1947), p. 203.
6. See Tim Snelson, *Phantom Ladies: Hollywood Horror and the Home Front* (New York: Rutgers University Press, 2015).
7. 'Chicago Psychiatrist Traces Aggressive Girls to Pix' Not-So-He-Men', *Variety*, 29 August 1945, pp. 1, 16.
8. See Snelson '"Bad Medicine"', pp. 93–107.
9. Robert Couglan, 'Modern Marriage', *Life* magazine, 24 December 1956, p. 109.
10. John Cotten quoted in Couglan, 'Modern Marriage', p. 110.

11. Ibid., p. 116.
12. Herman, *The Romance of American Psychology*, p. 280.
13. Kate Millett, *Sexual Politics* (New York: Doubleday, 1970), p. 189. See also Shulamith Firestone, *The Dialectic of Sex: The Case for Feminist Revolution* (New York: William Morrow, 1970).
14. Janet Walker, *Couching Resistance: Women, Film, and Psychoanalytic Psychiatry* (Minneapolis: University of Minnesota Press, 1993), p. 143.
15. Ibid., p. 144. Referring to the writing of Shulamith Firestone, Zaretsky identifies that consciousness-raising privileged 'that which had forbidden or suspended within psychoanalysis – "acting out"'. See Zaretsky, *Secrets of the Soul*, p. 328.
16. Walker, *Couching Resistance*, p. 159.
17. Justine Lloyd and Lesley Johnson, 'The Three Faces of *Eve*: The Post-war Housewife, Melodrama, and Home', *Feminist Media Studies* 3(1) (2002): 9.
18. Ibid., p. 20.
19. Ibid., p. 18.
20. Hervey Cleckley, *The Mask of Sanity: An Attempt to Clarify Some Issues About the So-Called Psychopathic Personality* (St Louis, MO: CV Mosby Co., [1941] 1955). The first edition of *The Three Faces of Eve* includes the line 'Author of the Mask of Sanity' under Cleckley's name on the cover.
21. See Robert Genter, '"We All Go a Little Mad Sometimes": Alfred Hitchcock, American Psychoanalysis, and the Construction of the Cold War Psychopath', *Canadian Review of American Studies* 40(2) (2010): 140–1.
22. Harold Merskey, 'The Manufacture of Personalities: The Production of Multiple Personality Disorder', *British Journal of Psychiatry* 160 (1992): 327.
23. Geoff Rolls, *Classic Case Studies in Psychology* (London: Routledge, 2014), pp. 223–4.
24. See Colin Ross, *Dissociative Identity Disorder: Diagnosis, Clinical Features, and Treatment of Multiple Personality Disorder* (New York: Wiley, 1997), p. 61.
25. Corbett H. Thigpen and Hervey M. Cleckley, *The Three Faces of Eve* (New York: McGraw-Hill, [1957] 1992), p. 5.
26. Ibid., p. 4.
27. Ibid., p. 141.
28. Ibid., p. 244.
29. Katie Joice, 'Mothering in the Frame: Cinematic Microanalysis and the Pathogenic Mother, 1945–67', *History of the Human Sciences* 34(5) (2021): 105–31.
30. Letter from Corbett Thigpen to Chris Costner Sizemore, 7 October 1953, Chris Costner Sizemore Papers, David M. Rubenstein Rare Book and Manuscript Library, Duke University (hereafter Costner Sizemore papers).
31. Thigpen and Cleckley, *The Three Faces of Eve*, pp. 107–8.
32. Letter from Corbett Thigpen to Costner Sizemore, 30 July 1956, Costner Sizemore papers.
33. Peter Shelley, *Joanne Woodward: Her Life and Career* (Jefferson, NC: McFarland, 2019), p. 26. As Thigpen explained to Costner, while Nunnally Johnson thought Garland was the 'best actress in Hollywood' and perfect for the role, he was

'somewhat concerned by her propensity for alcohol and sedatives'. Letter from Corbett Thigpen to Costner Sizemore, 3 August 1956, Costner Sizemore papers.

34. Shelley, *Joanne Woodward*, p. 28. In addition to Garland and Woodward, the long-list for the role of Eve featured many of classical Hollywood's biggest stars: Doris Day, Marilyn Monroe, Lana Turner, Rita Hayworth, Olivia de Havilland, Vivien Leigh and Susan Hayward. Hayward was reported to have taken the role prior to the announcement of Woodward. Casting memo, 21 June 1956. William 'Billy' Gordon papers, 71321912, Margaret Herrick Library, Beverly Hills, CA.

35. William Condon, William Ogston and Larry Pacoe, 'Three Faces of Eve Revisited: A Study of Transient Microstrabismus', *Journal of Abnormal Psychology* 74(5) (1969): 618.

36. Chris Costner Sizemore and Elen Sain Pittillo, *I'm Eve: The Compelling Story of the International Case of Multiple Personality* (New York: Doubleday, 1977), pp. 262–3.

37. Ibid., p. 300.

38. Ibid., p. 302.

39. Ibid., p. 453.

40. Corbett H. Thigpen and Hervey C. Cleckley, 'A Case of Multiple Personality', *Journal of Abnormal and Social Psychology* 495 (1954): 150.

41. While the book was inspired by Jackson's own mental health issues, the film's reception often identified it as being based on Costner's case history too.

42. When working on the manuscript of *The Last Face of Eve*, James Poling complained about Fox losing this archival material and tape recordings, stating: 'I can't help that regret a lot of so much that might have proved invaluable . . . As for the five tapes that got erased in Hollywood – well, that's typical of Hollywood.' Letter from James Poling to Costner Sizemore, 4 April 1957, Costner Sizemore papers.

43. Letter from James Poling to Costner Sizemore, 15 November 1957, Costner Sizemore papers.

44. Letter from Corbett Thigpen to Costner Sizemore, 28 March 1956, Costner Sizemore papers.

45. Costner Sizemore and Pittillo, *I'm Eve*, p. 343.

46. Ibid., p. 339.

47. Letter from Irmis Johnson to Costner Sizemore, 2 April 1956, Costner Sizemore papers.

48. Letter from Thigpen to Costner Sizemore, 16 May 1956, Costner Sizemore papers.

49. Letter from Thigpen to Costner Sizemore, 20 July 1956, Costner Sizemore papers.

50. Letter from Thigpen to Costner Sizemore, 3 August 1956, in Costner Sizemore papers.

51. Letter from Thigpen to Costner Sizemore, 9 January 1957, Costner Sizemore papers.

52. Letter from Nunnally Johnson (Twentieth-Century Fox) to Corbett Thigpen, 25 February 1957, Costner Sizemore papers.

53. Letter form Lionel Schreiber to Costner Sizemore, 3 April 1957, Costner Sizemore papers.
54. Letter from Nunnally Johnson to Costner Sizemore, 12 April 1957, Costner Sizemore papers.
55. Costner Sizemore and Pittillo, *I'm Eve*, p. 343.
56. Ibid., p. 343.
57. Letter James Poling to Costner Sizemore, 4 April 1957, Costner Sizemore papers.
58. Letter from Thigpen to Costner Sizemore, 29 April 1957, Costner Sizemore papers.
59. Letter from Thigpen to Costner Sizemore, 6 June 1957, Costner Sizemore papers.
60. Letter from Corbett Thigpen to Don Sizemore, 4 September 1957, Costner Sizemore papers.
61. In her later account, *A Mind of My Own*, Costner Sizemore blames Thigpen for her not going to Hollywood to film the prologue with Cooke, (mis)remembering him deciding it was 'not advisable for Jane to go. So the film was completed without anyone telling her that the cameo appearance had been scrapped'. Chris Costner Sizemore, *A Mind of My Own: The Woman Who Was Known as 'Eve' Tells the Story of Her Triumph over Multiple Personality Disorder* (New York: Willian Morrow, 1989), p. 70.
62. Gabbard and Gabbard *Psychiatry and the*, pp. 37–9.
63. Walker, *Couching Resistance*, p. 159.
64. Ibid.
65. Ibid., p. 160.
66. See Lloyd and Johnson, 'The Three Faces of Eve', pp. 7–25.
67. Letter from Thigpen to Costner Sizemore, 13 September 1955, Costner Sizemore papers.
68. Harry Brand, Synopsis (annotated), 29 April 1957, *The Three Faces of Eve* file, PCA collection.
69. Memo (undated) on Legion of Decency classification (5 September 1957), *The Three Faces of Eve* file, PCA collection.
70. Costner Sizemore and Pittillo, *I'm Eve*, p. 352.
71. Costner Sizemore, *A Mind of My Own*, p. 69.
72. Costner Sizemore and Pittillo, *I'm Eve*, p. 350.
73. Ibid.
74. Letter from Thigpen to Costner Sizemore, 24 September 1957, Costner Sizemore papers.
75. Costner Sizemore and Pittillo, *I'm Eve*, p. 353.
76. 'The Three Faces of Eve', *McCarthy Sheet*, 10 October 1957, McCarthy Film Distributor Critique Sheets, National Science and Media Museum collections, Bradford.
77. Hol, 'Three Faces of Eve', *Variety*, 21 August 1957, p. 6.
78. 'The Three Faces of Eve', *The Times*, 17 October 1957, p. 5.
79. London Film Critic, 'The Three Faces of Eve', *The Guardian*, 19 October 1957, p. 3.

80. Bosley Crowther, 'Women's Pictures', *New York Times,* 6 October 1957, p. 133.

81. Ibid.

82. Phillip Scheuer, 'Films "Appealing to Women" Show Sign of Returning', *Los Angeles Times,* 18 August 1957, p. 2.

83. Bosley Crowther, 'Screen: "3 Faces of Eve"', *New York Times,* 27 September 1957, p. 16.

84. See, Phillip Scheuer, 'Two New Films Concerned with Split Personality, *Los Angeles Times,* 17 May 1957, p. 2; Edwin Schallert, 'Split Personality Film Spotlights New Talent', *Los Angeles Times,* 12 October 1957, p. 2.

85. Hol, 'Three Faces of Eve', p. 6.

86. Costner Sizemore, *A Mind of My Own,* pp. 70–1. A number of articles, most titled 'The Three Faces of Joanne', celebrated Woodward's performance of the three personalities, 'any one of which could have pegged her as an Oscar nominee'. Woodward responded to the question of how she achieved it by stating, 'I don't like to talk too much about it. I might talk those Eves right out of existence – just as the real-life girl did during her emergence as a normal personality. E. Forrest, 'The Three Faces of Joanne', *Picturegoer,* 2 November 1957, p. 34. The *New York Times* discussed her psychologically rich performance in the context of her method-acting training and positioned her as the 'female Brando'. Liza Wilson, 'Three Faces of Joanna', *Washington Post,* 21 April 1957, p. 16.

87. Costner Sizemore, *A Mind of My Own,* p. 73.

88. Ibid., p. 152.

89. Ibid., p. 153.

90. Nadine Brozan, 'The Real "Eve" Sues to Film the Rest of Her Story', *New York Times,* 7 February 1989, p. 13.

91. Ralph Slovenko, 'Multiple Personality: Perplexities about the Law', *Medicine and Law* 14(1995): 627.

92. Brozan, 'The Real "Eve"', p. 13.

93. Hacking, *Rewriting the Soul,* p. 39.

94. Ibid., p. 41.

95. Ibid.

96. Ibid., p. 43.

97. Ibid., p. 34.

98. Costner Sizemore, *A Mind of My Own,* pp. 208–9.

99. Staff Writer, 'The Millers Tale', *Augusta Chronicle,* 23 September 2007, available at: https://eu.augustachronicle.com/story/opinion/editorials/2007/09/09/edi-142885-shtml/14699560007, last accessed 6 January 2023.

100. Ross' claims included that Thigpen, 'attended her husband's funeral uninvited, was her son's godfather and engaged in sexual misconduct with her. He arranged for her to have an abortion, and during the procedure she was sterilised without her or her husband's consent.' Bruce Weber, 'Chris Costner Sizemore, Patient Behind "The Three Faces of Eve", Dies at 89', *New York Times,* 5 August 2016, p. 20.

101. Ibid.

102. Lloyd and Johnson, '*The Three Faces of Eve*', p. 10.

103. Friedan, *The Feminine Mystique*, p. 96.

104. Nathan G. Hale, *The Rise and Crisis of Psychoanalysis in the United States: Freud and the Americans, 1917–1985* (Oxford: Oxford University Press, 1995), p. 346.

105. Ibid.

106. Friedan, *The Feminine Mystique*, p. 95.

107. Herman, *The Romance of American Psychology*, p. 292.

108. Zaretsky, *Secrets of the Soul*, p. 328.

109. Jessica Grogan, *Encountering America: Humanistic Psychology, Sixties Culture and the Shaping of the Modern Self* (New York: Harper Perennial, 2013), p. 261.

110. Herman, *The Romance of American Psychology*, p. 297.

111. Bonnie Moore Randolph and Clydene Ross-Valliere, 'Consciousness Raising Groups', *American Journal of Nursing* 79(5) (1979): 294

112. Ibid.

113. Carol Hanisch, 'The Personal is the Political', in Shulamith Firestone and Anne Koedt (eds), *Notes from the Second Year* (New York: Published by Editors, 1970), p. 76.

114. Jeanne Marecek, 'Mad Housewives, Double Shifts, Mommy Tracks and Other Invented Realities', *Feminism & Psychology* 13(2) (2003): 259. See also, Jacqueline Foertsch, 'Tools of the Trade: Working Women in Texts from the Sexual Revolution', *CEA Critic* 81(2) (2019): 100–16.

115. Kay Loveland and Estelle Changas, 'Eleanor Perry: One Woman in Film', *Film Comment*, Spring 197,: p. 65.

116. The extremely heartful and psychologically engaged *Time* magazine review began '*David and Lisa* is a tribute much more deeply touching: a story of two terrified children, lost in the deep black mine of the mind, who are found there by the means that Freud discovered and are led back to life by the bright red thread of love', and concluded that the film expressed 'the sense for what is specifically human in human beings, the sense of the heart.', 'Cinema: Children in Darkness', *Time*, 28 December 1962. Eleanor Perry wrote reviewer Darrick a long letter thanking him for the review, expressing that more than just a matter of positive film reception, she experienced a 'feeling of being completely understood of total empathy another human being'. Letter from Eleanor Perry to Mr Darrick, 1962, Eleanor Perry files, Margaret Herrick library, Beverly Hills, CA. Bosley Crowther, on the other hand, wrote a lukewarm review of the film that highlighted that its depiction of mental illness 'was a stumbling block in this film'. Bosley Crowther, 'Odd Romance Involves Mentally Ill Children', *New York Times*, 27 December 1962.

117. Loveland and Changas, 'Eleanor Perry', p. 66.

118. Ibid.

119. Ibid.

120. Ibid., p. 68.

121. Ibid.

122. Ibid.
123. Ibid.
124. Roger Ebert, 'Diary of Mad Housewife', *Chicago Sun Times*, August 1970, available at: https://www.rogerebert.com/reviews/diary-of-a-mad-housewife-1970, last accessed 10 April 2023.
125. Jay Cocks, 'Marital Pulp', *Time* magazine, 17 August 1970, p. 34.
126. Murf, 'Diary of a Mad Housewife', *Variety*, 5 August 1970, p. 16.
127. Grace Glueck, 'A Funny and Incisively Human "Housewife"', *New York Times*, 23 August 1970, p. 11.
128. Ibid.
129. 'Diary of a Mad Housewife', *Independent Film Journal* 66(5), 5 August 1970, p. 1313.
130. Cocks, 'Marital Pulp', p. 34.
131. Murf, 'Diary of a Mad Housewife', p. 16. The *Variety* review makes an interesting observation, that the *Diary*'s 'promotion will have to overcome possible misconception that film is a thriller, since the "mad" housewife is a "furious" one, not deranged'. Murf appears to be refereeing the ongoing cycle of 'New Gothic' thrillers, discussed in the book's introduction, featuring 'psychologically disturbed' heroines; recent examples were Roman Polanski's *Rosemary's Baby* (1968) and Robert Altman's *That Cold Day in the Park* (1969). While some are more 'schlocky', others focus on (and validate) mothers' horrific experiences of post-natal trauma, bereavement and insecure attachment.
132. Arthur Knight, 'In Conversation with Eleanor Perry', 28 October 1974, available at: https://pastdaily.com/2018/03/25/eleanor-perry-discusses-writing-film-feminism-1974-past-daily-gallimaufry, last accessed 10 March 2023. This assertion that she would have gone 'much further' in the feminist politics of the film was made earlier in a 1973 *Los Angeles Times* article titled 'Screenwriter Eleanor Perrys Consciousness-Lifting Crusade'. Discussing her ongoing commitment to enhancing women's roles in films, she states, 'In these days when you hear on all sides that nobody's writing good roles for women. It's all I've ever done.' Perry quoted in Eve Sharbutt, 'Screenwriter Eleanor Perry's Consciousness-Lifting Crusade', *Los Angeles Times*, 30 June 1973, p. 36.
133. Mary Murphy and Cheryl Bentsen, 'Coming to Grips with the Issue of Power', *Los Angeles Times*, 16 August 1973, p. 30
134. Lawson, 'Eleanor Perry Dies, p. 14
135. 1972 *Chicago Tribune* news report quoted in Paula Mejia, 'Summer and Swimmers', *Paris Match*, 16 June 2017, available at: https://www.theparisreview.org/blog/2017/06/16/summers-and-swimmers, last accessed 10 April 2023.
136. Loveland and Changas, 'Eleanor Perry, p. 69.
137. Lawson, 'Eleanor Perry Dies, p. 14.
138. Ebert, 'Diary of Mad Housewife.'

Chapter 5: Radical collaborations

1. Merete Bates, 'In Two Minds', *The Guardian*, 18 May 1972, p. 16.
2. See, R. D. Laing and Aaron Esterson, *Sanity, Madness and the Family* (London: Penguin, 1964).
3. Crossley, *Contesting Psychiatry*.
4. The interview with Tony Garnett was conducted at his home on 23 January 2018. The interview with Ken Loach was recorded over Zoom for the 'Locating Medical Television: The Televisual Spaces of Medicine and Health in the 20th Century International Conference', on 13 November 2020.
5. Jeremy Hornsby, 'In Two Minds', *Daily Express*, 2 March 1967.
6. 'NY Film Fest Firms Panel Sideshow', *Variety*, 27 September 1972, p. 20.
7. John Hill, *Ken Loach: The Politics of Film and Television* (London: British Film Institute, 2011); Sherryl Wilson, 'Dramatising Madness: *In Two Minds* and 1960s Counter-cultural Politics', *Transgressive Cultures* 2(1) (2012): 147–65.
8. Adrian Chapman, 'Re-Coopering Anti-psychiatry: David Cooper, Revolutionary Critic of Psychiatry', *Critical Radical Social Work* 4(3) (2016): 421–32; Oisin Wall, 'Villa 21: The Anti-Psychiatry Movement', *Contemporary Psychotherapy* 7(1) (2015), available at: https://www.contemporarypsychotherapy.org/volume-7-issue-1-summer-2015/villa-21.
9. Staub, *Madness is Civilization*; Sarah Marks, 'Psychotherapy in a Historical Perspective', *History of the Human Sciences* 30(2) (2017): 3–16; Wall, *The British Anti-Psychiatrists*; Jonathon Toms, 'MIND, Anti-Psychiatry, and the Case of the Mental Hygiene Movement's "Discursive Transformation"', *Social History of Medicine* (33)2 (2020): 622–40.
10. Crossley, *Contesting Psychiatry*, p. 29.
11. See Szasz, *Anti-psychiatry*, pp. 25–68.
12. Crossley, 'Transforming the Mental Health Field', p. 78
13. Wall, *The British Anti-Psychiatrists*, p. 2.
14. Ibid., p. 52.
15. Ibid., p. 165.
16. Crossley, *Contesting Psychiatry*, p. 101.
17. See Miller, 'David Stafford-Clark (1916–1999)'.
18. Chapman, 'Re-Coopering Anti-psychiatry'.
19. Crossley, *Contesting Psychiatry*, pp. 97–8.
20. The term mental hygiene was used from the nineteenth century, with its use to describe a movement pushing for the medicalisation of mental health beginning in America in the early twentieth century, instigated by one-time patient Clifford Beers. The movement began by pushing for better conditions in mental asylums, but evolved to prevention and early treatment of mental health issues. In the United Kingdom, the first organisation to be associated with the movement was the Central Association for Mental Welfare (CAMW), founded in 1913 in association with the creation of the 1913 Mental Deficiency Act and the associated board of control who would oversee British mental health institutions.

The CAMW merged with two interwar organisations that shared their mental hygiene principles – the National Council for Mental Health (1922) and the Child Guidance Council (1927) – following the recommendations of the Feversham Commission (1939). See Crossley, 'Transforming the Mental Health Field'.

21. Crossley, *Contesting Psychiatry*, p. 82.
22. Toms, 'MIND, Anti-Psychiatry', p. 634.
23. 'A Home of Their Own', *Mental Health* 25(4) (1966): 46–8. See 'About Anglia' television report from 1964, available at: https://player.bfi.org.uk/free/film/watch-care-in-the-community-a-very-new-idea-1964-online, last accessed 12 March 2021.
24. Crossley, *Contesting Psychiatry*, p. 80.
25. Public Information Committee terms of reference, 1956, Mental Health Information, Education and Public Attitudes. PPROS/C/8/1, Wellcome Library, London.
26. See, for example, the review of Mary Adams' 1958 lecture on 'Medicine on Television' for the Royal College of Surgeons in *British Medical Journal*, 29 November 1958, pp. 1351–2.
27. Toms, 'MIND, Anti-Psychiatry', p. 622.
28. NAMH Public Information Committee Minutes, 7 December 1956. Mental Health Information, Education and Public Attitudes, PPROS/C/8/1, Wellcome Library, London.
29. W. A. Belson, Senior Psychologist, BBC Audience Research Department, 'Some Effects of the Hurt Mind Series: An Interim Report, 4 June 1957', S322/117/2, BBC Written Archives, Reading.
30. William Sargant, 'The Hurt Mind', *British Medical Journal*, 1 March 1958, p. 517.
31. BBC Audience Research Report, 4 June 1957, p. 5, S322/117/2, BBC Written Archives. The BBC report actually reported a decrease in the number of audience references to psychoanalysis from 31 per cent before to 20 per cent post-broadcast, highlighting the significant awareness-raising for physical methods, p. 7.
32. 'Disease Education by the BBC', *British Medical Journal*, 15 February 1958, p. 389.
33. *Mind out of Balance* leaflet, 1957, Mental Health Information, Education and Public Attitudes, PPROS/C/8/1, Wellcome Library.
34. Mark Duguid, *The Human Jungle, 1963–64*, BFI Screen Online, 2019, available at: http://www.screenonline.org.uk/tv/id/1260403, last accessed 20 November 2019.
35. NAMH Public Information Committee Minutes, 14 June 1963, Mental Health Information, Education and Public Attitudes, PPROS/C/8/1, Wellcome Library.
36. Hugh Freeman, 'Maybury: Drama Series on Mental Health', *Bulletin of the Royal College of Psychiatrists* 5(7) (1981): 133.
37. Madeleine MacMurraugh-Kavanagh, 'The BBC and the Birth of "The Wednesday Play", 1962–66: Institutional Containment versus "Agitational Contemporaneity"', *Historical Journal of Film, Radio and Television* 17(3) (1997): 367–81.

38. The drama-documentary differs from the 'documentary-drama' which incorporated elements of fictional reconstruction into the documentary mode and was a genre employed by the BBC documentary department.

39. Hill, *Ken Loach*, p. 62.

40. Tony Garnett, 1968, quoted in Hill, *Ken Loach*, p. 63.

41. R. Roy Levin, *Documentary Explorations: 15 Interviews with Filmmakers* (New York: Doubleday. 1971), p. 106.

42. Crossley, *Contesting Psychiatry*, p. 1.

43. Tony Garnett to R. D. Laing, 22 January 1966, *In Two Minds* files, BBBWACT5/1522/1, BBC Written Archives.

44. Interview with authors, 2018.

45. R. D. Laing, *The Divided Self: An Existential Study in Sanity and Madness* (London: Penguin, [1960] 1965).

46. Ibid.

47. See Berkenkotter, *Patient Tales*.

48. Laing and Esterson, *Sanity, Madness and the Family*, p. 25.

49. F. Post, 'Sanity, Madness and the Family', *Mental Health* 24(4) (1965): 179.

50. Tony Garnett to R. D. Laing, 22 January 1966; Tony Garnett to David Cooper, 22 January 1966, *In Two Minds* files, BBBWACT5/1522/1, BBC Written Archives.

51. Tony Garnett to R. D. Laing, 23 February 1966, BBBWACT5/1522/1, BBC Written Archives.

52. Tony Garnett to R. D. Laing, 23 February 1966; Tony Garnett to David Cooper, 23 February 1966; Tony Garnett to Aaron Esterson, 24 February 1966, *In Two Minds* files, BBBWACT5/1522/1, BBC Written Archives.

53. R. D. Laing to Mr and Mrs Davis, 18 March 1966, *In Two Minds* files, BBBWACT5/1522/1, BBC Written Archives.

54. Both sets of parents subscribe to a shared narrative of an 'out-of-nowhere' shift in Ruth/Kate from 'very good child' to 'bad' adult daughter, with the 'principal signs of [their] "illness" [being their] abuse and resentment at [their] parents, and uncontrollable behaviour'. Laing and Esterson, *Sanity, Madness and the Family*, p. 162. This designation of fairly healthy generational conflict as pathological has 'never been called into question by psychiatrists who have "treated" [them] for this "condition"' over several years. Ibid., p. 163.

55. Interview with the authors, 2020.

56. Hospital administrators asked the producers to 'avoid any mention of Middlesex Hospital in the play . . . in case some of the material was not handled in a way that reflected our own approach to psychiatry'. Dr John Hinton to Stephany Marks, 8 August 1966, BBBWACT5/1522/1, BBC Written Archives.

57. Interview with the author, 2018.

58. Ibid.

59. Ibid.

60. The first line of *Sanity, Madness and the Family* is 'For five years now we have studying the families of schizophrenic patients', p. 15.

61. Hill, *Ken Loach*, p. 69.

62. Interview with the author, 2018.

63. Tim Boon, *Films of Fact: A History of Science in Documentary Films and Television* (London: Wallflower, 2008), pp. 209–32.
64. Tim Boon and Jean-Baptiste Gouyon, 'The Origins and Practice of Science on British Television', in M. Conboy and J. Steel (eds), *Routledge Companion to British Media History* (London: Routledge, 2014) p. 477.
65. Letter from BBC to Tony Garnett, 29 July 1966, *In Two Minds* files, BBBWACT5/1522/1, BBC Written Archives.
66. The scene also has a parallel in *The Divided Self*, of Kraepelin's questioning of a semi-catatonic woman with dementia praecox. The dehumanisation of the patient and the institutional inability/unwillingness to understand the patient maps perfectly onto this scene (Laing, *The Divided Self*, 1960, p. 29).
67. Boon, *Films of Fact*, p. 195.
68. See Sealey, 'The Strange Case of the Freudian Case History', pp. 36–50.
69. See G. Bateson, D. Jackson, J. Haley and J. Weakland, 'Toward a Theory of Schizophrenia', *Behavioural Science* 1 (1956): 251–64.
70. Andrew McDonald and Garry Walter, 'Hollywood and ECT', *International Review of Psychiatry* 21(3) (2009): 202; Edward Shorter and David Healy, *Shock Therapy: A History of Electroconvulsive Treatment in Mental Illness* (New Brunswick, NJ: Rutgers University Press, 2007), p. 9.
71. Boon, *Films of Fact*, p. 215.
72. *In Two Minds* Audience Research Report, 29 March 1967, BBBWACT5/1522/1, BBC Written Archives.
73. William Sargant, 'Treating Schizophrenia', *The Times*, 8 March 1967, p. 13.
74. David Mercer, 'Treating Schizophrenia', *The Times*, 11 March 1967, p. 11.
75. Henry Yellowlees, 'Treating Schizophrenia', *The Times*, 14 March 1967, p. 13.
76. Mary Dalison, 'Discharged But Not Cured', *The Times*, 11 March 1967, p. 13.
77. William Sargant, 'Treating Schizophrenia', *The Times*, 28 March 1967, p. 9.
78. Crossley, *Contesting Psychiatry*, p. 133. For example, *Mental Health*'s 1967 dismissive review of *Politics of the Family* begins: 'Deja vu . . . plus pa change . . . all the old clichés spring to mind as the familiar Laing aphorisms unroll yet again.' Robert Ferguson, 'The Politics of the Family', *MIND* (1971): 23.
79. Both Mercer in the article and Laing in the revised preface of *The Divided Self* (1965) use the metaphor of the military minds that sanction/drop the atom bomb to question the distinction between sanity and madness.
80. David Mercer, 'In Two Minds', *Mental Health* 26(2) (1976): 26.
81. 'Mental Health Scene: Debating Schizophrenia', *Mental Health* 26(2) (1967): 30.
82. Peter Black, 'We Can Learn a Lot from Kate', *Daily Mail*, 2 March 1967, the Ken Loach collection, BFI National Archive, Berkhamsted (hereafter Loach collection).
83. Nancy Banks-Smith, 'Not So Much a Case History as a Murder', *The Sun*, 2 March 1967, Loach collection.
84. Stanley Reynolds, 'Television', *The Guardian*, 2 March 1967.
85. Black, 'We Can Learn a Lot from Kate.'
86. Kenneth Eastlaugh, 'The Superbly Told Story of a Girl Deprived of Love', *Daily Mirror*, 2 March 1967, p. 14.

87. Reynolds, 'Television'.

88. Sylvia Clayton, 'In Two Minds', *Daily Telegraph*, 2 March 1967, Loach collection.

89. Jeremy Hornsby, 'In Two Minds', *Daily Express*, 2 March 1967, Loach collection.

90. See Gavin Miller, 'Psychiatric Penguins: Writing on Psychiatry for Penguin Books Ltd, c. 1950–c. 1980', *History of the Human Sciences* 28(4) (2015): 76–101.

91. Wilson, 'Dramatising Madness', p. 152.

92. Hornsby, 'In Two Minds'.

93. M. Wiggin, 'Convictions or Ill', *Sunday Times*, 5 March 1967.

94. J. Thomas, 'Getting a Bit Blurred on TV … Drama and Real-Life', *Daily Express*, 8 March 1967, p. 8.

95. Anthony Burgess, 'Television', *The Listener*, 9 March 1967, p. 335.

96. Dr M. E. Ward to Ken Loach, 6 March 1967, *In Two Minds* files, BBBWACT5/1522/1, BBC Written Archives.

97. David Mercer to D. M. Ward, 11 March 1967; J. B Parry to G. Savory, 8 March 1967; Prof. Tom Burns to Tony Garnett, 13 March 1966, *In Two Minds* files, BBBWACT5/1522/1, BBC Written Archives.

98. Margaret Mawer to R. D. Laing, 18 October 1968. MS Laing 7321/4, R. D. Laing Archive at the University of Glasgow.

99. Adrian Laing, *R. D. Laing: A Life* (Stroud: Sutton, 1994), p. 139.

100. David Mercer, *Family Life* script, 1971, Loach collection.

101. Wall, *The British Anti-Psychiatrists*, p. 80.

102. Tony Garnett to Stephen Murphy (BBFC), 17 September 1971, *Family Life* file, BBFC Archives, London.

103. Ken Loach quoted in Graham Fuller, *Loach on Loach* (London: Faber & Faber, 1998), pp. 44–5.

104. Irving Teitelbaum to Joy Simson, 28 July 1971, MS Laing L238/133, R. D. Laing Archive at the University of Glasgow, Glasgow.

105. Wall, *The British Anti-Psychiatrists*, p. 65.

106. Mercer, *Family Life* script.

107. Anglo-EMI, *Family Life Pressbook, 1972. Family Life Press Files*. London: BFI Reuben Library.

108. Alexander Walker, 'Unhappy Families', *Evening Standard*, 13 January 1972.

109. Derek Malcolm, 'Who's For Sanity? *The Guardian*, 12 January 1972.

110. Ray Connolly, 'The Ray Connolly Interview', *Evening Standard*, 27 November 1971.

111. David Robinson, 'Family Life', *Financial Times*, 14 September 1972.

112. J. Illman, 'Jan: Trapped between Two Schools of Psychiatry', *General Practitioner*, 14 January 1972.

113. 'Adolescent Identity Crisis on Film', *British Hospital Journal of Social Service Review*, 8 January 1972.

114. Crossley, *Contesting Psychiatry*, p. 126.

115. Toms, 'MIND, Anti-Psychiatry'.

116. This was also provoked by the interventions and infiltration of Scientologists who characterised the NAMH as a criminally motivated 'psychiatric front group'. MIND website at: https://www.mind.org.uk/about-us/what-we-do/our-mission/a-history-of-mind, last accessed 10 December 2019.

117. Film reviews were usually one occasionally two pages.
118. Richard Fox and John Payne, 'Right of Reply', *MIND* (Spring 1972), p. 34.
119. John Payne, 'Under Control', *MIND* (Winter 1971), p. 13.
120. Ibid., p. 16.
121. Ibid.
122. Fox and Payne, 'Right of Reply', p. 34.
123. Ibid., p. 35.
124. Ibid., p. 38. Fox says he saw Sargant as the 'model' for Dr Caswell in *Family Life*, explaining 'they even looked the same'.
125. Payne, 'Under Control', p. 16.
126. 'Like Other People', *MIND* (Summer 1972), p. 12.
127. 'Death in the Family', *International Times* 121, 13–27 January 1971, p. 8.
128. M. Finch to Stephen Murphy, 14 November 1973, *Family Life* files, BBFC Archive. The film also came under attack from the Left, in particular from Peter Sedgwick of the *Socialist Worker* who was a prominent voice of the parent–patient pressure group the National Schizophrenic Fellowship (NSF). He stated that, 'Unwittingly, the authors of this film have created a climate of opinion in which their audiences will no longer be so keen to resist the massive Tory attack on the psychiatric facilities of the Health service' (p. 30). Sedgwick's attack on the film must be understood in the context of his wider battle against Laing and anti-psychiatry, which he saw as 'conservative' and detrimental to the lives working-class people. See M. Cresswell and Z. Karimova, 'Ken Loach, Family Life and Socialist Realism: Some Historical and Theoretical Aspects', *Journal of British Cinema and Television* 14(1) (2017): 19–38.
129. T. Palmer, 'Unholy Family', *The Spectator*, 7 January 1972.
130. Michael Billington, 'Films', *Birmingham Post*, 20 November 1971. Others have suggested that Laing's credibility and celebrity was on the decline in the United Kingdom by this point anyway, so the connection might not have been so valuable as in the United States or France.
131. 'NY Film Fest Firms Panel Sideshow', *Variety*, 27 September 1972, p. 20.
132. Interview with the author, 2018.
133. Ibid.
134. Ken Loach quoted in 'Tony Garnett: Tributes to Kes, Cathy Come Home and This Life Producer', *BBC News*, 13 January 2020, available at: https://www.bbc.co.uk/news/entertainment-arts-51089420, last accessed 14 January 2020.
135. Loach quoted in Fuller, *Loach on Loach*, p. 25.
136. Wall, *The British Anti-Psychiatrists*.
137. Laing, *R. D. Laing*, p. 161.

Chapter 6: Aetiology of a murder

1. Karl Menninger, 'Verdict Guilty: Now What', *Harper's* magazine, August 1959, p. 4, *In Cold Blood* research (Menninger clinic), F658, Richard Brooks papers, Margaret Herrick Library, Los Angeles (hereafter Brooks papers).

2. Ibid., p. 5.
3. Abraham S. Goldstein, *The Insanity Defense* (New York: Yale University Press, 1967), p. 3.
4. Ibid.
5. Ibid., p. 9.
6. Ibid., p. 93.
7. Ibid., p. 9. In 1960, *R. v. Byrne* (2 QB 396), set a precedent in UK courts by applying the irresponsible impulses rule to the case of a sexual psychopath who murdered a young woman, successfully proving lack of criminal responsibility due to 'abnormality of mind', in contrast to the M'Naghten rules 'defect of reason'.
8. The court-appointed expert does not have to be qualified psychiatrist, they can be any physician irrespective of any specific expertise in mental health.
9. Letter from Otto Preminger to Geoffrey Shurlock, 29 April 1959, *Anatomy of a Murder* file, PCA collection.
10. The Catholic Legion of Decency concurred with the Chicago court that the film's clinical language was 'so explicitly and frankly detailed is judged to exceed the bounds of moral acceptability and propriety in a mass medium of entertainment', but gave it a 'C' (condemned) rating rather than outright rejection. Memo, 9 July 1959, *Anatomy of a Murder* files, PCA collection.
11. Bosley Crowther, 'Attempted Murder: Chicago Censors Try to Kill a Fine Film', *New York Times*, 12 July 1959, p. 1.
12. Powe, 'Anatomy of a Murder', *Variety*, 26 June 1959, p. 6. *Time* magazine joked that 'it is a courtroom melodrama that seems less concerned with murder than with anatomy', 13 July 1959.
13. 'Anatomy of a Murder', *Cue*, 4 July 1959, *Anatomy of a Murder* files, PCA collection.
14. Bosley Crowther, 'A Court Classic', *New York Times*, 3 July 1959, p. 10.
15. Roger Lane, *Murder in America: A History* (Columbus: Ohio State University, 1997), pp. 268–9.
16. Jean Murley, *The Rise of True Crime: 20th-Century Murder and American Popular Culture* (Westport, CT: Praeger, 2008), p. 47.
17. Ibid., p. 51.
18. Ibid., p. 154.
19. Truman Capote, *In Cold Blood* (London: Penguin Classics, [1966] 2000).
20. Kenneth Tynan, 'The Kansas Farm Murders', *The Observer*, 13 March 1966, p. 20.
21. Capote, *In Cold Blood*, pp. 286–94.
22. Svein Atle Skålevåg, 'Truth, Law and Forensic Psychiatry in Truman Capote's *In Cold Blood*', *Law and Humanities* 6(2) (2012): 255
23. Sara Sligar, '*In Cold Blood*, the Expansion of Psychiatric Evidence, and the Corrective Power of True Crime', *Law & Literature* 31(1) (2019): 38.
24. Capote, *In Cold Blood*, pp. 286–7.
25. Ibid., pp. 288–9.
26. Ibid., p. 289.
27. Ibid., p. 290.
28. Ibid.

29. See Joseph Satten, Karl Menninger, Irvin Rosen and Martin Mayman, 'Murder without Apparent Motive: A Study in Personality Disorganization', *American Journal of Psychiatry* 117 (1960): 48–53.

30. Capote, *In Cold Blood*, pp. 290–92. Quoted from Satten et al, 'Murder without Apparent Motive', p. 48.

31. Capote, *In Cold Blood*, p. 292.

32. Ibid., p. 293.

33. Ibid.

34. Ibid., p. 294.

35. Ibid.

36. Ibid.

37. Skålevåg, 'Truth, Law and Forensic Psychiatry', p. 258.

38. Brooks quoted in Douglas Daniel, *Tough as Nails: The Life and Films of Richard Brooks* (Madison: University of Wisconsin Press, 2011), p. 171.

39. Production Code records for *In Cold Blood* show that initial reports of the film being made triggered a negative response by at least one psy professional who had a high-profile ally. On 10 August 1966, Senator Robert Kennedy forwarded a letter from clinical psychologist Dr Paula Elkisch to Geoffrey Shurlock, then Director of the Motion Picture Production Code. Elkish's letter called on Kennedy to try to block the production on the grounds of its 'glorification [. . . of the] deeds of the insane' and potential impact on the 'psychology of adolescents, in fact [on] the emotional health of our nation'. The senator's letter to Shurlock is non-committal in his opinion on the proposed production, but Shurlock forwarded the letters from Elkisch and Kennedy to Robert Brooks on 16 August with the equivocal statement that the letters 'speak for themselves'. Whether this initial negative professional (and political) response had any bearing on Brooks' decision to seek high-profile technical advice is unclear. Letter from Paula Elkisch to Robert Kennedy, 13 January 1967, *In Cold Blood* Production files, PCA collection.

40. Daniel, *Tough as Nails*, p. 174.

41. Ibid., p. 181.

42. Capote, *In Cold Blood*, p. 292.

43. David Devonis and Jessica Triggs, 'Prison Break: Karl Menninger's *The Crime of Punishment* and its Reception in US Psychology', *History of Psychology* 20(1) (2017): 93.

44. James E. Carney, 'The Freudians come to Kansas: Menninger, Freud, and the Émigré Psychoanalysts', *Kansas History* 16 (1993): 91.

45. Devonis and Triggs, 'Prison Break', p. 92. See Karl Menninger, *The Crime of Punishment* (New York: Viking, 1968).

46. Menninger, *The Crime of Punishment*, p. 96.

47. 'Schedule for Mr Richard Brooks, 16 and 17 January, 1967', F658, Brooks papers.

48. 'Meeting at Menninger Clinic: 16–17 January 1967', interview transcript, F659, Brooks papers (hereafter 'Menninger Clinic' transcript).

49. In addition to Menninger's chapter and the aforementioned article (n. 1), these are: Karl Menninger and Joseph Satten, 'The Development of a Psychiatric

Criminology', *Bulletin of the Menninger Clinic* 25(4) (1961): 164–72; Sydney Smith, 'The Adolescent Murderer: A Psychodynamic Interpretation', *General Psychiatry* 13 (1956): 310–19; Sydney Smith, 'Delinquency and the Panacea of Punishment', *Federal Probation*, September 1965; Joseph Satten, 'Correctional Institutions and Psychiatry' and 'Crime and Mental Disorders', in *The Encyclopaedia of Mental Health* (New York: Franklin Watts, 1963), pp. 367–80, 402–14.

50. Satten quoted in 'Menninger Clinic' transcript, tape 3, p. 1.
51. Brooks quoted in 'Menninger Clinic' transcript, tape 3, p. 17.
52. Satten quoted in 'Menninger Clinic' transcript, tape 3, p. 19
53. Satten quoted in 'Menninger Clinic' transcript, tape 5, p. 21.
54. Satten quoted in 'Menninger Clinic' transcript, tape 3, p. 13.
55. Ibid.
56. Ibid., p. 37.
57. Ibid., p. 5.
58. Speaker quoted in 'Menninger Clinic' transcript, tape 1, p. 24.
59. Ibid., p. 25.
60. Brooks quoted in 'Menninger Clinic' transcript, tape 1, p. 25.
61. Satten quoted in 'Menninger Clinic' transcript, tape 4, p. 5.
62. Menninger, *The Crime of Punishment*, draft chapter, p. 27, F659, Brooks papers. In this draft chapter, Brooks has marked up the section on 'Displacement', which he discusses a hunter who displaces his anger for his father onto the animals he hunts and dreams of them with his father's face substituted for the animal prey. Brook's marked this up with note 'S' for Smith).
63. Brooks quoted in 'Menninger Clinic' transcript, tape 6, p. 3.
64. Ibid., p. 9.
65. Ibid., p 12.
66. Speaker quoted in 'Menninger Clinic' transcript, tape 4, p. 10–11.
67. Satten quoted in 'Menninger Clinic' transcript, tape 4, p. 11.
68. Brooks quoted in 'Menninger Clinic' transcript, tape 4, p. 9.
69. Satten quoted in 'Menninger Clinic' transcript, tape 5, p. 25.
70. Satten quoted in 'Menninger Clinic' transcript, tape 5, p. 1.
71. Satten quoted in 'Menninger Clinic' transcript, tape 4, p. 30.
72. Ibid.
73. Brooks quoted in 'Menninger Clinic' transcript, tape 5, pp. 9–10.
74. Satten quoted in 'Menninger Clinic' transcript, tape 4, p. 16.
75. Jane Howard, 'A Nightmare Lived Again', *Life Magazine*, 12 May 1967, pp. 98–101.
76. Ibid., pp. 103–4.
77. William Cotter Murray, 'Returning to the Scene of the Crime', *New York Times*, 16 April 1967, p. 15.
78. Murf, 'In Cold Blood', *Variety*, 13 December 1967, p. 6.
79. Richard Schickel, 'Cold Blood Shouldn't be that Simple', *Life Magazine*, 12 January 1958, *In Cold Blood* files, PCA collection.
80. Murf, 'In Cold Blood', p. 6.
81. John Mahoney, 'In Cold Blood', *Hollywood Reporter*, undated, *In Cold Blood* files, PCA collection.

82. Richard Gertner, 'In Cold Blood', *Motion Picture Daily*, undated, *In Cold Blood* files, PCA collection.

83. Arthur Knight, 'Cold Blood, Calm Reflection', *Saturday Review*, 30 December 1967, *In Cold Blood* files, PCA collection.

84. Ibid.

85. Schickel, 'Cold Blood Shouldn't be that Simple'.

86. Joseph Morgenstern 'Two for the Road', *Newsweek*, 25 December 1967.

87. Raymond Haberski, *Freedom to Offend: How New York Remade Movie Culture* (Lexington: University Press of Kentucky, 2007), p. 195. In Roger Ebert's article, he explained the pressure more traditional critics were facing to revise their opinions on *Bonnie and Clyde*: 'Bosley Crowther of the *New York Times* attacked the film on three different occasions. Last week, it was announced that Crowther will retire.' Roger Ebert, 'Bonnie, Clyde and the Critics', *Chicago Sun Times*, 10 December 1967.

88. Haberski *Freedom to Offend*, pp. 177–88.

89. Barbara Klinger, *Melodrama and Meaning: History, Culture, and. the Films of Douglas Sirk* (Bloomington: Indiana University Press, 1994), p. 72.

90. Bosley Crowther, 'Ten Best Films', *New York Times*, 28 December 1947. Although it is the source for *Crossfire*, Brooks' novel actually dealt with homophobia rather than anti-Semitism.

91. Bosley Crowther, 'Of Color, Crime and Punishment', *New York Times*, 17 December 1967, p. 99.

92. Renata Adler, 'Cold Blood, Cheap Fiction', *New York Times*, 28 January 1968, p. 1.

93. Ibid.

94. Nicholas McDonald, 'Chilling Enough', *New York Times*, 24 March 1968, p. 11; Tom Andrews, 'What It's About', *New York Times*, 24 March 1968, p. 11; Gary B. Claps, 'To the Editor', *New York Times*, 24 March 1968, pp. 11, 13.

95. Roger Ebert, 'In Cold Blood', *Chicago Sun Times*, 6 February 1968.

96. Andrew Sarris, 'The Graduate; In Cold Blood', *The Village Voice*, 28 December 1967, p. 329.

97. Menninger, *The Crime of Punishment*, p. 162.

98. Crowther, 'Of Color, Crime and Punishment', p. 99.

99. Patrick Gallwey, 'Truman Capote's In Cold Blood', *Mental Health* 27 (1968): 40–1.

100. 'Yes to Hanging Scene in Film', Motion Picture Export Association press release, 16 January 1968, *In Cold Blood* files, PCA collection.

101. Tim Snelson, '"The Horror Film to End all Horror Films": *10 Rillington Place* (1971) and the BBFC's Policy on Recent Murder Cases', in Anne Etienne, Benjamin Halligan and Christopher Weedman (eds), *Adult Themes: British Cinema and the 'X' Rating, 1958–1972* (New York: Bloomsbury Academic, 2023) pp. 199–216.

102. John Trevelyan, Notes to Martin Ransohoff 'On Proposal from Filmways Productions to Film 10 Rillington Place', 12 March 1970, *10 Rillington Place* files, London, BBFC Archive.

103. Stella Bruzzi, 'Making a Genre: The Case of the Contemporary True Crime Documentary', *Law and Humanities* 10(2) (2016): 278.

104. Satten quoted in 'Menninger Clinic' transcript, tape 4, p. 10.
105. Brooks quoted in 'Menninger Clinic' transcript, tape 5, p. 10.

Conclusion: aftershocks

1. 'NY Film Fest Firms Panel Sideshow', *Variety*, 27 September 1972, p. 20.
2. Derek Malcolm, 'Grave Business: Derek Malcolm on the Week's Film', *The Guardian*, 29 July 1972, p. 8.
3. Derek Hill, 'Peeping Tom', *The Tribune*, 29 April 1960. The psychological thriller *Peeping Tom* about a young filmmaker, driven psychopathic by his psychologist father's experiments on him when a child, received vitriolically negative reviews that were seen to end lauded British director Michael Powell's career. The most famous of these reviews was Derek Hill's for *The Tribune*, that railed: 'The only really satisfactory way to dispose of *Peeping Tom* would be to shovel it up and flush it swiftly down the nearest sewer. Even then, the stench would remain.' However, almost across the board the British critics hated the film, with C. A. Lejeune of *The Observer*, who walked out of the film, stating 'It's a long time since a film disgusted me as much as *Peeping Tom*.' C. A. Lejeune, 'Peeping Tom', *The Observer*, 10 April 1960. Dilys Powell was also appalled by the film's new and more concerning psychological approach to horror, saying that while 'wast[ing] much indignation on the Draculas and Mummies and Stranglers of the last few years, *Peeping Tom* is another matter'. Dilys Powell, 'Peeping Tom', *Sunday Times*, 10 April 1960.
4. John Mahoney, 'The Trip', *Film Daily*, August 1967.
5. Pauline Kael, 'El Topo', *The New Yorker*, 20 November 1971, p. 212
6. Harry Benshoff, 'The Short-lived Life of the Hollywood LSD-Film', *The Velvet Light Trap* 47 (2001): 29–44.
7. *Who's Afraid of Virginia Woolf?* (1966) was the first film to receive the PCA's short-lived 'M' rating, so bearing the 'Suggested for Mature Audiences' tag on its promotion.
8. James Monaco, 'The Waning Production Code and the Rise of the Ratings System', *The Sixties: 1960–1969* (Berkely: University of California Press, 2001), pp. 56–66.
9. Stephen Farber, *The Movie Rating Game* (Washington, DC: Pubic Affairs Press, 1972), p. 72.
10. Ibid., p. 94.
11. Samuel Z. Arkoff quoted in ibid., p. 90.
12. Sam Peckinpah, 'Did They Rate the Ratings Board Unfairly?' *New York Times*, 7 May 1972, p. 11.
13. Michael Bernstein, *Controlling Hollywood: Censorship and Regulation in the Studio Era* (New Brunswick, NJ: Rutgers University Press, 1999). Valenti implied in later accounts that he forced Stern out: 'I once made a mistake of putting a psychiatrist in charge . . . How he viewed certain things, the stance he was taking in the press . . . was not consonant with the motives of the ratings

system.' Moira Hodgson, 'Movie Ratings: Do They Serve Hollywood or the Public? The Movie Ratings', *New York Times*, 24 May 1981, p. 1.

14. McDonald and Walter, 'Hollywood and ECT', pp. 200–6.
15. Thomas Szasz, 'Toward the Therapeutic State', in T. S. Szasz, *Law, Liberty, and Psychiatry: An Inquiry into the Social Uses of Mental Health Practices* (New York: Macmillan, 1963), pp. 212–22.
16. Murf, 'One Flew Over the Cuckoo's Nest', *Variety*, 18 November 1975.
17. Ibid.
18. Vincent Canby, 'Jack Nicholson, the Free Spirit of "One Flew Over the Cuckoo's Nest"', *New York Times*, 28 November 1975.

Index

A Case of Multiple Personality
   (documentary), 99–102, 110
A Child is Waiting (1963), 34–6
A Clinical Lesson at the Salpêtrière
   (Brouillet), 74
A Clockwork Orange (1971), 4, 90
Adams, Mary (BBC), 128
Adler, Alfred, 76
Adler, Renata, 172–3
A Fine Madness (1966), 30–2
Allied Artists, 30
Altman, Robert, 4
American Psychiatric Association (APA),
   26, 71, 76, 102
American Psychoanalytic Association
   (APsA), 70, 71, 78
A Mind of My Own (Costner Sizemore),
   112, 113–14
Anatomy of a Murder (1959), 4, 152, 153–4,
   157
anti-psychiatry, 4, 8, 45, 124–50, 191n
A Suitable Case for Treatment (television),
   131
anti-psychotic drugs, 3, 54
Asylum (1972), 4, 177
Asylum (documentary), 177
authoritarianism and obedience, 4

Bad Seed, The (1956), 4, 16–18
Balio, Tino, 5
Bartlett, Hall, 53–5
Bates, Norman (character), 1–3, 5

Bergman, Ingmar, 32–3
Beguiled, The (1971), 4
Behind Locked Doors (1948), 46
Berkenkotter, Carol, 79
Bewitched (1945), 27
Bewitched (television series), 91–2
Bier, Reverend William C., 16, 76–7
Big Cube, The (1969), 4
Billy Liar (1963), 132
Black, Stephen, 23, 44, 56–64
Blanton, Smiley, 71
Bliss of Mrs. Blossom, The (1968), 143
Blood of Dracula (1957), 14–15
Blue Pages (Perry), 121–2
Bogdanovich, Peter, 4
Bonnie and Clyde (1967), 172–3, 174, 176
Borderlines (1965) *see Caretakers, The* (1963)
Boston Strangler, The (1968), 4, 42, 44,
   62–3, 155, 175
Bouhoutsos, Jacqueline C., 181
Bowlby, John, 129
brainwashing, 21–2
Breen, Joseph, 10, 27
Breuer, Joseph, 68, 80
British Board of Film Censors (BBFC), 6, 7,
   23, 42–64, 87–8, 149, 175, 178, 180
   independence from State, 43, 47, 52–3,
   64
British New Wave, 4, 48
Brooks, Richard, 159–76
Bunny Lake Is Missing (1965), 4, 5
Burgess, Anthony, 142

Cape Fear (1962), 4
capital punishment, 167–9, 171–2
Captive Wild Woman (1943), 67
Caretakers, The (1963), 4, 42, 43, 49–56, 93, 178, 182, 192–3n
Cathy Come Home (television), 131
Cat People (1942), 96
Catholics and psychiatry, 11–13, 70
censorship, 10–41, 42–64
Chapman Report, The (1962), 196n
Charcot, Jean-Martin, 74–6
child development and attachment, 3, 4
Children of the Damned (1964), 4
Child's Play (1972), 4
Christie, John, 58, 175
circuits of mass communication, 8
Citizen Kane (1942), 88
Classification and Rating Administration (CARA), 6, 93, 181
Clayton, Jack, 4
Cleckley, Hervey, 94–5, 98–116
Clift, Montgomery, 78, 89
Cold War, 65, 72
Collector, The (1965), 4, 5, 42, 43–4, 56–8, 151
Compulsion (1959), 4, 153
consciousness raising (CR), 117–18, 120–1, 123
Cooke, Alistair, 104–5, 106–7, 110
Cooper, David, 54, 124–5, 126, 127, 133–4, 141, 145, 148
Costner Sizemore, Christine, 94–5, 98–116, 122–3, 179, 202n
Cotton, John, 97
counterculture, 45, 127, 143, 148–9, 179
Coward, Noel, 4
Crime of Punishment, The (Menninger), 161, 162, 174
Crossfire (1947), 172
Crossley, Nick, 44–5, 125–6, 150
Crowther, Bosley, 87, 113, 154, 172–3, 174
Curran, Charles, 72
cycles (film), 5, 178

Dark Mirror, The (1946), 96
Darwinism, 14–15
David and Lisa (1962), 4, 5, 33–4, 49, 93, 95, 118, 178, 204n

DeAngelis, Michael, 45
Deinstitutionalization movement, 45, 49, 126, 178
Demons of the Mind (1972), 4, 9, 182n
Diary of a Lost Girl, The (1929), 67
Diary of a Mad Housewife (1970), 94–5, 116–23
    reception of, 120–1
dissociative identity disorder, 2, 4, 9, 94–5, 98–116, 122–3
Divided Self, The (Laing), 132, 209n
Durham rule (1954), 152–3

Eckstein, Rudolf, 78
Edison, the Man (1940), 67
electroconvulsive therapy (ECT), 45, 46, 51, 54–5, 126, 129–30, 132, 134, 137–8, 141–1, 144–6, 147, 182
Erikson, Eric, 71
Esterson, Aaron, 124–5, 127, 132, 133–4
Exorcist, The (1973), 4
Eysenck, Hans, 141

Family Life (1971), 4, 7, 48, 64, 124–5, 143–9, 150, 179, 182
    reception of, 146–9
Farber, Stephen, 5, 181
Farrow, Mia, 4
Ferman, James (BBFC), 43
Feminine Mystique, The (Friedan) *see* Friedan, Betty
Firestone, Shulamith, 97
Fleischer, Richard, 62, 175
Foucault, Michel, 44
Fox, Richard, 128, 147
Freeman, Hugh, 130–1
Friedan, Betty, 94, 116–17, 118, 123
Freud, Sigmund, 11, 14, 16, 24, 25, 65–93, 102–3, 160;
    feminism, 117
    infantile sexuality, 68, 70, 77, 80
    Oedipus conflict, 68, 70, 77, 80, 85
Freud, Anna, 68–9
Freud (1962), 4, 7, 15–16, 19, 24–5, 32, 39, 65–93, 132, 179, 180
    dream sequences, 76–7, 81–6
    reception of, 86–91
    therapy scenes, 82–6
Fuller, Samuel, 29

Gabbard, Krin, and Gabbard, Glen O., 5–6, 66, 107
Gallwey, Patrick, 174
Garland, Judie, 101, 200–1n
Garnett, Tony, 124–5, 131–50
genetic determinism, 15–18
Goffman, Erving, 49
Goldstein, Abraham, 152, 153
Goldwyn, Samuel, 66
Goodbye Gemini (1970), 4
Gordon, William, 70–1, 78, 85
Gorsky, Doreen, 129
gothic, 5, 205n
Grimes, Stephen, 81–4
Grotjan, Martin, 71–2, 196n

Hacking, Ian, 95, 115
Hanisch, Carol, 118
Harrison, Lyman, 78
Hays Office *see* Production Code Administration
Hepburn, Audrey, 4
historical reception studies, 8–9
Hitchcock, Alfred, 2, 4, 26–8, 170
Horney, Karen, 117
Human Jungle, The (television), 130–1
Hurt Mind, The (television), 53, 129–30, 136, 138, 145
Huston, John, 5, 65–6, 67–93, 195n
Hyatt Williams, Arthur, 62
Hypnotic Eye, The (1962), 18
hypnotism, 13–14, 18–21
hysteria, 73–6

Images (1972), 4
I'm Eve (Costner Sizemore and Pittillo), 102, 105, 114–15
In Cold Blood (1967), 4, 8, 152, 159–76, 179
    reception of, 170–5
In Cold Blood (Truman Capote) (1966), 155–9, 168, 171–2
Innocents, The (1961), 4, 198n
insanity defence, 4, 116, 151–4
Inside Daisy Clover (1965), 4, 5
insulin shock therapy, 46
In Two Minds (1967), 4, 6, 124–5, 131–42, 145, 149–50, 179, 182
    reception of, 138–42
I Was a Teenage Werewolf (1957), 13–15

Jackson, Sheila, 103
Jane, Topsy, 132
Joker (2019), 4, 41
Johnson, Irmis, 103–4
Johnson, Nunnally, 101, 103, 104–5, 111
Jones, Ernest, 67–8
Jones, Quincey, 160
Jung, Carl, 76

Kaufman, Charlie, 68, 69
Kaufman, Sue, 118, 119
Kingsley Hall, 126, 134, 146
Kuhn, Annette, 44

Laing, Adrian, 143
Laing, Ronald D., 45, 52, 54, 124–5, 126–7, 132, 133–4, 139, 140, 141, 142–3, 145, 146–9, 150, 177, 192n
Lector, Hannibal (character), 4
Legion of Decency, 7, 10–41, 72, 81, 84–5, 111, 179–80, 212n
Lifeline (television), 53, 130
Life of Emile Zola, The (1937), 67
Like Other People (1942), 148
Lilith (1964), 4, 5, 49, 83, 178
Linder, Robert M., 82
Lizzie (1957), 4, 103
Loach, Ken, 48, 124, 131, 133, 135, 143–4, 148, 149
Lodger, The (1927), 4
Lola Montes (1955), 88
Loneliness of the Long Distance Runner, The (1962), 132
Look Back in Anger (1959), 48
Loomis, Earl, 24, 72–8
Lord of the Flies (1963), 4
Losey, Joseph, 4
LSD *see* psychotropic drugs

Madame Currie (1943), 67
Man Alive (television), 134, 148
Manchurian Candidate, The (1962), 21–2
Maniac (1963), 5
Man in the Middle (1964), 153
Man Who Loved Cat Dancing, The (1973), 121
Mark, The (1961), 15
Marnie (1964), 4, 26–8
Marwick, Arthur, 3, 7

Index **221**

Mask of Sanity, The (Cleckley), 98
Maslow, Abraham, 117
Matters of Life and Death (television), 128
Mayer, Arthur, 87
Mayman, Martin, 157
Menninger Clinic, 72, 151, 160–1, 176
Menninger, Karl, 151, 157, 160–1, 169
Mental Health and Mental Retardation
   Act, 1963 (US), 49
Mental Health Act, 1959 (UK), 51
Mental Health Film Council (NAMH),
   51, 128
mental hospital (as setting), 46–7, 51–5, 63
mental hygiene movement, 50, 206n
Mercer, David, 48, 124, 139, 140
Micales, Mark, 74–5
Miller, Derek, 62–3, 195n, 78
Millett, Kate, 97
MIND, 147–8, 150
Mind Benders, The (1963), 22
Mind of Mister Soames, The (1970), 4
M'Naghten rule (1843), 152–4, 155–6,
   159, 172
Modern Woman: The Lost Sex (Lundberg
   and Farnham), 95–6
Modlin, Herbert, 162, 166
Monitor (television), 128
Monroe, Marilyn, 69
Morgan: A Suitable Case For Treatment
   (1966), 4, 132
Motion Picture Production Code, 10, 19
multiple personality disorder, 2, 4, 9, 94–5,
   98–116, 122–3
Murley, Jean, 155

National Association for Mental Health
   (UK), 7, 45, 50–6, 125, 127–31, 142,
   150
National Association for Mental Health
   (US), 72
National Catholic Office of Motion
   Pictures (NCOMP) *see* Legion of
   Decency
Newman, Sydney, 131, 135, 139
Now Voyager (1942), 67

Olivier, Lawrence, 4
One Flew Over the Cuckoo's Nest (1975),
   138, 182–3
Other, The (1972), 4

Pabst, G. W., 66–7
Paramount Pictures, 19–20
Paranoiac (1963), 5, 9
Payne, John, 147–8
Peeping Tom (1960), 4, 177, 216n
Penrose, Lionel, 129
People, Not Psychiatry (PNP), 148
Performance (1970), 4
Perry, Eleanor, 95, 118–23
Perry, Frank, 118
Petley, Julian, 43
Phantom Lady (1944), 96
Philadelphia Association, 126
Pink Panther Show, The, 91
Polanski, Roman, 42, 6061
Poling, James, 103, 105, 201n
Pope Pius XII, 12–14, 40
Possessed (1945), 12
Preminger, Otto, 4, 152, 159
Pressure Point (1963), 4, 82–3
Prince, Morton, 1023
Production Code Administration, 7, 10,
   17, 19, 23, 28, 65, 69–70, 92–3, 111,
   180–1, 213n
psychiatric essentialism, 15–18
psychiatry, biomedical approaches to, 45,
   51, 126, 129
Psycho (1960), 1–3, 4, 5, 26–7, 39, 98, 151,
   162–3, 177, 179
psychogenetics, 3, 4, 15–18
psychopathy, 2, 4–5, 56–8, 62–3, 98, 153,
   174
Psychopath, The (1966), 4, 5
psychotherapy, 4, 45, 143–4, 178
psychotropic drugs, 3, 4, 62, 143, 178–8
Psych Out (1968), 4
psychosurgery (e.g. lobotomies), 45, 126
Pumpkin Eater, The (1964), 36–8, 142
Punishment Park (1971), 4

Rees, T. P., 126, 128, 129
Reinhardt, Wolfgang, 69
Reisz, Karel, 4
Repulsion (1965), 4, 23–4, 43–4, 58–62,
   151, 179
Riddall, Mike, 144–5
Roma (1972), 122
Room at the Top (1959), 48
Rosemary's Baby (1968), 4, 194n
Rosen, Irwin, 157, 164

Rosenzweig, Saul, 90
Rowan and Martin's Laugh-In, 91

Sachs, Hans, 67
Sanity, Madness and the Family (Laing and Esterson), 124, 132–4, 208n
Sargant, William, 53, 129–30, 138, 139–40, 148, 193n
Sartre, Jean Paul, 66, 69, 199n
Satten, Joseph, 152, 157–8, 160–9, 171, 176
Saturday Night, Sunday Morning (1960), 48
schizophrenia, 2, 4, 32, 60, 125, 132–3, 134–8
Sealey, Anne, 79
Search for Bridey Murphy, The (1956), 19–21
Second World War, the
    psychological effects, 46
    women's roles, 95–6
Secret Ceremony (1968), 4
Secrets of a Soul (1926), 67
Sedgwick, Peter, 211n
Servant, The (1963), 84
Seven-Percent Solution, The (1976), 197n
Seventh Seal, The (1945), 12
Shock (1945), 67
Shock Corridor (1963), 28–9, 32, 48, 49, 138, 178, 182
Shock Treatment (1964), 48, 49, 138, 178
Sigler, David, 86
Sisters (1973), 4
Sleep, My Love (1948), 18
Slocombe, Douglas, 84
Slovenko, Ralph, 161–2
Smith, Sydney, 162, 165
Snake Pit, The (1948), 46–7, 57, 63, 67
Snodgress, Carrie, 119–21
sociopathy, 4
Spacek, Sissy, 114
Spellbound (1945), 12, 26, 67
Stafford-Clark, David, 53–4, 78, 130, 197n
Stern, Aaron, 181, 216–7n
Story of Louis Pasteur, The (1936), 67
Straw Dogs (1971), 181
Studies in Hysteria (Freud), 67, 73, 79, 80
Sybil (1976), 98, 115
Szasz, Thomas, 45, 49, 182

Tavistock Clinic, 42, 62
10 Rillington Place (1971), 4, 175

Thigpen, Corbett, 94–5, 98–116
Third Secret, The (1964), 4
Three Faces of Eve, The (1957), 4, 7, 94–116, 122–3, 132, 179, 183
    reception of, 111–13
Three Faces of Eve, The (Thigpen and Cleckley), 94, 98–9, 100
Through a Glass Darkly (1961), 32–3
Tomkinson, Harvey, 76–7
trends (film), 5, 178
Trevelyan, John (BBFC), 42–4, 47–64, 88, 180, 194n
    What the Censor Saw (biography), 48, 62
Trip, The (1967), 4, 62
Trog (1970), 4
Twentieth Century Fox, 95, 103, 114–15
Twisted Nerve (1968), 4, 64

United Artists, 49–56
Universal-International Pictures, 1, 16, 24–5
Unman, Wittering and Zigo (1971), 4

video nasties, 43
Villa 21, 126, 127, 133–4, 143–4

Walker, Janet, 97, 109
Wall, Oisín, 126
Watkins, Arthur (BBFC), 46–7
Wednesday Play, The (BBC), 131–2
Wicker Man, The (1973), 4
Winnicott, Donald, 3
What's New Pussycat? (1965), 143
Whelden, Huw, 128–9
Women's Liberation Movement, 4, 94–5, 117–18, 119, 121–2, 123
Woodward, Joanne, 101, 104, 107–11, 114, 115, 203n
Wyler, William, 4, 56
Wyndam Goldie, Grace, 129, 131

York, Susannah, 80, 89–90
Your Life in their Hands (television), 128, 136, 138

Zaretsky, Eli, 65, 71, 91, 92